iPad® and iPad® mini

ABSOLUTE BEGINNER'S GUIDE

James Floyd Kelly

que®

800 East 96th Street,
Indianapolis, Indiana 46240

iPad® and iPad® mini Absolute Beginner's Guide

ISBN-13: 978-0-7897-5099-0
ISBN-10: 0-7897-5099-6

Library of Congress Control Number: 2013935265

Printed in the United States of America

Second Printing: January 2014

Trademarks

Warning and Disclaimer

Bulk Sales

Que Publishing offers excellent discounts on this book when ordered in quantity for bulk purchases or special sales. For more information, please contact

U.S. Corporate and Government Sales
1-800-382-3419
corpsales@pearsontechgroup.com

For sales outside the United States, please contact

International Sales
international@pearsoned.com

Editor In Chief
Greg Weigand

Executive Editor
Rick Kughen

Development Editor
Rick Kughen

Managing Editor
Sandra Schroeder

Project Editor
Mandie Frank

Copy Editor
Bart Reed

Indexer
Lisa Stumpf

Proofreader
Paula Lowell

Technical Editor
Karen Weinstein

Publishing Coordinator
Cindy Teeters

Designer
Anne Jones

Compositor
Mary Sudul

Contents at a Glance

Table of Contents

About the Author

James Floyd Kelly is an author and blogger from Atlanta, Georgia. He has a B.A. in English (University of West Florida) and B.S. in Industrial Engineering (Florida State University). He has worked in technology for more than 15 years, including work as a technical trainer, a network systems administrator, and a technology outsourcing consultant. Jim has written books and articles on numerous subjects, including LEGO Robotics, building a CNC machine and a 3D printer, and open source software. When not writing books, he can usually be found tinkering in his workshop or spending time with his wife and two young boys.

Dedication

I'd like to thank my wife, Ashley, for all her support and patience of the crazy-husband as delivery dates and deadlines loomed.

Acknowledgments

I'd like to thank the team at Pearson—Rick, Mandie, Karen, and Bart—for all their help in getting this book ready for print.

A special thanks also goes to my wife, Ashley, and my two little boys. I was writing two Pearson books simultaneously, and jumping back and forth between the two was a bit crazy at times...resulting in a husband/father who was a bit crazy at times. Everything worked out, the books were done, and now I get to spend a little time with the family before the next writing assignment lands.

We Want to Hear from You!

As the reader of this book, *you* are our most important critic and commentator. We value your opinion and want to know what we're doing right, what we could do better, what areas you'd like to see us publish in, and any other words of wisdom you're willing to pass our way.

We welcome your comments. You can email or write to let us know what you did or didn't like about this book—as well as what we can do to make our books better.

Please note that we cannot help you with technical problems related to the topic of this book.

When you write, please be sure to include this book's title and author as well as your name and email address. We will carefully review your comments and share them with the author and editors who worked on the book.

Email: feedback@quepublishing.com

Mail: Que Publishing
       ATTN: Reader Feedback
       800 East 96th Street
       Indianapolis, IN 46240 USA

Reader Services

Visit our website and register this book at quepublishing.com/register for convenient access to any updates, downloads, or errata that might be available for this book.

INTRODUCTION

The iPad and iPad mini are the world's bestselling tablets. The original iPad was released in 2010, and numerous updates to both the hardware and software continue to make it the number-one selling tablet in the world. Apple never sits still with any of its products, so new features and capabilities are always appearing with each new version of the iPad.

As with all previous versions of the iPad, the current iPad and iPad mini both run the iOS operating system. This is the same operating system found on its popular iPhone and iPod touch products. As this book is heading to the printer, the most current version of operating system is iOS 6. The iOS operating system was designed for touch-based products, and the iPad and iPad mini are most definitely touch-based tablets.

Apple has another operating system called OS X that is found on its desktop and laptop products. While iOS and OS X have historically been two separate products that differ in both look and function, this distinction between operating systems is starting to blur. Apple continues to develop those features that users of its iDevices (iPod, iPhone, iPod touch, iPad mini, and iPad) and its mainstream computing hardware (desktop computers and laptops) use and enjoy to work on both iOS and OS X. What this means to you is that many of the tools you use on the iPad will look and work identically on a new MacBook

Air, for example. Features such as a calendar application or a contact database not only look the same, but in many instances they're actually shared between devices, so when you move from one device to another there is no disruption.

This capability is part of Apple's iCloud service, something you'll learn how to use later in this book if you're not already familiar with it. With iCloud, Apple is giving those users with multiple Apple products the ability to have all their applications and data stored in such a way that any Apple device—iPad, iPhone, or computer—can access them. If you add an appointment for tomorrow to the calendar on your iPad, your iPhone can be configured to receive that update (and much more). Later in the evening, when you're out with your friends and your iPad is sitting at home on the couch, if someone asks you about your schedule tomorrow, you pull out your iPhone and check your calendar. (And much of your data stored in iCloud can be accessed from any web browser, so if you have a Windows computer or an Android tablet, you're still able to access the calendar, notes, and contacts features.)

Although the iCloud service is available across all Apple devices, this book is all about the iPad and iPad mini. As a matter of fact, both the iPad and iPad mini run the exact same version of the operating system, so when I say iPad in this book, you can read that as iPad or iPad mini—the only difference between the two being the smaller size of the iPad mini's screen. There is no assumption made in this book that you have any previous experience with the iPad tablet. You're going to learn about all its features, both hardware and software related. Along the way, you'll also pick up advice and tricks for using the iPad with other devices (such as mobile phones and computers), but ultimately the book's primary goal is to give you answers to all those questions you may have about how to use the iPad.

If you have experience using a previous version of the iPad, you'll take to the newest versions of the iPad fast. One of the great things about the design of the iPad and its operating system is the familiarity maintained between versions, so experienced iPad users can scan the chapter layout and jump to new topics and skip those subjects they have mastered already.

Those new to the iPad, however, are encouraged to take each chapter in order. The chapters and their respective subjects have been ordered in such a way that new users will be able to apply what they've learned in early chapters to later, more complex subjects. (For example, using the touchscreen and many of its interface features are covered early on in the book because so many later subjects depend on a solid understanding of the user interface.) This isn't to say you can't skip around to subjects that interest you, but if you truly want to learn all the bells and whistles that the iPad offers up, you'll get the best results if you take each chapter in order.

How This Book Is Organized

This book is organized into six main parts as follows:

- Part I, "Get Acquainted with iPad Hardware and iOS Basics," provides you with an overview of the iPad's buttons (there aren't many), ports (only two of them!), speaker, and charger; you'll also be introduced to the touchscreen and gestures. You'll also learn about the basics of the iOS operating system (including the concept of apps and screen navigation) as well as iCloud. You'll also be introduced to the Settings app so you'll know where to go later in the book for specific settings related to apps you'll be learning about and using.

- Part II, "Using the iPad's Basic Productivity Apps," introduces you to a number of apps that come standard with the iPad, such as Notes, Calendar, Contacts, and the Safari web browser.

- Part III, "Camera, Video, and Communication Apps," introduces you to using your iPad for taking photos, shooting video, using FaceTime for video chats, and more social apps.

- Part IV, "Movies, Books, Music, and Apps," shares with you all the features of the iPad related to entertainment. Coverage of iTunes, iBooks, the App Store, and the Newsstand and more will be provided.

- Part V, "Everything Else," wraps up the book with a mix of topics such as Maps, the Notification Center, add-ons, cases, Wi-Fi and data plans, and additional resources. You'll also be introduced to some great free apps as well as some apps that aren't free but provide great service for the price.

Again, you do not have to read the chapters in any particular order, but if you are new to the iPad, you'll find that the structure provided here and the order in which topics are introduced has been done to familiarize you with concepts earlier in the book that will help you master other concepts in later chapters.

Conventions Used in This Book

The *Absolute Beginner's Guide* series is written to be as easy to read and follow as possible. New iPad users should find that instructions provided in the chapters will include plenty of figures for following along. But unlike other computer books that tell you to "move your mouse so that the mouse pointer is over the OK button and right-click to select that option," you'll find that using the iPad makes some slightly different demands on its users.

First, there are gestures. You'll learn all about gestures in Chapter 1, "Overview of the iPad," but you've probably already noticed the iPad lacks a keyboard and a mouse, two items that are still fairly common in today's computing world. Gestures are how you work with your iPad. You drag one or more fingers up, down, left, or right to perform tasks. And there are plenty more (such as pinching gestures).

Computers with mice and keyboards also have their share of shortcuts. Instead of selecting a bit of text and then choosing Copy from the Edit menu, you can often press ⌘+C (on a Mac) or Ctrl+C (on a Windows computer) to copy the text. This is a shortcut. And believe it or not, the iPad, without a keyboard or mouse, also has shortcuts. (Well, the iPad actually does have a keyboard, but it's probably not what you think.)

Shortcuts

Shortcuts do exist on the iPad—some are specific to certain apps that you'll learn about and others are shortcuts that can be used at any time, no matter what you are doing with the iPad. Shortcuts are just that—methods for shaving a few seconds (or less) off a repetitive task. Where these are available in the book, you will be given an example of how to use them. It's up to you to remember how to use a shortcut because it will likely only be mentioned once or twice, and then the assumption will be that you know it exists. Most shortcuts involve a gesture or a certain sequence of button presses, but watch out for them in the chapters because they can be extremely helpful as your iPad power skills develop.

Keyboard

The iPad has an onscreen keyboard that is kept hidden when you don't need it, and it pops up when the iPad thinks you can use it. There are other times you can call it up on demand. Throughout the book, when you need to use the onscreen keyboard, you will be told how to access it (and whether you should expect it to appear). Other than that, don't worry that the iPad lacks a keyboard. You're going to find that not having a keyboard attached to the iPad is one of its numerous best features.

Special Elements

Throughout the chapters, you'll find a number of items that aren't included in the standard text. These items are there to provide you with additional information that can make using the iPad more friendly, more efficient, or more safe. There are three special elements to watch for: tips, notes, and cautions.

TIP A *tip* is a bit of information about an app or a feature on the iPad that can give you a bit more control or at least improve how you use the iPad. Tips can be little tricks (such as undocumented shortcuts) that can make the tablet experience more enjoyable.

 NOTE A *note* is meant to provide you with additional information related to a topic. Notes will often offer links to websites that can offer you more details about an app or a capability that isn't crucial to using the iPad.

 CAUTION A *caution* is exactly that—a small warning to be careful with the information you've just been provided. It could be related to the iPad's hardware or maybe something that could put your data at risk. Watch for cautions and learn about what they say so that your iPad, your apps, and your data have many healthy days ahead.

Let Me Know What You Think

Authors aren't perfect. We try to write the best books we can, but sometimes errors can find their way into the text. At other times, we might miss answering a question that has popped into your head. Keep in mind that cutting-edge technology such as the iPad and the iOS operating system are moving targets, with updates and improvements that might make something you read in this book obsolete or at least slightly inaccurate.

Authors also love to hear from their readers. We take suggestions and polite criticism well, but we also just like to know when we've provided our readers with some great content.

For all these items, you can email feedback@quepublishing.com. Send in your praise, your concerns, your complaints, and your questions (including the book's title and my name—James Floyd Kelly) and the publisher will happily forward these on to me so I can respond.

IN THIS CHAPTER

- What is the iPad?
- How does the iPad differ from a laptop or desktop computer?
- What are the benefits of an iPad?
- What are the iPad's weaknesses?
- A closer look at the iPad hardware

1

OVERVIEW OF THE iPAD

What Is the iPad?

For folks who own a previous version of the iPad, this question may seem a bit silly. With as much media coverage that has been given not just the iPad, but tablets in general, it's hard to imagine that anyone out there doesn't know about this device.

However, some people have never picked up, let alone seen an iPad up close. And even those of us who are quite familiar with the best-selling device were once complete novices when it came to using one. And that's the reason not only behind this chapter, but behind the entire book. It's not called *iPad and iPad mini Absolute Beginner's Guide* to reach out to iPad gurus!

Even if you're an expert at using the iPad (either the 10" version or the 7" mini version), I'm betting there's something you don't know about the new iPad... maybe a lot of things. It's a completely new version of the iPad, meaning there are new bells and whistles that even the most advanced user might not know about at first glance.

And if you're not an expert? If this is the first iPad you've ever owned? Well, you've picked up the right book, because I'm not going to make any assumptions about what you do or do not know regarding the iPad. Take, for example, it's classification as a device—a tablet. That may be a completely new technology term to you, so let's start right there and talk about exactly what the iPad is...and what it is not.

First, the iPad is a tablet. You've heard of stone tablets, right? Well, the iPad and iPad mini both weigh considerably less than a stone tablet used by early man to record information, but in a nutshell that function still holds true. The iPad is used to store and present information. What kinds of information? All kinds! If you collected a dozen iPads from a dozen different users, you'd find all or some of the following:

- Recipes
- Games
- Address lists
- Spreadsheets
- Chapters for the next Great American Novel
- Photos of last summer's vacation
- Videos of that first birthday
- To-do lists
- Calendars with appointments
- eBooks (digital versions of print books)
- Maps with directions to the new dentist office
- And much more!

It's a digital tablet, most definitely. The iPad is a lightweight device that's meant to be portable so you can take it with you when you're out and about, or you can simply hold it with a single hand to read over the latest news headlines while sitting on your couch at home. It's an electronic device, so it has an internal battery and has to be charged in order to keep functioning. It can play music, show movies, and display books you've purchased (or downloaded for free—more on that in Chapter

13, "iBooks and the iBooks Store"). It's thin, so you can squeeze it into a backpack. It's capable of connecting to the Internet, so you can send and receive email messages and browse online stores and websites that interest you. And it has its own internal memory storage, so you can load it up with the stuff you want to keep with you (such as photos, videos, songs, and books) without worrying about losing it when the battery needs charging.

If these descriptions of the uses of the iPad are causing you to wonder why it's not simply called a laptop or a computer, you'd be right to ask that question. A tablet does share some things with its larger cousins (especially the laptop), but there are actually more differences than there are similarities.

However, before we go into more detail about the differences between the iPad tablet and a desktop or laptop computer, let's get a few of the nitty-gritty details about the physical aspects of the iPad and iPad mini tablets out of the way.

 NOTE   Feel free to skip ahead to the next section if you're not interested in stuff such as the dimensions or weight of the iPad. However, some folks like to know this information, especially those who may have purchased this book to learn about the iPad before actually buying one.

First, there's its size. If you hold the 10" version of the iPad so that it is longer than it is wide, that's called Portrait view. When held in Portrait view, the 10" iPad is 9.5 inches tall (24.12 cm), 7.31 inches wide (18.57 cm), and 0.37 inches thick (9.4 mm). When held so that the 10" iPad is shorter than it is long, this is called Landscape view, and the iPad is used in both views depending on what you are doing with it. The iPad mini is even smaller (obviously), and its dimensions are 7.87 inches tall (20 cm), 5.3 inches wide (13.47 cm) and 0.28 inches thick (7.2 mm)!

As for weight, the 10" iPad comes in at a measly 1.44 pounds (652 grams). Try to find a laptop or desktop computer that weighs less than the iPad! The iPad mini's weight is only 0.68 pounds (308g)—yes, just over half a pound. I've got paperback books that weigh more than that!

All in all, the 10" and 7" iPads' small sizes and low weights are major reasons they are listed as portable devices such as a mobile phone or a small handheld game unit.

 CAUTION   Although mobile phones such as the iPhone can also be used for many of the same functions as the iPad (functions you'll be learning about in this book), their small screen is their major drawback. You can certainly create a spreadsheet, read a book, or watch a video on the iPhone, but your eyes may pay for it later.

There's one final thing about the iPad you should know, and it has to do with the versioning that Apple uses. As you can probably guess, there have been three versions of the iPad prior to the release of the iPad 4. The first iPad was simply called iPad. It was released in 2010.

The next version came out in 2011, and it was called iPad 2. It was a little thinner, a camera was added for taking photos and shooting video, and some hardware and software changes were added that were considered major improvements. Sales were higher than for the original iPad, and most users agree that the iPad 2 was a huge improvement and a nice update to the iPad.

In 2012, the next version was released. However, instead of calling it iPad 3, Apple chose to label it the New iPad. There are marketing and sales reasons behind the name change, but folks still call it the iPad 3. It had a much improved screen (called a Retina Display) and larger battery (to power that new screen, but no real change in battery life) among other improvements—and if sales figures are any indication, it was also a huge success.

And then, in 2013, Apple announced the New New iPad—or what everyone else called it, the iPad 3.

As a bonus, Apple released the iPad mini in 2012. It runs the same operating system (iOS), but it was (as the name implied) smaller in size.

What's next after the New/iPad? Well, it's probably a safe bet the iPads will be called one thing by Apple and *iPad X* by everyone else. As for any changes to the hardware and software, by the time you're reading this, rumors will probably already be swirling around the Internet, so just google "iPad 5" or "iPad mini 2" if you're curious.

One final note: For the rest of this book, instead of writing *iPad or iPad mini*, I'm going to just write *iPad*. If I reference a previous version, I'll make certain to use its version number, like this: The iPad 1 came out before the iPad 2 and the iPad 3. Apple may cringe, but it sure will make my job easier!

How Does the iPad Differ from Laptops and Desktops?

The iPad's dimensions are definitely smaller than the standard laptop or desktop computer. There are laptops with screens this small, but they're traditionally called *netbooks*. When talking about the iPad, however, it's acceptable to lump laptops and netbooks together with the larger desktop units (or tower/mini-tower units that sit on the floor). I'm going to do just that and call all these things *computers*.

NOTE Netbooks were all the rage around 2010, but they're definitely dropping in popularity. Slow speeds were one complaint, and so was the tiny keyboard. You can purchase a full-size keyboard to connect to the iPad via Bluetooth or a keyboard that has a small stand built in to it where the iPad docks. Also, some iPad cases have keyboards built in to them so they open and close like a laptop. Netbooks had their chance, but the iPad and other tablets are quickly putting them to bed.

Computers (that is, laptops, netbooks, desktops, towers, and mini-towers) have one obvious difference when compared to an iPad, and that's the keyboard. The iPad doesn't have one. Well, that's not completely true—it does, but it is displayed onscreen. (I'll talk about this more in Chapter 2, "Overview of the iOS.")

Other differences between laptops/netbooks and the iPad is the lack of a mouse or touchpad. The iPad doesn't use a mouse or touchpad. Instead, the iPad has what's called a *touchscreen*, which can detect when one or more fingers are touching it. Almost all actions on the iPad are done using nothing more than one or two fingers tapping or dragging across the screen. I'll also get into this in more detail in Chapter 2, but for now all you need to know is the iPad lacks an external keyboard and has no mouse or touchpad. In fact, the entire screen can be considered one giant touchpad, but it's simply called the touchscreen.

Also, a laptop has an internal battery that makes it possible for you to lug it to a coffee shop or on an airplane, but laptop batteries are often heavier than the iPad's internal battery (they're typically much larger), meaning you've got a lot of added weight to carry.

The iPad also lacks items such as a CD or DVD drive, USB port(s), memory card slot, cables, and even a fan! These are all things found in laptops and some netbooks (as well as the nonportable desktop/tower/mini-tower computers), making them not as easy to tote around.

All computers as well as the iPad run a special piece of software called the *operating system*. You've probably heard of Windows, Linux, and Mac OS X, which are the names given to the operating systems found on laptops and larger computers. These are designed specifically for computers that have mice, external keyboards, and large screens that are not touch sensitive (although some are, by the way). However, the software found on the iPad is different—it's called iOS and is specially designed to work with the iPad and its touchscreen.

Because the iPad uses a unique operating system, it won't run the applications (games, spreadsheet, word processor, and so on) you're used to seeing on a computer. Instead of applications (or *programs* as they're frequently called), the iPad runs *apps*. You're going to learn all about iPad apps in the rest of this book, but I just wanted to point out that using an iPad requires a slight change in the way you think about using a digital device. With that said, I believe that learning to use the iPad is much easier than learning to use a laptop or desktop, with all its added complexities.

What Are the Benefits of an iPad?

I could write a number of chapters on all the great things I do with my iPad. And my list will differ from those of other iPad owners you ask. But one thing is for certain: What one person likes about the iPad will be something someone else hates. So in this section, I'm going to do my best to touch on the following things I believe most users would say the iPad does right (which is open to debate, of course):

- **Portability**—Yes, laptops are portable, but they're still heavy compared to the iPad. With Wi-Fi or a data connection, the iPad can provide access to the Internet, to email, to books and movies, and much more…and with less stress on your shoulders and back.

- **Long battery life**—Compared to laptops, the battery life on the iPad is a dream. My MacBook Air's battery can give me about 4 or 5 hours when it's not plugged in, but my iPad easily hits 7 or 8 hours (or more), depending on what I do with it. For example, I can watch about three 2-hour movies before a recharge is needed. Just searching the Web, checking email, and reading books? Easily 10+ hours before I need to charge that battery!

- **All-in-one media device**—There's nothing like carrying all my books, movies, music as well as my calendar and contacts on one lightweight iPad. My laptop can do this, too, but the iPad lets me do it more comfortably in the car, on a plane, in a boat, or on a train (apologies to Dr. Seuss).

- **Instant On**—My desktop computer takes about 3 minutes to completely turn on before I can do anything with it. My laptop takes about a minute. My iPad? I turn it on and it's ready to go. No waiting. The same goes for applications. Some of the games and productivity applications that I have to double-click to open on my desktop or laptop can take 15 seconds, 30 seconds, or even a minute (or longer) to open up. Contrast that with a single tap on an iPad app, which typically opens in less than 3 seconds. (The app I have that takes the longest to load opens in about 10 seconds—I can live with that.)

- **Games**—There are technology purists out there who would never admit to using an iPad for games, but the honest truth is that there are folks who buy the iPad simply for the games! With the excellent graphics and the big multitouch screen (meaning a game can take advantage of the screen being touched in two or more different locations simultaneously), it's no surprise that the game apps for the iPad pretty much outnumber all other categories. If you've got a favorite type of game (shooter, logic, RPG, and so on), you can rest assured that there are games in that genre available for you to play!

What Are the iPad's Weaknesses?

I don't consider the differences between how computers operate and how the iPad operates to be weaknesses. For example, whereas some users consider the lack of an external keyboard a weakness, others consider it a benefit. Users often want all the functionality they're used to having from their computers squeezed into their iPads. But in a sense, having all that functionality (including portability) would simply make the iPad a laptop. And in that case, why wouldn't you just buy a laptop? This is an argument that will go on and on.

No, when I speak of weaknesses, I'm talking about actual limitations in either the hardware or software that can reduce the iPad's usefulness to its user from the standalone view of the iPad, not via a comparison to a laptop.

For example, the iPad comes with a fixed amount of internal memory. When you purchase an iPad, you can choose from three different memory amounts: 16GB, 32GB, and 64GB. As you add apps, photos, videos, and eBooks to your iPad, that memory gets used—and eventually you run out. Because the iPad has no way to increase that memory (using a memory card, for example), you're forced to delete some stuff off your iPad if you want to free up some memory.

Another weakness that many iPad users have encountered is the lack of a USB port. USB devices are everywhere, and all of us are quite used to how easy it is to plug in a USB printer, camera, or other device to our computers. Because the iPad lacks a USB port, users are forced to purchase special cables or apps that allow them to work around this limitation. These are often called just that—*workarounds*.

What about software weaknesses? Well, I encounter a big one every time I want to use my iPad for my job. I write for a living, and my publishers expect me to deliver my chapters using the Microsoft Word application. But guess what? There is no Microsoft Word app for iPad (yet). Although some apps try to deliver some (not all) of Word's features, I've yet to find one that does everything I need it to do. This is not Apple's fault, and it's not Microsoft's fault (well, maybe a little bit). It's simply the reality I face when I want to write on my iPad. I can do so, but I can't use the application I prefer or that is required by my job. (Rumor has it that Microsoft may be releasing a version of Office for the iPad in 2013, so you may very well be using Word or Excel by the time you're reading this.)

Whether you're talking about hardware or software, one thing is for certain: The iPad is constantly being pushed to its limits. This means that although a weakness may exist today, there's a possibility someone will come up with a fix in the near future. It may be an update from Apple or it might be a piece of hardware or an app from a third party that fills the need. Ultimately, today's iPad limitations may not exist tomorrow.

A Closer Look at the iPad Hardware

Before ending this chapter, I want to take you on a quick tour of the actual hardware of the iPad . This won't take long at all, mainly because the iPad's design keeps things simple.

 NOTE   Keep in mind that the iPad mini has identical external features as its big brother, so while I'll be showing you the items on the 10" version, the buttons are in the same locations on the iPad mini.

Take a look a Figure 1.1. This is a photo of the front of the iPad taken in Portrait view (with the touchscreen facing up).

FIGURE 1.1

The iPad in Portrait view with the touchscreen visible.

As you can see, the iPad in Portrait mode shows only three things: the touchscreen, the webcam (used for taking photos and talking to friends and family using a special app called FaceTime—see Chapter 10, "Apps for Instant Communication," for more information), and the Home button. I'll go into more detail about the function of the webcam and Home button later, but I just wanted you to know where they were located.

Next, Figure 1.2 shows the backside of the iPad (still in Portrait view). Once again, the list of hardware visible is short: just the camera lens and speaker. What the speaker does is obvious—sounds come out of it. The camera lens is used for taking pictures and shooting video—you'll learn how in Chapter 9, "Apps for Photos and Videos."

Camera lens

FIGURE 1.2

The iPad reverse side in Portrait view.

Figure 1.3 shows the iPad in Portrait view, but from a unique angle. If you look along the top edge, you'll see the headphone port (for plugging in a set of headphones) and the Sleep/Power button. (Chapter 2 explains how the Sleep/Power button works.) And near the top of the right-edge of the iPad you'll see a small toggle switch, which can serve as either a mute button or a lock button for keeping the screen from changing views when you rotate the iPad between Portrait and Landscape views, and the volume buttons (the top one increases the volume and the bottom button decreases the volume).

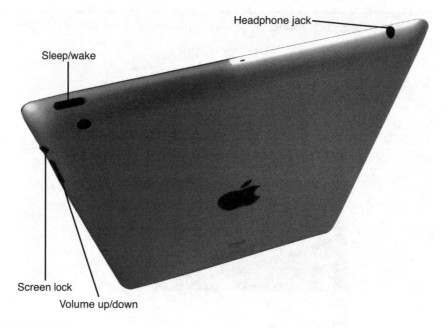

FIGURE 1.3

The top edge of the iPad in Portrait view.

Finally, Figure 1.4 shows the bottom edge (in Portrait view) and the docking port. The docking port sits right beneath the Home button and is used not only to charge the iPad but to plug in third-party hardware to provide other functionality (such as a special cable used to transfer photos and videos from a camera to the iPad or a special keyboard to dock the iPad upright and charge it while you type).

FIGURE 1.4

The bottom edge of the iPad in Portrait view.

What did you not see? That's easy. There's no access panel to pull out the battery. And there's no USB port or memory card slot for adding more memory. And unless Apple increases the thickness of the iPad in a later version, you'll also not see a CD/DVD drive of any sort.

Yes, the iPad's frame/shell is super-simple. And that makes complete sense, in a way: The more hardware features are added to the iPad, the shorter the battery life *and* the more complex the software and operating system must be to use those additional features.

2

OVERVIEW OF iOS

Say Hello to iOS!

Before you start learning how to use your iPad, you're going to need to turn it on and go through a basic setup routine. Don't worry—it's extremely easy to follow and understand. But just in case you're a bit nervous, I'm going to walk you through some of the steps.

Keep in mind that Apple does update the setup routine occasionally, so by the time you're reading this, there might be an additional screen added or an existing screen might look a bit different. The main point is that the setup routine deals with one thing at a time. Go slow, read all the instructions on the screen, and you'll be fine. If you choose to skip something (such as setting up the Wi-Fi connection), you can always reconfigure your iPad later.

NOTE Earlier iPad versions (1 and 2) required you to connect the iPad to your computer to sync with the iTunes application. You even had to install iTunes on your computer prior to setting up your iPad if you didn't already have it installed! But since the iPad 3's release, the iPad can now be set up without needing to connect to a computer. All that's needed is a Wi-Fi signal, so make certain you have Wi-Fi set up in your home or office before turning on the iPad for the first time. If you don't have Wi-Fi available at your home or office, find a local coffee shop that offers free Wi-Fi and get yourself a cup of coffee or tea while you're at it. (Likewise, you can skip some of the setup steps if you don't have access to Wi-Fi and do them later once you have an Internet connection.)

1. Press and hold the Power/Sleep button on the top-right edge of your iPad, as shown in Figure 2.1.

FIGURE 2.1

Press and hold the Power button for 5 seconds.

2. Release the Power button when you see the Apple icon in the center of the screen. This may take a few minutes of your time, as the iPad is unpacking and installing some files so that you can begin using the tablet. Be patient, and when you see the screen shown in Figure 2.2, continue to step 3.

FIGURE 2.2

Slide the button to the right to begin.

3. Next, you're going to need to select the language you want to use (I'm assuming English, but there are other options), and tap the right-arrow button in the upper-right corner of the screen as shown in Figure 2.3.

FIGURE 2.3

Select the language you wish to use for your iPad.

4. Next, you'll select your country and tap the Next button.

5. You should now see the screen asking for the Wi-Fi network you want to join as shown in Figure 2.4. Tap it with your finger, and then use the onscreen keyboard that appears to type in the password. Press Done to connect to the network.

 TIP You can skip the Wi-Fi network selection if you want and configure it later. (Likewise, if you purchased an iPad that supports a data connection via a cellular network, this will automatically work once the iPad finishes the setup routine.)

FIGURE 2.4

Select the Wi-Fi network you want to use with your iPad, and enter a password if needed

6. The iPad Activation step will begin, requiring you to wait a few minutes while it does some software configuration. When that's completed, you'll be asked whether you want to enable Location Services. I recommend against enabling Location Services until you understand more about how it works. Choose the Disable Location Services button.

7. Now you will choose whether you are setting up your iPad as a New iPad or if you want to restore settings that are saved by Apple or in the iTunes software. Because you're just starting with your iPad, select the Setup as New iPad option shown in Figure 2.5, and then tap the Next button.

 NOTE iPad no longer requires you to connect to a computer running iTunes, but if you are already a user of iTunes, you can connect your iPad after the setup routine is completed and synchronize your iPad's various settings in case your iPad is lost or stolen; you can connect a replacement iPad to iTunes and get all your settings and data back.

FIGURE 2.5

Configure your iPad as a New iPad.

8. Up next, you'll need to login with an Apple ID or create one as shown in Figure 2.6. Log in or tap the Create a Free Apple ID button and follow the on-screen instructions.

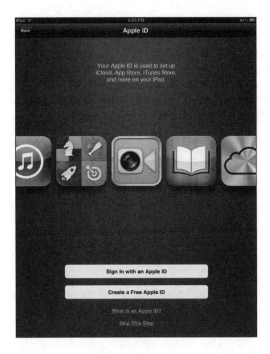

FIGURE 2.6

Login with an Apple ID or create one.

9. The next step requires you to accept Apple's Terms & Conditions. Read through the text and tap the Agree button to continue. (If you Disagree, you won't be able to use your iPad, so you really have no choice but to accept the Terms & Conditions if you want to use your new iPad.)

10. You'll next be asked whether you want to use iCloud. Go ahead and click the Use iCloud button shown in Figure 2.7. You'll learn about iCloud later in the book, and can disable it if you want, but for now there's no real harm in enabling it for your iPad.

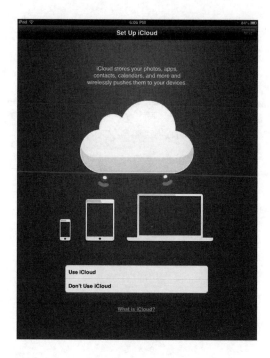

FIGURE 2.7

Choose to use iCloud for backing up your iPad's information.

11. Enter an email address to be used with FaceTime, the iPad's video chat feature. You'll learn more about FaceTime in Chapter 10, "Apps for Instant Communication," but for now go ahead and enter an email address and tap the Next button.

12. Siri is a voice-activated feature that allows you to press and hold the Home button to ask questions ("What is the weather for Atlanta, Georgia, today?") and get Siri to provide answers. It's a fun feature, so tap the Enable Siri button unless you don't think you'll use it.

13. Next, you'll be asked to allow or disallow diagnostic information to be sent to Apple. I recommend allowing this option—it requires no additional work on your part, and it does help Apple locate and troubleshoot bugs with the iPad's software so it can release updates.

14. And the last screen will ask you to register your iPad.

15. When the setup routine is done, you'll see a screen like the one in Figure 2.8.

FIGURE 2.8

The setup routine finishes and you're ready to start using your iPad.

16. Tap the Start Using iPad button and that's it! You've now set up your iPad, and it's ready to be used.

In the remainder of this chapter, I'll explain more about what you're actually seeing on the iPad's screen and give you additional background on the software that has just been installed on your new iPad. The software you just installed and configured is called iOS. Although the iPad hardware is certainly important, without iOS, that hardware is pretty much useless to you.

What Is iOS?

If you're familiar with any computer system, then you probably know about Microsoft Windows, Mac OS X, and Linux. Every computer has an operating system (OS), and it's the OS that makes it easy for us humans to get work done with digital devices. Without an OS, computers would be almost useless to us. We'd have no way to type documents, move files around, email photos to our friends, and a thousand other tasks.

In the early days of computing, an operating system was nothing more than a blinking cursor on the screen and required typing cryptic commands such as `del *.*` and `rm *`. Do those look fun to use? Believe it or not, some folks out there prefer this old style of control, but for most of us this method of communicating with a computer just isn't feasible.

The next step for operating systems came when those confusing, text-based commands were replaced with a graphical "desktop"—a new way to visualize our data as well as the work we did on that data. No longer did we need to type `copy jim.txt jim2.txt` to copy a file with a new name. Now, we could move the mouse pointer over the file, click it, select Copy from a menu on a toolbar, and type in the name of the new file. There were arguments that this method was slower because you had to click here, drag there, click here, type there. But even if typing `copy jim.txt jim2.txt` got the job done 2 seconds faster, it wasn't intuitive or easy to remember for most people. The graphical user interface (GUI) was born, and it continues to be the one used for today's modern operating systems, including Apple's Mountain Lion (Mac OS X), Microsoft's Windows 8, and Linux.

Now we've reached a point in time when our mobile devices are doing almost as much work for us as our computers and laptops. Maybe even more! I certainly use my iPad and my iPhone for more of my day-to-day duties than ever before. I read and send emails, I take digital photos, I check news and weather, and I even read my eBooks on these devices. About the only thing I use my MacBook Air laptop for these days is typing up chapters like this one! (Oh, and I do play some fun games on my laptop that are much easier on the eyes with the larger screen.)

Because our mobile devices can do many of the same things as their older cousins (the desktop and laptop computers), it makes sense that they also have an equally useful operating system—some method for you to perform your work (or play games), check your email, send files, and much more. For tablets and phones not made by Apple, the operating system typically is either Microsoft's Windows 8 or some version of Google's Android OS. But for the iPad and iPhone, that operating system is called iOS.

iOS is a GUI (pronounced *gooey*), which is short for *graphical user interface*. Users of both iPads and iPhones use this operating system instead of Mac OS X because iOS is designed to work with touch screens. From this point forward, I'm going to be talking specifically about the iPad and iOS, but just keep in mind that the iPhone also uses iOS, but with a smaller screen and some specialty apps designed for mobile phones. Other than that, iOS works the same for iPad and iPhone—it even shares the same version number. When iOS is upgraded, this upgrade is pushed out to both iPhone and iPad at the same time. You can see the lock screen of iOS in Figure 2.9, but keep in mind that this is only one possible home screen—iOS can have many, as you'll learn later in this chapter. To see the home screen on your own iPad, press the On button on the top-right edge for just a second and release it—tap and hold your finger on the little slider near the bottom of the screen (where it says Slide to Unlock) and drag it to the right.

Now let's talk about iOS and the iPad. As I'm writing this, the current version is iOS 6. Between now and when iOS 7 is (inevitably) released, Apple will provide smaller updates to fix bugs, make improvements in how the operating system works with the hardware, and add new software features. Rest assured, Apple doesn't sit still between releases of iOS, so as you use your iPad, just keep in mind that at some point an update (maybe even two or three) will come your way.

iOS is also one of the easiest operating systems to use because it requires the use of tools you're very familiar with—your fingers. Everything you do with your iPad involves using one or more fingers to interact with the touchscreen. You'll use your fingers to drag files, type email, play games, and much more. I'll show you later in this chapter all the various ways you use your fingers to control your iPad.

And, finally, iOS is a very stable operating system. I used my iPad 3 for over a year, and it never crashed or locked up on me. Never. Not once. And it's extremely fast. When you turn on the iPad, it starts immediately. There's no 30- to 60-second delay as it prepares itself to be used. It's ready to go when you are. Don't believe me? Well, it's time to take your iPad for a spin and see for yourself.

Take a Quick Tour of iOS

If your iPad isn't already on, go ahead and press the On button on the upper-right edge of the device. You will see a small slider bar that needs to be unlocked near the bottom of the screen, as shown back in Figure 2.1. Press your finger on the slider's arrow and move it to the right without lifting your finger from the screen (shown in Figure 2.9).

FIGURE 2.9

Slide your finger to unlock the iPad.

If you did this correctly, you should be presented with the iPad starting home screen, as shown in Figure 2.10. If the home screen isn't visible, try unlocking the iPad again. Doing so might require that you turn off the iPad (press and release the On button) and then turn it on again.

FIGURE 2.10

The iPad starting home screen.

Congratulations—you just performed your first gesture! I'll explain gestures in the next section, but in a nutshell they're a collection of movements performed by one or more fingers. What you just did is called the basic swipe. A swipe uses a single finger and can be done left-to-right or right-to-left. In this instance, you did a left-to-right swipe using the drag bar. Trust me, there are a *lot* more gestures that do some amazing things. Again, more on that shortly.

So now that you're looking at the iPad's home screen, I want point out a few things to you (see Figure 2.10).

First, along the top of the screen are the Wi-Fi signal strength (or the data connection strength if you're using your mobile carrier's service), the current time, and the battery meter. I'll show you in a later chapter how to set the time if it's not correct, but the iPad is fairly good at determining your current location using Wi-Fi or a data connection, so it's a good bet that the time is already correct.

The battery meter offers you two pieces of information: One is a percentage value of remaining battery power. In Figure 2.10, you can see that I have 94% left. To the right of the percentage value is a battery icon. As the battery drains, the outline of the battery change to appear more empty. I'm not certain why iOS offers both items; the percentage meter is more useful in my opinion, but you get both and there doesn't appear to be a way to turn either one off.

Let's continue down the screen. See all those small squares filling up most of the screen? Each of those is an *app*, the iPad version of an application. These are the tools you'll use to get things done, such as playing games, sending email, taking photos, reading eBooks, and much more. We'll get into these apps in more detail throughout the rest of the book, but before we continue with the home screen, tap the app labeled Calendar. When you do, you should see a screen similar to the one shown in Figure 2.11. (It'll be different because you're reading this on a different day than I took the screenshot.)

FIGURE 2.11

The Calendar app open to the current date.

I had you do this for two reasons. One, to teach you a new gesture—the simple Tap-to-Open gesture. And two, to show you how fast an iPad app typically opens. If you've never opened an app on an iPad or iPhone before, this probably surprised you. It's quick!

I'm not going to have you do anything with the Calendar app right now, so go ahead and close it down by pressing the Home button at the bottom of the iPad. Remember, it's the small black circle just below the touchscreen. Pressing this button once will close Calendar and return you to the home screen.

Continuing down the page, you'll notice one small dot underneath the collection of apps. If you look closer, you'll see that the dot on the far left is actually a small magnifying glass. The other dot represents a home screen, and you can have more than one home screen (11, actually). Each white dot indicates which home screen you are currently viewing relative to the other home screens so you can tell here that I've got additional home screens on my own iPad. Figure 2.11 shows an empty dot to the right of the white dot—this means there's a home screen to the "right." To view it, place a single fingertip on the screen (but not on an app) and flick your finger to the left like you're turning the page of a book. This swipe gesture will take you to the other home screen, shown in Figure 2.12.

FIGURE 2.12

Another home screen on the iPad.

This home screen doesn't have as many apps on it as the previous one. Go ahead and return to the previous home screen by performing another swipe gesture, but this time swipe to the right. Notice how the current home screen pulls to the right and is then replaced. It's like turning pages in a book!

 TIP I'll show you later how to add more home screens; this is a useful method for organizing your iPad as you add more and more apps to it. You can easily create a home page that has all your games, another that holds tools related to work, and another that has apps related to your personal life. Each home screen you add, by the way, adds another dot to the screen.

What happens if you swipe again from left to right? Go ahead and try it! You'll end up on the Search screen, shown in Figure 2.13. I cover this tool in Chapter 16, "Finding Things."

FIGURE 2.13

The iPad's Search screen.

Return to the iPad's primary home screen—I call it the *primary* home screen because any time you press the Home button while on any other home screen or on the Search screen, you'll be taken back to *this* home screen. I put all my favorite apps on the primary home screen for just this reason—rather than swiping, I can tap the Home button once to return to it (or twice if I'm in an app that's located on a home screen other than the primary home screen.)

Okay, we're almost done with our tour of the home screen. Just below the dots that represent your home screens you'll find what's called the Dock. Any apps stored on the Dock are always visible on any other home screen (but not the Search screen). You can always change the apps that are stored in the Dock as well as add two additional apps, for a total of six apps on the Dock. I keep my most used apps here—this includes my email, photo gallery, and web browser, among others. I'll show you how to move apps around on the screen as well as on and off of the Dock in the next section.

Moving Apps and Creating Folders

Apps can be moved easily around a home screen, but they can also be moved between home screens, allowing you to customize the primary home screen and the Dock to hold those apps that you use most often. You may have noticed that a home screen can only hold 20 apps (not including the Dock), but I'm also going to show you how to create folders that can hold many more apps, allowing you to store more than 20 apps per home screen.

First, return to the primary home screen by either swiping to it (if you're on a different home screen or the Search screen) or pressing the Home button. Now, tap and hold on the Calendar app until you see it start to dance. Seriously! It will begin to wiggle along with the other apps on the screen, as shown in Figure 2.14.

FIGURE 2.14

Dance of the iOS apps.

 NOTE Apps that don't have the small X are considered required iOS apps that cannot be deleted. They can be moved but not deleted from the iPad.

To move an app around on the home screen, simply tap anywhere on it and hold until it begins to wiggle (other than on the X) and then drag it with your finger. Go ahead and try it. As you move the app around, the remaining apps will shift location to let you squeeze in the app you are currently dragging.

While still holding down on the app, drag it all the way to the right edge of the screen and hold your finger there for a moment. After a brief pause, the home screen to the right will appear—this is how you can drag an app from one home screen to another. You can drag apps left or right, but they will not move to the Search screen; the primary home screen is as far left as you can place an app.

Drag the app you're holding back to the left and hold it until the primary home screen appears again. Lift your finger, and the app will drop where you place it. The dancing will continue until you press the Home button to cancel the move operation, but don't do that just yet.

While the apps are still dancing, tap and hold the Calendar app one more time and drag it directly over the Reminders app. Doing this will create a folder that contains both the Calendar and Reminder apps. You will see the two dancing apps underneath a text bar, as shown in Figure 2.15.

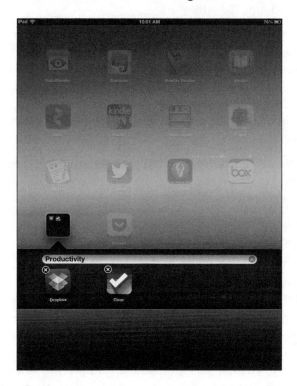

FIGURE 2.15

Creating a new folder containing multiple apps.

Tap on the text bar and use the onscreen keyboard to give the folder a name that suits the collection. Figure 2.15 shows that the folder is named Productivity. Other apps I'll probably drop in here include the Notes, Maps, and Contacts apps.

After typing in the folder name, tap on the Done button on the keyboard. Tapping anywhere outside the text bar and area where the wiggling apps appear will return you to the current home screen; you can select additional apps to drop into your new folder or just tap the Home button to stop the dancing apps. Easy!

Using Gestures with iOS

So far, you've used three gestures—swipe, tap-and-release, and tap-and-hold. However, you'll want to learn many more gestures to make using the iPad so much easier and fun. Here they are:

- **Reverse pinch**—This gesture uses your thumb and pointer finger. Place them together at a point on the screen, and if the app supports this gesture, pulling your fingers apart will cause anything visible on the screen to enlarge and zoom in. This is a useful gesture for working with photos or maps, for example. When you want to see more detail (such as zooming in on a street or a face in a crowded picture), the reverse pinch allows you to zoom in on an image.

- **Pinch**—With this gesture, you tap your thumb and pointer finger on the screen and pull them together. This allows you to zoom in on an image that has been expanded.

- **Five-finger collapse**—If you have an app open and want to close it quickly, just spread your fingers and touch the screen with five fingers and pull them together like you're squeezing a bit of dough.

- **Four-finger swipe (left/right)**—I haven't mentioned this yet, but when you open an app and then return to a home screen, the app hasn't really closed—it's running in the background, making it faster for the iPad to open it and display the exact spot where you left it (useful for games, for example). Because apps you've opened are all running in the background (it's called *multitasking*), you can easily move back and forth between these open apps by place four fingers on the screen and swiping left or right.

- **Four- or five-finger Multitask Viewer**—You can use the four-finger swipe (left/right) to move back and forth between open apps, but if you'd like to see the order in which the apps will open (depending on a left or right swipe), place four or five fingers on the screen and slide them up. This will open the Multitask Viewer near the bottom (where the Dock would normally sit) that shows all open apps. Use a single-finger swipe to move left or right to view all the open apps. The order in which you see them is also the order they will open when you use the four-finger swipe (left/right) gesture.

TIP After you've been using your iPad for a while, you'll have opened quite a number of apps. These are running in the background and eventually can impact the speed with which the iPad operates. Granted, you have to open a *lot* of apps for things to get sluggish, but it can and will happen. When this happens, open up the Multitask Viewer and press and hold on a single app. You'll once again see the dancing apps, but instead of an X to delete an app you'll see a minus sign (–). Tap the minus sign on an app to close that app completely and remove it from the Multitask Viewer. I do this at least once a week just to close down those apps that I'm not using regularly—I leave running those I like to use frequently.

Gestures can make using the iPad more enjoyable. You'll find yourself zipping between apps, checking email, sending a fast Tweet (via Twitter—see Chapter 11, "Social Apps"), and much more, all in seconds using a series of gestures. Spend some time practicing them and they'll quickly become second nature to you.

What About Typing?

Earlier in the chapter you did a single finger swipe all the way from the left to the right, revealing the Search screen. You probably saw the small onscreen keyboard that appeared, but if not jump back and take a look at Figure 2.13.

The onscreen keyboard will appear when it is needed and stay hidden when it is not. When does it appear? Basically any time some text needs to be entered—typing in an address while ordering something online via the web browser or creating an email message, for example.

Figure 2.13 showed the keyboard in Portrait view—the keys are smaller, but still fairly easy to use. You'll most likely use a single finger to type in Portrait view, but should you want some larger keys so you can type with your hands together as they would be on a typical keyboard, rotate the iPad to Landscape view when you see the onscreen keyboard appear. The keyboard will increase in size, as shown in Figure 2.16.

FIGURE 2.16

A larger keyboard is available in Landscape view.

Notice in Figure 2.16 that you can hide the keyboard by tapping the Hide Keyboard key in the lower-right corner (small keyboard icon with an arrow pointing down below it). You can tap the button to its left to gain access to numbers and special characters, as shown in Figure 2.17.

FIGURE 2.17

Access numbers and special characters on the keyboard.

Return to the letters on the keyboard by tapping the ABC button shown in Figure 2.17.

You can also choose to speak what you wish to type by using the Dictation button indicated in Figure 2.16. It's available on both the letters and numbers key screens (Figure 2.16 and Figure 2.17). Tap it once, and it will listen for you to speak. Tap it again when you're done. It's fairly accurate, but you may have to tap the text where you need to make corrections.

 NOTE The Dictation button is not Siri. Siri is always available by pressing and holding the Home button (see Chapter 16), but the Dictation button is available only when the onscreen keyboard is visible.

You'll also find the keyboard available whenever you are in an app that requires you to input your name, address, or other bit of information. The best thing about the onscreen keyboard is that it just seems to know when it's needed, and disappears when it's not needed. But just in case, you can always tap the Hide Keyboard key to make it go away. If you need it again, just tap anywhere you see a text box or place where text is required, and it will reappear.

iCLOUD AND SETTINGS

Customization and Backup

Both the iPad and the iPad mini are pretty much ready to go right out of the box. However, using certain features on these devices, you can perform some minor customizations to your iPad, making it feel a bit more like, well, *your* iPad.

One of the most important apps that comes preloaded on all iDevices is the Settings app, which I'll introduce you to in this chapter. The Settings app lets you tweak a setting here and tweak a setting there, further pushing the device to behave as you desire it to and less like a clone of every other iPad tablet out there.

And while the Settings app is specific to your iPad, there's another service I want to introduce to you that allows you to not only back up certain information from your iPad, but also allows you to move seamlessly between iDevices (such as your iPad and iPhone) when you're using certain apps. It's called iCloud, and you're going to want to use it, I'm certain.

Settings, Settings, Settings

Believe it or not, just after you turn on your iPad and follow the onscreen wizard that walks you through connecting it to the Internet, your iPad still has hundreds of settings you can tweak to customize your tablet. Fortunately, most of these settings aren't critical to your using and enjoying your iPad. Even better, many of the settings that relate to security are set to the more "locked down" option, making your device secure immediately—it'll be up to you to turn on or off certain settings that may or may not make your iPad more susceptible to risks.

All of these settings related to security are found in the Settings app, but hundreds more are not necessarily related to security, as you're about to find out.

 NOTE When you first turn on your iPad, you're going to want to have either a data service subscription from a carrier (such as Verizon or AT&T, for example) or access to a Wi-Fi connection. When you first turn on your iPad, it will try to connect to the Internet—but don't worry if you don't have a connection because you'll be able to connect at a later time using the Settings app.

Take a look at Figure 3.1 and you'll see the Settings app icon.

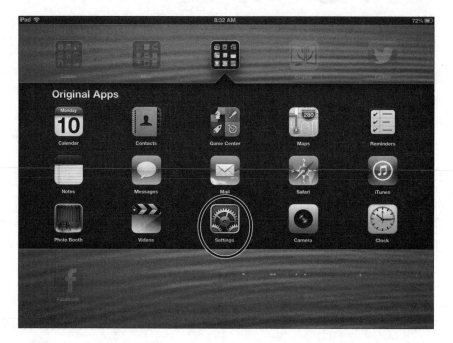

FIGURE 3.1

The Settings app icon.

When you tap the Settings app icon, it opens up the app immediately, and you'll see a screen similar (but not identical) to the one in Figure 3.2.

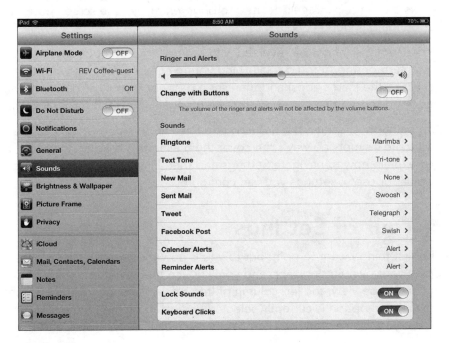

FIGURE 3.2

The Setting app is open and ready for you to explore.

Your screen won't look exactly like this because it's possible you have a 3G/4G/LTE version of the iPad that allows you to access the Internet using a data service provided by a mobile carrier such as Verizon or AT&T. As you can see, I have the Wi-Fi–only iPad, and I'm connected to my favorite coffee shop's free Wi-Fi.

 NOTE As I show you around the Settings app, keep in mind that you may see an occasional item in the figures that you don't see on your screen. This could be due to an update to iOS or an app that I have installed on my iPad that you currently do not have. The Settings screen is an ever-changing tool.

In the Settings app, you'll find all sorts of strange, unusual, and eye-catching items just begging to be touched and examined. Feel free to do so! Very few options in the Settings app cannot be undone; reversing a setting is often as easy as tapping it again (such as flipping a toggle switch from On to Off).

Often what I find works best when dealing with the various items that can be configured in the Settings app is to make a single change and then see how it affects the iPad. One example of this is turning on or off the clicking sound the keyboard makes as you type. Yet another example is a simple On/Off button that allows the Auto-Brightness feature to brighten or dim the screen based on the surrounding lighting conditions.

Other settings cannot be reversed with a simple tap of a button. For example, if you turn on the Auto-Lock (allowing you to set a screen password to gain access to the iPad's apps) and then set a password, you'll also need to enter that password to turn the Auto-Lock feature off again. So don't forget your password!

As I mentioned earlier, the Settings app has hundreds of settings you can tweak, and there's simply no way I can cover them all in this chapter. Instead, I want to first explain how to navigate Settings and then I'll show you some of the more popular or useful settings you can configure.

Take a Tour of Settings

The first thing I want to point out to you is how the Settings app is organized. Open your own Settings app and you'll notice that whether the iPad is in Portrait or Landscape view, the left column of items never changes. Figure 3.3 shows that the General option is currently selected (indicated by the blue bar that highlights it), but you can see many more options, such as Privacy, Notes, and Reminders.

FIGURE 3.3

The setting options run down the left side of the screen.

This list is scrollable; a simple swipe of your finger up or down will let you see additional options not currently visible. You'll see more of the list in Portrait view, but I prefer Landscape view.

 NOTE The remaining figures in this chapter are shown in Landscape view, so if you don't see an option on your screen that is referenced in the book, try scrolling up or down a bit.

When you tap an option in the left column, the right column will change to display items related to the settings option you selected. Figure 3.4 shows some of the options I can configure on the right side of the screen that are related to the General option I tapped in the left column.

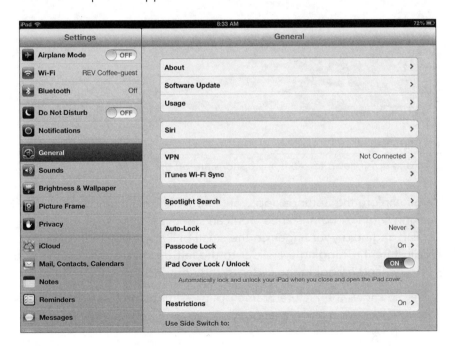

FIGURE 3.4

A selected option's configurable items appear on the right side.

Just as with the list of settings options on the left, the right side of the screen is often scrollable, so swipe a finger up or down to see if any configuration options are hidden just off the screen. As you can see in Figure 3.5, I scrolled down a bit for the General option (by swiping a single finger up—don't worry, you'll get the hang of this real quick) and there are even more configurable options available.

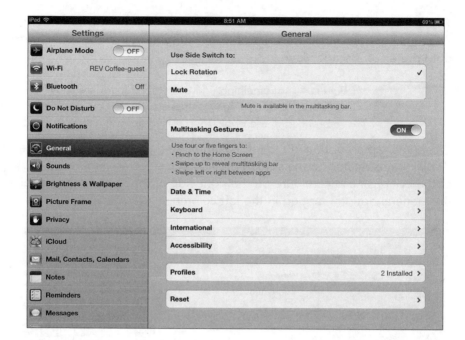

FIGURE 3.5

Be sure to scroll down to see if any options are off the screen.

As you explore the Settings app, you'll notice a small number of methods for tweaking settings. For instance, you can see the slider bar at the top of Figure 3.2. Tap and hold your finger on the small ball and drag it left or right to make an adjustment. Dragging the slider to the left decreases the volume of the ringers and alerts, and dragging the slider to the right increases the volume.

Figure 3.6 shows the Picture Frame option settings on the right and offers three other methods for making changes.

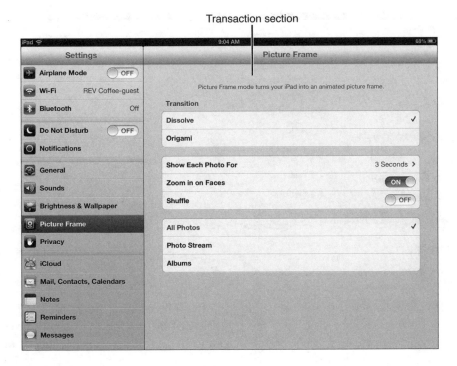

FIGURE 3.6

Methods for making changes in Settings.

First is the simple check mark seen in the Transition section. The check mark is on the Dissolve option, but a tap on the Origami option will move the check mark to that transition option. With a check mark, one option must always be selected within each group of options. If you look at the bottom group of options shown in Figure 3.6, you'll see a check mark next to All Photos. If you don't want the selected transition (Dissolve) to be applied to All Photos, tap the Photo Stream or Albums option to place the check mark there, but one of those three options must have the check mark next to it. (You'll learn all about photos, Photo Stream, and albums in Chapter 9, "Apps for Photos and Videos.")

Second is the On/Off toggle switch, which is also shown in Figure 3.6. If it's set to On, a single tap of your finger will move the switch to the Off position (and vice versa).

Figure 3.7 shows the final method for configuring options in Settings. It's the right-pointing arrow (or chevron).

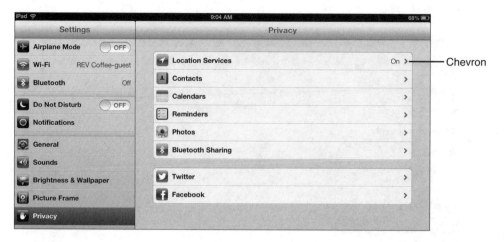

FIGURE 3.7

The right-pointing arrow (or chevron).

Here, I've selected the Privacy setting in the left column; the various options that can be tweaked are visible on the right side of the screen. Tap any right-pointing arrow (chevron), and you'll be taken to another page that has additional options that can be configured.

Now let's return to the left column for a moment. I want you to scroll down a bit until you see the list of apps that come preinstalled on your iPad, as shown in Figure 3.8.

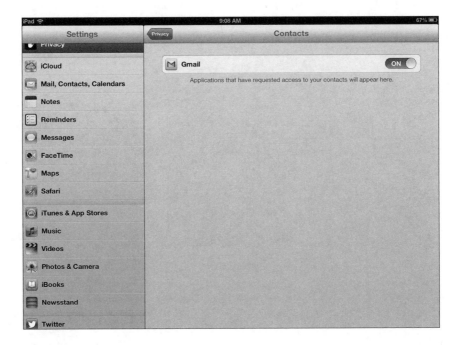

FIGURE 3.8

Preinstalled apps also have settings that can be tweaked.

Your list may look different (especially if there has been an update to iOS since I wrote this chapter), but the ones you'll most likely see are iCloud, Reminders, Messages, Safari, Music, and Photos & Camera, among others.

The list of options near the top of the left column are what you might call iOS-specific options. These settings are related to the operation of your iPad and are always in effect. The options for a preinstalled app are for making changes that only affect the specific app selected.

If I select In Kilometers instead of In Miles in the Distances option section, other apps I open may still show distances in miles; in other words, this setting is specific *only* to the Maps app.

At this point, you've probably not installed any additional apps on your iPad. (You'll learn how to do this in Chapter 12, "Apps for the iPad.") But once you start installing more apps, you'll find that many of them add a listing in the left column.

I haven't covered the Safari app yet (jump to Chapter 8, "The Safari App," for more details), but for now, just tap the Safari app icon shown in Figure 3.9.

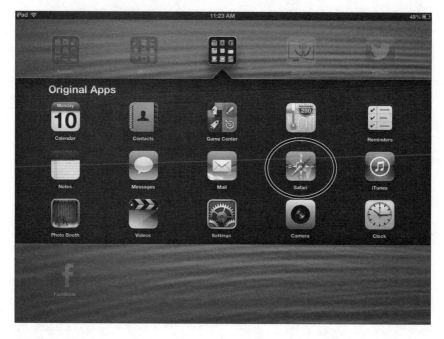

FIGURE 3.9

The Safari app icon.

Don't worry about all the stuff you see on your screen at the moment; instead, I want you to tap the Bookmarks button indicated in Figure 3.10 and then tap the iPad User Guide option in the menu that appears.

FIGURE 3.10

Access the iPad User Guide in Safari.

When you tap the iPad User Guide, it opens as shown in Figure 3.11. Scroll down the list on the left. When you tap on an item in that list, you'll find everything you need to know about configuring it on the right side of the screen.

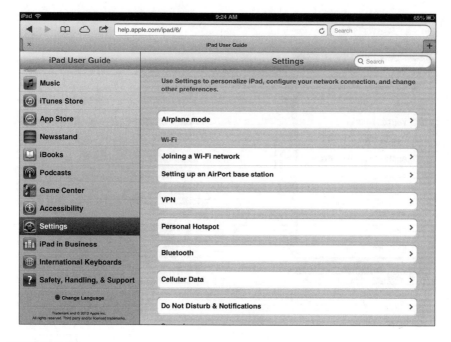

FIGURE 3.11

Search the iPad User Guide for help.

You'll find details for every one of the preinstalled apps on your iPad, including much more coverage of the Settings app than I can provide in this chapter.

 TIP   For third-party apps, you may have to visit the company's website for help. If you're lucky, the app developer has included documentation inside the app that may be accessed with a Help button or menu option. Look around or just contact the app developer and ask where you can get additional help if you need it.

Fun and Easy Settings to Tweak

I'm going to start at the top of the left column in the Settings app and mention some settings you might want to investigate. I won't be able to show all of them to you with figures, but they're not difficult to figure out. Remember, most settings are not destructive! You can undo almost any setting with ease.

Do you fly often? If so, the Airplane Mode button is your fast way to disable the wireless data feature on your iPad. Tap the button shown in Figure 3.12 to toggle it between On and Off. It's a quick method for disabling your electronic device, including Wi-Fi, Bluetooth, and cellular/mobile data signals. Any apps that depend on these signals won't work until you turn the Airplane Mode toggle switch back to the On position.

FIGURE 3.12

The Airplane Mode toggle switch.

If you're like me and you frequent coffee shops or other places where free Wi-Fi exists, you'll want to tap the Wi-Fi option and select the name of the Wi-Fi network (and provide a password, if necessary) so your iPad will have Internet access.

 TIP   I cover the Do Not Disturb and Notifications options in Chapter 17, "The Two iPad Centers," but for a quick way to disable your iPad's beeps and boops, tap the Do Not Disturb toggle switch to turn it to the Off position. This is very useful when you're heading into meetings, and I also like it when it's time for bed and I just don't feel like walking my iPad downstairs to charge it; I won't have to worry about a reminder or incoming email waking me up with a loud ding!

Tap the Brightness & Wallpaper option and then tap the image shown on the right to select a new wallpaper for your iPad. You can choose some images provided by Apple, or you can even choose an image from the Camera Roll, which contains photos you've taken with your iPad. (More on using the Camera app in Chapter 9.)

The Picture Frame options are fun to tinker with. When you first turn on your iPad, you'll see the Slide to Unlock slider, but look to the right and you'll see a small icon of a flower, as shown in Figure 3.13.

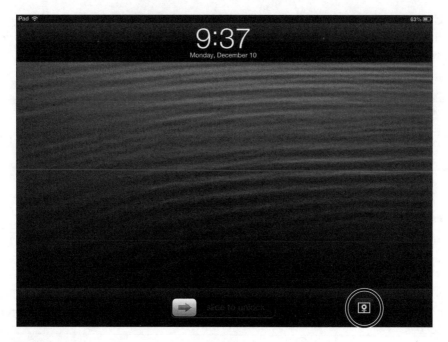

FIGURE 3.13

Launch the Picture Frame feature on your iPad.

Tapping this icon will turn your iPad into the most expensive Picture Frame you've ever owned (maybe). But rather than display a single photo, the Picture Frame feature cycles through all the photos you've saved on your iPad in the Camera Roll album. (Again, refer to Chapter 9 for more details on the Camera Roll album.)

 TIP The iCloud option is covered in the next section, but just know that the Settings app is the only place where you can configure iCloud options.

You'll be learning about the various preinstalled apps throughout the remainder of this book, so just remember to tap each of those apps in the left column and examine the options available on the right side of the screen.

You can easily spend an hour or two looking through every option in the Settings apps. Fortunately, you don't have to do this all at once. Instead, I recommend an occasional visit to the Settings app when you have a moment and picking a setting on the left and examining its options on the right. There are some options in the Settings app that I've never used, but I do know where they are located. The only way you'll know about all the options available is to take the time and investigate.

The Power of iCloud

Before I get into the features of iCloud, you may actually be wondering just what is iCloud? Good question! I could go into a detailed, technobabble-filled explanation of cloud-based storage, but I'd rather just give you a clear, easy-to-follow explanation by telling you what iCloud can do for you. So here goes...

You're probably familiar with how your computer stores files on a hard drive; the hard drive is installed in your computer and has a certain amount of storage space—250 gigabytes (250GB) or 500 gigabytes or maybe event 1 terabyte (1,000 gigabytes!). Your iPad or iPad mini also has a certain amount of storage built in to it—8GB, 16GB, 32GB, or 64GB. If you have a photo stored on your computer or iPad, that photo is taking up some of that storage space. With me so far?

Let me stick with the photo for a few moments, but all of the following discussion relates to any data you use—email, contacts, music, video, and so on.

Now, that photo stored on your iPad can be shared with your family and co-workers, but only if they're sitting with you *and* only if you've got your iPad with you. In other words, that photo is "location locked."

Here's another problem with that photo (and all the other photos stored on your iPad)—if your iPad is lost, stolen, or damaged, that photo is gone. Unless you are able to recover your iPad, that photo is unrecoverable (unless you made a backup somewhere).

And here's yet another problem—photos start to really add up in terms of storage space. If you have 4GB of free storage space left on your iPad mini, it only takes about 1,250 photos to wipe that out! (My photos average about 3MB–4MB each, so 1,000 photos equals 4,000MB, or 4GB.) Once you've reached your iPad's storage limit, you'll have to start deleting photos, songs, videos, and apps.

Three big limitations or problems! Wouldn't it be nice if you had a way to circumvent these three issues? Imagine if you could share a photo with someone, even if you didn't have your iPad handy. Imagine knowing that your photos were backed up and available should the worst happen to your iPad. And imagine not having to worry about storage limitations. Sound good? Well, you're going to love iCloud.

iCloud is a service offered by Apple that makes the preceding problems disappear. And there are many more benefits to it that I'll explain shortly. In a nutshell, iCloud is a service offered by Apple that allows you to access photos, videos, contacts, and much more from any iOS or Mac computing device that also supports iCloud. iCloud also allows you to store your photos, contacts, and other items with Apple, reducing the demand on your iPad's storage space. Apples gives you an automatic 5GB of free storage space, and you can buy more if you need it with a yearly subscription fee. And by using iCloud, you reduce the risk to your data by storing it with Apple; if your iPad is stolen, for example, you can easily download your data right back onto a new iPad—photos, contacts, calendar events, and anything else you choose to back up to iCloud.

 CAUTION iCloud uses your Apple ID and password to recognize, provide, and back up your data. This means you're going to want to create a strong password that isn't easy to figure out. Don't use "password" or "123456," for example.

Figure 3.14 shows the iCloud settings options in the Settings app.

FIGURE 3.14

The iCloud settings options.

First, you'll always see your Apple ID account name at the top. If you never created an Apple ID, you're going to have to create one if you want to use iCloud (it's also required if you wish to download third-party apps to your iPad or buy music, videos, and eBooks).

If you need help creating an Apple ID, visit Apple.com/itunes for more information. Apple does just about everything via iTunes, and it's the easiest way to create an account and password. Please note also that iCloud does not require that you have a credit card stored on file with Apple, but for any purchases you make with your iPad (music, eBooks, videos, apps, and so on), Apple will require you to provide credit card information or have iTunes credit on file. (You can get iTunes gift cards that can be redeemed for credit to be used for purchases from Apple.)

 TIP For assistance on creating an Apple ID without a credit card on file, point your web browser to http://support.apple.com/kb/HT2534.

As you can see on the right side of Figure 3.14, a number of apps can be turned on or off for iCloud. Options include Mail, Contacts, Calendars, Reminders, Safari, Notes, Photo Stream, Documents & Data, and Find My iPad.

Any app that is turned on will have its data sent to iCloud. This creates a backup of that app's information as well as makes it available on other iDevices. For example, I have an iPhone with the Contacts app turned on in iCloud. This means that if I add a contact to the Contacts app on my iPad (see Chapter 4, "Contacts"), that contact will be stored with iCloud, and that update will be pushed to my iPhone's Contacts app as well.

The process works in the other direction, too. If I take a photo with my iPhone, that photo is sent to iCloud. When my iPad is connected to the Internet, that photo will be pulled down from iCloud and stored on my iPad because I have the Photo Stream service turned on (see Figure 3.14).

Want another example? Sometimes I don't have my iPad with me when I'm out running errands. If I open the Safari web browser app on my iPhone to check Amazon.com for the price on a book and then close down the app, when I get home and open the Safari app on my iPad, guess what happens? Yep, because I have the Safari app backing up its data to iCloud, when I open the Safari app, the last web page I was viewing on my iPhone (in this case, Amazon.com) will appear on my iPad. It's seamless, and it makes moving from one iDevice to another extremely easy. I'm using a MacBook Air laptop, and because I have iCloud running on it as well, I can move between my iPhone, iPad, and MacBook with ease. My contacts list is always updated and synchronized across all devices. Any new songs I purchase with iTunes (see Chapter 14, "Movies, Music, and More") will be visible on all three devices. If I buy an eBook, it is available on all three devices so I can read no matter which device I have in my hands at the moment.

iCloud is amazingly easy to use, but it does have some limitations.

First, obviously, is the 5GB of storage space provided to you. Believe it or not, that space runs out quickly, especially when you start adding new apps that can store their data on iCloud. As you can see in Figure 3.14, I don't have the Mail app backing up to iCloud because it quickly eats up my 5GB of space. I choose to use iCloud for my Contacts, Calendar, Reminders, Safari web browser, photos, and the Find My iPad option (which I'll explain shortly).

What do you do if you find you need more storage space from iCloud? Tap on the Storage & Backup button, shown in Figure 3.14, and you'll be taken to a screen like the one in Figure 3.15.

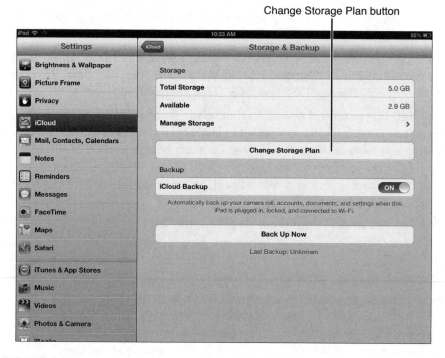

FIGURE 3.15

The iCloud Storage & Backup settings screen.

I'll explain a few items of interest on this screen. First, you can view how much storage space you currently have access to (I have 5.0GB) and how much is currently available (I have 2.9GB left). I can tap the Manage Storage option if I wish to view a more detailed breakdown of just how much data each app is using.

Tap the Change Storage Plan button to purchase additional iCloud storage.

Keep in mind that this purchase is good for 1 year—you're not buying this extra storage space permanently. Tap the Buy button and follow the instructions if you wish to purchase additional storage space.

TIP You may have noticed that music isn't an option for backing up to iCloud. That's because Apple does not charge you storage space for songs you purchase from iTunes. This means if you only have 3GB of iCloud storage space left and you purchase 8GB of music from iTunes, you're still left with 3GB of free space because Apple will store your 8GB of iTunes music for you at no charge. Nice!

Notice the iCloud Backup toggle button set to On in Figure 3.15. I can turn that to the Off position and disable the automatic backup that occurs whenever my iPad connects to the Internet. I prefer to leave it on, but you might prefer to manually back up your iPad's data to iCloud.

NOTE If you wish to disable the automatic backup of your data to iCloud, toggle this button to Off and your iPad will only back up to iCloud (and grab any updates from another iDevice) when you synchronize your iPad with iTunes by connecting it to your computer with a USB cable.

You can also tap the Back Up Now button to immediately send any updates (such as a new contact in your Contacts app) to iCloud. The option is waiting for iCloud to automatically start the synchronizing process, which can take anywhere from 15 minutes to a few hours, depending on the size and quantity of data you need to back up.

I mentioned earlier that iCloud offers more services than just backing up your data, and the Find My iPad option is one great example. Should your iPad get lost or stolen, you'll want to open a web browser and point it to iCloud.com, tap the big Find my iPhone button shown in Figure 3.16, and then log in with your Apple ID and password.

FIGURE 3.16

Log in to iCloud.com and open the Find My iPhone service.

Don't worry—the Find My iPhone service will also find your iPad (and you may not even own an iPhone).

Figure 3.17 shows the map and the location of my iPad. (Fortunately, that's exactly where I happen to be at the moment.)

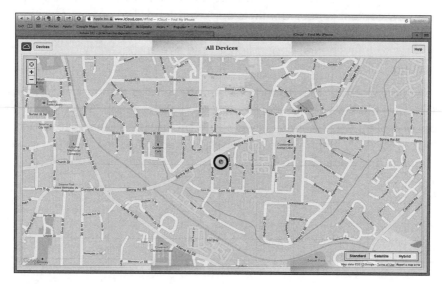

FIGURE 3.17

The map shows where my iPad is currently located.

If I tap the Devices button in the upper-left corner of the screen, I can select my iPhone or my iPad. When I tap on one of the devices, I'm given three options, as shown in Figure 3.18.

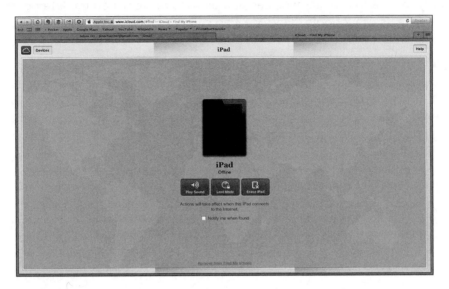

FIGURE 3.18

I have three options when trying to locate my iPad.

I've used the first option, Play Sound, more times than I can count. I have two small boys, and occasionally my iPad finds itself under a couch or into another room. When I tap the Play Sound button, as long as my iPad has Internet connectivity (and it does when it's at home), a minute or two later I'll hear a loud and distinct pinging sound.

The Lost Mode button will immediately lock your iPad so that it can only be unlocked with your Apple ID password. This is useful if you think your iPad has been lost or stolen. If you truly suspect your iPad is stolen and you don't have a password lock on it, you can use the Erase iPad button to wipe it clean. This is not reversible, so use this option with care!

 TIP Why aren't you using a password lock on your iPad? Open the Settings app, tap the General option on the left, and on the right side of the screen turn on the Passcode Lock option and create one! Yes, you'll have to type it in every time you turn on your iPad, but should a bad guy get your iPad, that password lock will keep your data secure.

I cannot recommend iCloud strongly enough. Even if you don't wish to back up your data (such as contacts and photos) to iCloud, do use the Find My iPad feature, if only to find your tablet should it become lost or stolen. It's such an easy feature to use, and you can find all sorts of stories on the Internet that will validate its use (google "Find My iPad success story" to read some great tales of recovered iPads, including stolen ones).

Remember, you get 5GB of free iCloud storage. Music, videos, and eBooks that you purchase from Apple are not charged against that 5GB of space. If you have an iPhone or Mac computer, enabling iCloud on these devices will allow you to share and synchronize data across all devices. And, should you run out of space, Apple is happy to sell you some more.

CONTACTS

Say Hello to the Contacts App

You've been learning about gestures and home screens and iCloud, but so far you haven't actually used any of the productivity apps on your new iPad. That's about to change. The best way for you to learn to use your iPad is to actually do something, and that means opening apps. I'll start you out slow by introducing you to the Contacts app, the standard iOS application for storing information such as phone numbers, addresses, birthdays, and much more, for your friends, family, co-workers, and miscellaneous contacts.

NOTE If you own an iPhone, you're probably already quite familiar with the Contacts app. The iPad and iPhone versions of the Contacts app work in an identical manner, so it's quite possible you may find your Contacts already synced from your iPhone to your new iPad via the iCloud service discussed in Chapter 3, "iCloud and Settings." If that's the case, you may still want to read through this chapter because it will show the Contacts app as displayed on the iPad's screen, and you might discover a feature or two you didn't know were available.

Take a look at Figure 4.1, which shows the icon for the Contacts app. For the remainder of this chapter, we'll be working in the Contacts app in Landscape view, but the Contacts app also works just fine in Portrait view.

FIGURE 4.1

The Contacts app icon as seen on the iPad screen.

Go ahead and tap the icon to open Contacts app.

Your contacts list running down the left side of the screen will not look like the one in Figure 4.2. Probably the only contact you and I will share at the start is the Apple Inc. listing—Apple has provided its 800 number, web address, and corporate address for you.

FIGURE 4.2

Use the + button to create a new contact.

If you've never used the Contacts app before, you'll probably have the Apple Inc. listing and nothing else. (iPhone users may see their contacts listed here, especially if iCloud has been enabled—refer to Chapter 3.)

Running down the left side of the screen, you'll see an index of letters and the # symbol. Unless you have dozens contacts in the list, tapping a letter or the # symbol won't do anything; however, they are provided for jumping to the letter of either a contact's last name (if you provided one) or first name. For example, take a look at Figure 4.2 and you'll see that I have five contacts entered using only their first names. They are each listed under the letter that corresponds to their first name.

I also have a contact entry for John Smith, but because he has a last name, his contact information is filed under the letter *S*, not *J*.

But that's enough about my contacts. I want to walk you through adding a new contact to the Contacts app.

Adding a New Contact

Adding a new contact is super-simple—simply click the + button at the bottom of the left page, as indicated in Figure 4.2.

Tapping the + button opens a blank Info window and the onscreen keyboard, as shown in Figure 4.3.

FIGURE 4.3

The onscreen keyboard and a blank Info page.

Name—A blinking cursor will be placed in the First text box, but you can tap in another box (such as Last, Company, or Phone) to enter information elsewhere. I'm going to start by entering a new contact named Sally Mason.

Mobile Number—Next, I'll enter the contact's mobile phone number. I don't have to tap the hyphen (-) key because the hyphen is automatically provided as I type out the number.

iPhone or Custom Number—After you enter a phone number, the Contacts app automatically adds a new phone number field labeled iPhone. Don't worry—you can change this label by simply tapping it. A list of custom options appears, which allows you to choose Home, Work, Mobile, and other options.

Take a look to the left of each of the new phone numbers you've added and you'll see two red circles with a minus sign inside. Tap one of these, and a red Delete button appears to the right of the number, as shown in Figure 4.4. Only tap the Delete button if you're absolutely certain you want to remove the entry— you will not be asked to confirm the deletion.

> **TIP** If you tap to place the cursor on an existing bit of text, you'll also see a small gray circle with an X inside. Tapping this will delete the existing text but will not remove the new label you've selected.

Figure 4.4 shows that I've continued to add more numbers, including a Twitter name and an extension number for this contact's work number. This additional information will show up on a contact's information page when you tap a contact's name in the Contacts app.

FIGURE 4.4

Finishing out the phone numbers.

Add Photo—To add a photo, simply tap the Add Photo button to the left of the contact's name. You'll be given two options: Choose Photo and Take Photo.

If your new contact is currently with you, simply ask them for permission to take the photo, press the Take Photo button, and hold the iPad up so you can see your contact's smiling face on the screen. Tap the green button with the camera icon on it, as shown in Figure 4.5.

FIGURE 4.5

Take a photo to add to your new contact's Info page.

If you're happy with the photo, tap the Use Photo button that now appears in place of the green button or tap the Retake button to try again. After tapping the Use Photo button, the new image will be added to the left of the contact's name.

If you already have a photo of your contact stored on your iPad, tap the Choose Photo button and then select the Camera Roll option that appears. A collection of thumbnails will appear, as shown in Figure 4.6.

FIGURE 4.6

Select an existing photo to add to a contact's entry.

Tap a thumbnail to select that image and then move it around with your finger to center it in the box. Tap the Use button in the upper-right corner, as shown in Figure 4.7, and your selected photo will be added to the contact's Info page.

FIGURE 4.7

Center your selected photo and tap Use.

Email Address—Adding an email address works just like adding a phone number—when you add one, another blank text box will appear below it. In this manner, you can add email addresses for home, work, and other. You can even create a custom label.

Figure 4.8 shows that I've added a home and work email as well as a custom label (tap Add Custom Label to create your own).

FIGURE 4.8

Additional email addresses can be added as needed.

Once again, red dots appear to the left of the email addresses so you can delete any or all if necessary.

Ringtone and Text Tone—Scroll down a little more, and you'll see the Ringtone and Text Tone boxes. These allow you to assign specific sounds that are heard when that contact calls you or sends you a message. (I'll cover the Messages app in Chapter 10, "Apps for Instant Communication.") To be honest, these aren't all that useful for the iPad, but they are great if you're an iPhone user. Feel free to experiment with them by tapping the current selection; a pop-up window will appear like the one shown in Figure 4.9 that you can scroll up and down. Tap a ringtone name to select it and hear it play; Marimba is the default, if you want to switch back to the original sound.

FIGURE 4.9

Change ringtones for individual contacts.

Website—Does your contact have a website? If so, you can enter that information in the Home Page text box.

As with phone numbers and email addresses, you can add more than one website, including changing the label to home, work, or other. You can even create your own custom label.

Mailing Addresses—Scroll down the Info page a little more and you'll reach the Add New Address text box. Here's where you can enter your contact's mailing address (street, city, state, ZIP code, and country). Once you enter the first street address, a second Street text box will appear below it should you need it.

Below the first mailing address you'll see a green circle with a plus sign inside. Tap it to add another mailing address. You can always tap the existing label to view a pop-up list that offers additional labels, plus the ability to create a custom label.

Add Field—Tap the green circle to the left of the Add Field button, and a scrollable list will appear like the one shown in Figure 4.10.

FIGURE 4.10

Additional fields can be selected or created.

Scroll through this list, and you'll see many options—birthday, related people, date (this one is used for an anniversary), and more.

When you choose to add a new field, the new field doesn't always appear at the bottom of the Info page. For example, when I selected Job Title from the Add Field list, a new field was added below this contact's last name, as shown in Figure 4.11.

FIGURE 4.11

New fields are placed in different locations.

Figure 4.12 shows where I scrolled back down to the bottom of the Info page so that you can see I've added this contact's anniversary date. Below that, I've tapped the Add Field button and selected Instant Message from the scrolling list. This adds a new field that can hold a username for any of the popular instant messaging services such as AIM or MSN Messenger. You can tap the service name and get a scrollable pop-up list of other services. I selected Skype as the Instant Messaging service and added a Skype user name. (Additional services include Facebook and Yahoo! Messenger, but you can also create a custom service name.)

FIGURE 4.12

Add more information, such as special services.

Notes—The Notes field is nothing more than a scratch pad of sorts—you can type anything you like inside. Type a bit of text and then tap the Return button to move to the next line. There doesn't seem to be a limit to how much you can type, but obviously the more concise the information is, the less scrolling you'll have to do when you're viewing the contact's Info page.

After tapping the Done button, I'm returned to the Contacts app and my new contact is displayed on the right side of the screen, as shown in Figure 4.13. (Alternatively, I can click the big red Delete Contact button to delete the entire listing.)

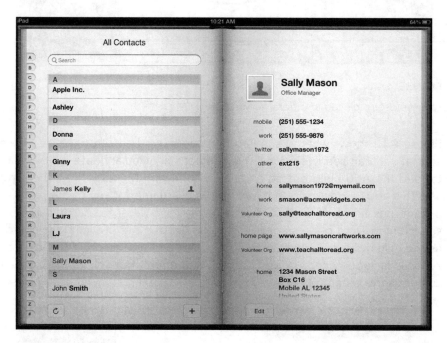

FIGURE 4.13

The new contact's Info page is displayed.

Depending on how much information you entered, the new contact's Info page might scroll up and down. I've entered quit a bit of info on this contact, so I have to scroll all the way up to see her phone numbers and email addresses and all the way down to see the notes.

Speaking of scrolling all the way down, notice the four new buttons at the very bottom of the contact's Info page: Send Message, FaceTime, Share Contact, and Add to Favorites, all shown in Figure 4.14. I'll go over these buttons in just a moment, but I'd also like to point you to the Edit button at the bottom of the same screen.

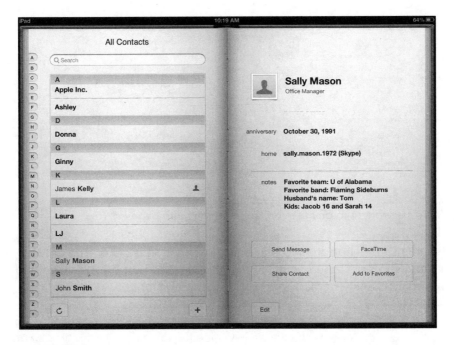

FIGURE 4.14

Five buttons are available at the bottom of a contact's Info page.

If you select a contact from the left side of the screen and scroll down the displayed Info page on the right, tap the Edit button to reopen the Info screen and make any changes you like, including deleting entries. Just remember to click the Done button when your edits are finished.

There is a shortcut, however, if all you wish to do is delete a bit of info on a contact's Info page. All you have to do is place your finger on the line containing the info you wish to delete and then swipe left. When you do this, a Delete button will appear to the right of the line you've swiped (see Figure 4.15).

FIGURE 4.15

There's a shortcut to delete information from an Info page.

Tap the Delete button, and that bit of information is gone. The only way to add it back is to select the contact again, tap the Edit button, and add the deleted information once more.

TIP If you change your mind about making a deletion using the swipe shortcut, simply swipe the same line but this time swipe to the right. The Delete button will disappear.

Okay, now let's return to those four new buttons at the bottom of a contact's Info page. I'll go over each of them in their own sections next.

Send Message

Because you haven't yet reached the chapters that cover the Mail and Messages apps, I'm not going to go into the Send Message option in much detail here. Instead, I'll remind you in Chapter 7, "The Mail App," and Chapter 10, where this button will come in handy.

Tapping the Send Message button opens a window that allows you to select a contact's phone number, email address, or other type of account (such as Twitter) to launch the matching app that will let you contact your, uh, contact. Again, the selection you make from the list will decide what other iOS app opens to let you continue.

FaceTime

Just like the Send Message button, the FaceTime button will launch its respective app and attempt to make a video call to your contact. I cover FaceTime in Chapter 10. There are some caveats about using this service that you'll need to know before using it, so just know that if you and your contact both have devices that support FaceTime (iPhone, iPad, iPod touch, iPad mini, Mac OS), you can make video calls and see and speak to one another.

Again, I'll cover FaceTime a bit later in the book, but just remember after you've gone through that chapter that you can select the FaceTime option when viewing a contact's Info page.

Share Contact

I cover the Mail app in Chapter 7. You're probably familiar with email already, which means you probably know about attachments. If not, an attachment is simply a file that you send along with an email message.

When you tap the Share Contact button, you'll have two options—Email or Message. I'll choose Email and the Mail app will open. The information for the contact you are currently viewing will be saved as an attachment that can be emailed to someone else. If you send this to someone else who has the Contacts app, tapping on the attachment will automatically add that information to their list of contacts. Figure 4.16 shows a new email message that will be sent to Donna Kelly. The Sally Mason information is appended to the bottom of the message—all I have to do is click the Send button and the information is on its way to Donna.

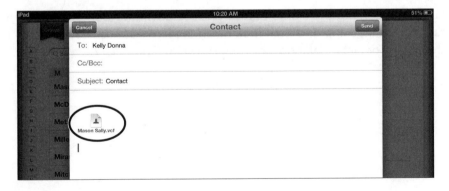

FIGURE 4.16

Share details of a contact with someone else.

Add to Favorites

Finally, tapping the Add to Favorites button really only does one thing—it allows you to add that contact's email address to the FaceTime app. The FaceTime app has a Favorites tab that saves you time having to hunt down a contact's email address (FaceTime uses email addresses to make the connection).

 TIP If you're an iPhone user and have iCloud syncing between your iPhone and iPad, you'll also be able to use this button to send a contact's phone number to the Phone app's Favorite tab.

FaceTime is covered in more detail in Chapter 10, so just remember that when you're viewing a contact's Info page, you can send that person's email address directly to the FaceTime app so it can be added to the Favorites tab.

Settings Tweaks

Back in Chapter 3, I introduced you to the Settings app. The Settings app can be a bit overwhelming if you've never used it before, so once again I'll ask you to just follow along with my instructions if you want to keep the information overload to a minimum. I'll continue to show you how to use the Settings app where it's applicable in each chapter. You'll be happy to know that the Settings app has a very short list of options for the Contacts app.

Go ahead and tap the Home button to close down the Contacts app. Find and tap the Settings app and then look down the left-side list of options until you see the Mail, Contacts, Calendars option, shown in Figure 4.17.

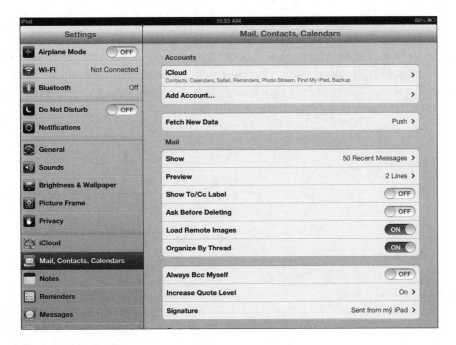

FIGURE 4.17

The Mail, Contacts, Calendars option in Settings.

Tap the Mail, Contacts, Calendars option and you'll see way more information on the right side of the screen than you probably care to view. Don't worry about all that stuff—just scroll down the right side (by swiping a single finger upward on the screen) until you see the section labeled Contacts.

There are three options here: Sort Order, Display Order, and My Info.

Sort Order—If you tap Sort Order, you can select between sorting your contacts by their first or last names. The default is to sort by last name and then to resort to first name if no last name exists. But if you prefer to view all contacts in your list by their first names, select First, Last as the option.

Display Order—Tap the Mail, Contacts, Calendar option to return to the Contacts section and then tap the Display Order option. Once again, you can choose between First, Last or Last, First for the order in which you want names displayed. If you choose Last, First, contact names running down the left side of the Contacts app will be displayed with the last name followed by the first name.

My Info—Once again, tap the Mail, Contacts, Calendar option to return to the Contacts section. This time, tap the My Info option. Here, you can select your own contact information in the Contacts app. If you haven't added yourself to the Contacts app, go ahead and do so—having your information in there is useful for other apps that can access this information. I go over this in more detail later in the book where this info will be useful.

5

NOTES AND REMINDERS

My iPad goes everywhere I do—I call it my personal assistant for a reason! It provides me with a lot of tools, including email, web browser, instant messaging, maps, and much more. I showed you in Chapter 4, "Contacts," how to use your iPad to keep all of your contacts in one place, and in the next chapter I'm going to show you how to use the Calendar app for keeping your appointments and important dates always at hand.

But between accessing my contacts and my calendar, there are two reasons I use my iPad often and cannot live without it. The first is the ability to take quick notes. Regardless of whether I'm on a phone call, in a face-to-face meeting, or stuck in traffic, I open the Notes app when I need to jot down some basic text so I won't forget.

And speaking of not forgetting, that's the other benefit I get from keeping my iPad handy—reminders. The Reminders app keeps me organized, reminding me of conference calls with my editor, chapters due, doctor and dentist appointments for my kids, and much more.

The best thing about the Notes and Reminders apps is that they're just so simple to use. Let me show you.

 NOTE iPhone owners who use iCloud will find that the Notes and Reminders apps share entries between the iPad and the iPhone. Create a reminder in your iPad and that reminder will be synced with your iPhone. Likewise, type up a note on your iPhone and later you can edit it on a larger screen by opening the same note on your iPad.

Takin' Some Notes!

The Notes app has been included with every version of iOS, and you'll be happy to know it's still available with the newest versions of iPad and iPad mini, as well as the iPhone 5. You can see the icon for the Notes app in Figure 5.1.

FIGURE 5.1

The icon for the Notes app.

Tap the icon to open the Notes app and you'll be greeted by a blank note page, as shown in Figure 5.2.

The Notes list only appears when the
iPad is turned on its side—or landscape view

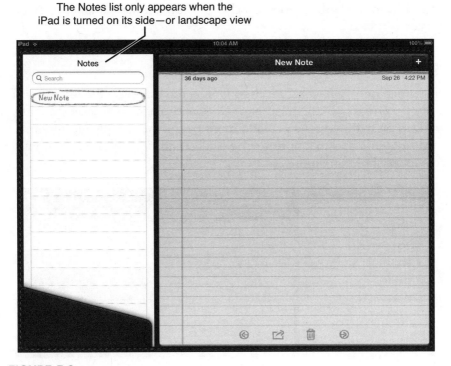

FIGURE 5.2

Opening the Notes app.

 NOTE As a reminder, I'll be using Notes in Landscape view in this chapter because it shows all the notes I have stored in the app. In Portrait view, the Notes list (or *pane,* as some call it) shown in Figure 5.2 on the left will not be visible until you tap the Notes button in the upper-left corner of the screen, as shown in Figure 5.3.

Tap the Notes button to see the Notes list shown in Figure 5.2

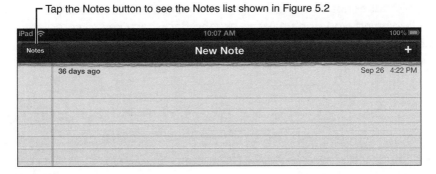

FIGURE 5.3

The Notes app in Portrait view.

Returning to the Notes app in Landscape view, let me explain the different sections and icons.

Creating Notes

First, because you haven't yet used Notes, the listing on the left side is blank, and the current page is called New Note and is circled to indicate that you are working on that page. As you add more pages, you simply tap the note you wish to view or edit and that note will be circled and displayed on the right side of the screen, as shown in Figure 5.4.

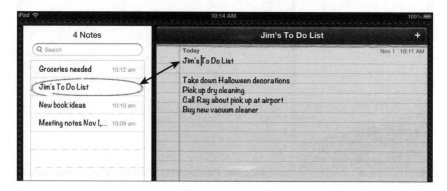

FIGURE 5.4

Tap a note to view it.

When you start using the onscreen keyboard to type up a note, the title of the note changes to whatever is entered on the first line. As you can see in Figure 5.4, the first line of the current note I'm viewing is "Jim's To Do List." I can edit that title by tapping at the end of that line with my finger and then using the keyboard's Backspace key to modify it.

If you'd rather not delete an entire line of text but maybe insert a bit of text at the beginning, you don't have to use the Backspace key to completely erase the existing line. Instead, press and hold your finger anywhere on the line, and a small magnifying lens will appear, as shown in Figure 5.5.

Press and hold to bring up a magnifying glass

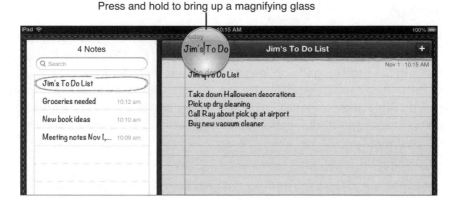

FIGURE 5.5

Editing a line of text using the magnifying lens.

While the magnifying lens is visible, move your finger left or right and place the cursor where you wish to begin editing. You can then use the Backspace key to delete some text or just type to add new text. Figure 5.6 shows that I've added my first name to the To Do List line, and this is also reflected in the title of the note.

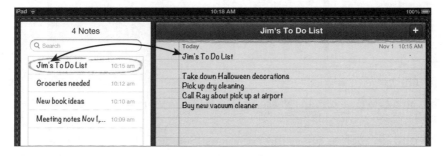

FIGURE 5.6

Editing the title of an existing note.

To add a new note, tap the plus sign (+) in the upper-right corner; a new, clean note page will appear, allowing you to type up a new page of notes.

Once you have a note typed, you have some tools available that aren't readily visible.

Editing Notes

First, the magnifying lens will work with any text you've typed into a note, so use it to make quick edits. Forget to capitalize a word? No problem! Tap and hold your finger so the magnifying lens appears and then drag the cursor just behind the letter that needs changed. Use the Backspace key, type in the uppercase letter to replace the deleted lowercase letter, and then tap elsewhere to move the cursor either to another location that needs editing or to the end of the note to add new text.

Now try this: Tap and hold on an existing word in a note until the magnifying lens appears and then remove your finger. A small pop-up toolbar will appear, as shown in Figure 5.7.

FIGURE 5.7

Tap, hold briefly, and then release on a word for three new features.

The pop-up toolbar offers three choices: Select, Select All, and Paste. If you tap Select, the word you tapped and held will briefly be selected, as shown in Figure 5.8.

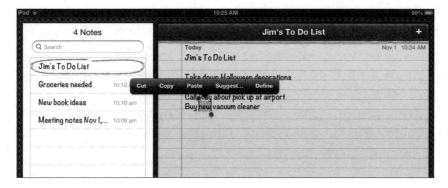

FIGURE 5.8

Select a single word to edit.

The word will be highlighted and a new toolbar will appear that offers five options: Cut, Copy, Paste, Suggest, and Define.

Before I explain these options, notice that the highlighted word has two small dots surrounding it. If you drag the dot in the upper-left corner of the word to the left, the selection can be expanded to include any words that occur before the single selected word. Likewise, dragging the dot in the lower-right corner to the right will allow you to highlight additional words to the right of the single selected word. As you can see in Figure 5.9, I've used these dots to select two words.

 NOTE Using the dots can take some practice. Fortunately, a rectangular magnifying lens will appear that can help you properly select the words you need.

Drag these dots to select additional words

FIGURE 5.9

Use the dots to select additional words.

Once I've selected the words to edit, I can use Cut, Copy, or Paste. In this case, I'll choose Copy. When I do, the small toolbar disappears.

Next, I'll tap on an empty line in the note (use the Return key to add additional blank lines if you need them) and a familiar toolbar appears, offering the options Select, Select All, and Paste. When I select Paste, the copied text is added.

Now let's revisit the Select All option. I'll tap and hold my finger and then release it so the toolbar shown in Figure 5.7 appears. This time, however, I'll tap Select All, which selects the entire word.

After making the text selection, you choose whether you want to Cut, Copy, or Paste. Cut removes the text completely, Copy stores a copy of the selected text on the clipboard, and Paste replaces any text currently selected (in this case, all of it) with whatever is currently stored on the clipboard (in this case, "Buy new"). You can also expand the current text selection using the dots as described previously.

 CAUTION Be careful with the Select All and Paste options because there is no Undo feature in the Notes app!

 NOTE The Notes app is extremely simple to use, but that means its text features are extremely simple as well. You won't find any font selections, larger or smaller font sizes, and formatting features such as tabs and bullet lists. It's basic text, and nothing else. If you want more advanced writing features, be sure to read Chapter 20, "Eight Great Paid Apps," where I give you a recommendation for a more powerful writing app called Pages.

Back in Figure 5.8, you saw that two other options are available when you select a word: Suggest and Define.

If you tap Suggest, you will be given a short list of replacement words—these aren't always synonyms, so be careful. Instead, Notes typically offers a pluralized form of the selected word or a different spelling option. Honestly, I've never found the Suggest feature to be of much use. If the iOS thinks a word is misspelled, the word will be underlined, as shown in Figure 5.10.

Suspected misspellings are marked with a dashed red line

FIGURE 5.10

Words that the Apple iOS thinks are misspelled have a dotted line underneath.

Tap the misspelled word and a suggested correction will appear above it, as shown in Figure 5.11. If you prefer the suggestion, tap it and the original (misspelled) word will be replaced.

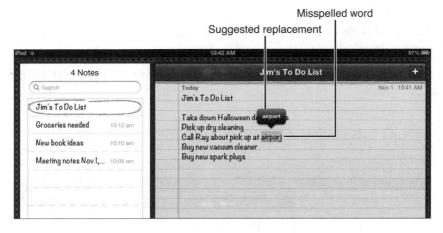

FIGURE 5.11

Replace a misspelled word with the suggested fix.

At the bottom of each note you'll see the four icons shown in Figure 5.12. If you cannot see the four icons, you may need to hide the keyboard by tapping the Hide Keyboard button in the lower-right corner of the on-screen keyboard. (It looks like a keyboard with a small arrow beneath it.)

Previous Note │ Delete Note
Share Note   Next Note

FIGURE 5.12

Four options for existing notes.

The Previous Note and Next Note buttons are self explanatory: Tap the Next Note button and the note below the current one in the Notes List will appear. If you're viewing the last note in the list, the Next Note button will be disabled. Tap the Previous Note button to view the note above the current one in the Notes List; the Previous Note button will be disabled when viewing the note at the top of the Notes List.

The Delete Note button looks like a trashcan; tap it and a Delete Note button will appear.

Tap the Delete Note button to delete the note, or tap elsewhere to keep the note. Deleting a note is permanent, so only tap the Delete Note button if you're 100% certain you won't need it again.

The Share button offers four options—Mail, Message, Print, and Copy—as shown in Figure 5.13.

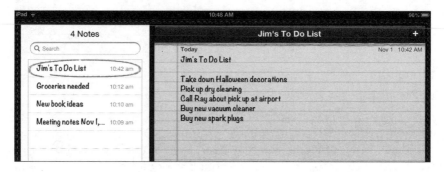

FIGURE 5.13

The Share button offers four options.

I cover the Mail app in Chapter 7, "The Mail App," and the Message app in Chapter 10, "Apps for Instant Communication," but just know that if you select either of these options, the matching app will open, allowing you either to email the contents of the note to a recipient (with the Mail app) or to instant message them to a contact (via the Message app).

The Print option will only work if you have a printer that has the AirPrint service built in. If you'd like a list of printers that offer this option, visit http://support. apple.com/kb/HT4356 and read the list of vendors that sell compatible printers as well as instructions for enabling the AirPrint feature on your iPad.

The Copy option allows you to place a copy of the note's contents on the clipboard so you can paste the text elsewhere in other apps (or simply in a new note). Not all apps have access to the clipboard, but if you find the Paste option in another app (such as Calendar), it's a good bet you'll be able to copy content from a note and paste it in the other app.

Before leaving the Notes app, I want to show you two more features the Notes app offers.

Searching and Deleting Notes

The first is the Search box that appears at the top of the Notes List, as shown in Figure 5.14.

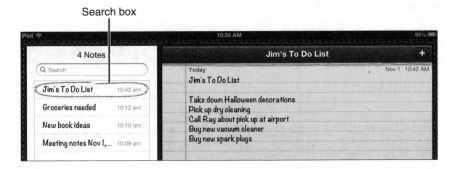

FIGURE 5.14

The Notes app Search box.

Over time, you're likely to build up quite a collection of notes in the Notes app. The title of a note doesn't always give you the best idea of what's inside, so type a word in the Search box and any notes that contain that word will be filtered and listed below the Search box, as shown in Figure 5.15. Notes that do not contain that word are not visible.

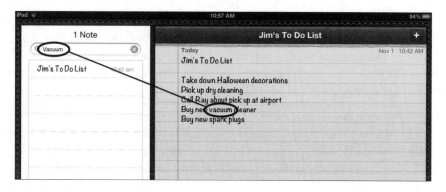

FIGURE 5.15

Filter your notes using a keyword typed into the Search box.

 TIP You can type in multiple words in the Search box, but only notes that contain every word you type will be visible. It's best to type one word at a time until you find the note you want. If more than one note appears in the list, type another word to see if notes start dropping off.

The second feature is more of a shortcut for the Delete Note button. If you tap and drag your finger left on the title of a note in the Notes List, a small red Delete button will appear, as shown in Figure 5.16. Tap the Delete button to permanently remove the note.

FIGURE 5.16

Quickly delete a note from the Notes List.

And that's the Notes app. Pretty simple, isn't it? But it's one of my go-to apps that I constantly use. I don't need fancy fonts and formatting most of the time, so the Notes app is fast and easy to use when I just need to type up some thoughts or ideas without risk of losing them.

TIP If you'd like to change the default font in the Notes app, open the Settings app, tap the Notes option in the left column, and on the right side of the screen select from Noteworthy, Helvetica, and Marker Felt.

Go ahead and press the Home button to close down the Notes app. Don't worry—any note you are currently working on will be saved instantly!

Using Reminders

Now open the Reminders app by tapping its icon once (see Figure 5.17).

FIGURE 5.17

The Reminders app.

The Reminders app looks the same in either Landscape or Portrait view, but in Portrait view the list of reminders displayed will be thinner so that longer descriptions will wrap to another line.

I'll start with the simplest task first: creating a reminder. Here are the steps to follow:

1. Tap the plus button (+) in the upper-right corner of the screen (or simply tap on the first line in the Reminders List) and the onscreen keyboard appears along with an empty check box on the selected line.

2. Type in a description of the reminder—keep in mind that you don't have to enter a time or date at this point. I'll show you how to set that information shortly.

3. Tap the Done button to add the reminder to the Reminders List.

4. Continue to add additional reminders either by tapping the plus sign or just tapping the Return button on the keyboard to move to the next line. Figure 5.18 shows that I've created three new reminders.

5. Tap and hold any Reminder item and drag it up or down to shift its location in the list.

FIGURE 5.18

Add more reminders to the Reminders List.

Choosing When You Want to Be Reminded

Adding reminders is easy, as you've just seen, but the real power of the Reminders app is actually having your iPad give you enough advanced notice about a reminder so that you can plan your day (or not forget an important item).

For instance, let's say I really need to remember to confirm the babysitter for Saturday evening, but rather than check with her on Saturday afternoon, I'd rather check on Friday. Here are the steps I would follow:

1. I start by tapping the reminder in the Reminders List. The Details window appears, as shown in Figure 5.19.

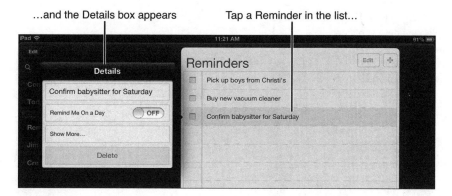

FIGURE 5.19

A reminder's Details window.

2. The first line is obvious: It matches the text of the reminder I created. I can tap in that text field, however, to edit the title if necessary.

3. As you can see, the Remind Me On a Day feature is turned Off, but I can simply tap the Off button to turn it to the On position, as shown in Figure 5.20. Turning on this option reveals more information that can be tweaked.

FIGURE 5.20

Turn on the Remind Me On a Day feature.

4. As you can see, the reminder date is set for today (Thursday, November 1, 2012 at 12 p.m.). The default reminder time will always be 30 minutes after you turn on the reminder, but this is easily changed. Just tap the date and time displayed, and four spinning columns will appear, as shown in Figure 5.21.

Adjust the date and time here

Tap the date and time

FIGURE 5.21

Set the day and time using the spinning columns.

5. I can now use my finger to adjust the date and time as necessary.

 NOTE The Reminders app allows you to fine-tune the reminder time in 5-minute increments.

6. When I'm happy with the selected day and time, I tap my finger on the title of the reminder to close the day/time selection tool.

7. I can also click the Done button if all I want is a single, one-time reminder.

Setting Recurring Reminders

Setting one-time reminders is very useful, but what if you want to set up a reminder that recurs at the same time each day, week, or month? Fortunately, your iPad can do just that. In this example, let's adjust a reminder so that it reminds us every Friday. Here are the steps to follow:

1. As you saw in Figure 5.20, the Reminder Details window shows the Repeat option. By default, it's set to Never. However, if you tap that line, you get the list of options shown in Figure 5.22.

FIGURE 5.22

The Reminder repeat options.

2. Several options are available: Every Week, Every 2 Weeks, Every Month, Every Year, and even Every Day (for those of you who need a constant daily reminder of something). In this example, we have chosen Every Week.

3. Once you've finished selecting a Repeat pattern, click the Done button, which takes you back to the previous screen.

4. If you want to set a specific end date, choose the End Repeat option, which allows you to select a day/time using the familiar columns that spin up and down.

5. Tap the Show More option, and you'll be given the ability to set the reminder's priority, select a list that holds the reminder, and add notes if you like. Figure 5.23 shows these three options.

FIGURE 5.23

Add additional information to a reminder.

- **Priority**—Tap the Priority option and you can set a reminder to None, Low, Medium, or High priority. Depending on your selection, the reminder will have one, two, or three exclamation points added its left, as shown in Figure 5.24.

FIGURE 5.24

A reminder's priority can contain a visual alert.

- **List**—Choosing the List option allows you to assign a reminder to the default Reminders List unless you tap the Create New List button shown just above the calendar. You can create new lists to organize reminders; you might create a work list and a home list to keep different reminders. Tap a list to only view reminders stored inside.

 TIP You'll also use the List option to move a reminder from one list to another. Simply place the checkmark next to a different List and the reminder will be moved to that list after you tap the Done button.

- **Notes**—Use the Notes field to type in information such as an address or gate code or other piece of information that will be relevant when the reminder opens. (I'll show you what a reminder on the iPad looks like when it pops up, in just a moment.)

TIP The calendar displayed in the lower-left corner of the Reminders app allows you to tap a day to view only reminders that have been set to trigger on that day. Use the Forward and Back arrows to change the month.

6. When you've completed a task, especially one you haven't configured to trigger at a certain day and time, simply tap the check box to the left of the item.

NOTE Reminders that are checked off will be moved to the Completed List. To permanently delete an item from the Completed List, simply swipe left on the item and click the Delete button that appears.

Receiving Alerts

Regardless of whether your iPad is sleeping or turned on, an alert box like the one shown in Figure 5.25 will appear, along with an audible warble (if you haven't turned off the speaker or turned the volume all the way down). An alert is triggered if you configured a Reminder app item (such as "Pick up Dan from airport") with a day and time to remind you (such as April 5, 2013 10:00AM).

FIGURE 5.25

Your reminder will pop up on screen.

Tap the Close button to remove the alert or tap the View button to open the Reminders app so you can place a check in the box.

 NOTE If you have iCloud turned on, your reminders will sync up with any other iOS device you are using (well, any other device that is configured with your Apple ID—refer to Chapter 2, "Overview of iOS," for more details). The default setting for Reminders to sync back with other iOS devices is one month, but you can go back as far as six months or choose All Reminders to synch with every reminder ever created on other iOS devices you own.

THE CALENDAR APP

I mentioned in Chapter 5, "Notes and Reminders," how I use my iPad as my own personal assistant; I can't afford a living, breathing human personal assistant, but a number of apps on my iPad provide me many of the same functions. Take the Reminders app I covered in Chapter 5, for example. I used to ask my wife and friends to "remind me to return this book" or "don't let me forget about the phone call this afternoon." Now I let my iPad do it for me.

Going hand-in-hand with the Reminders app is the Calendar app. This is the app I use to schedule appointments, create regularly occurring events (such as changing the air filters in my house), and find holes in my schedule to squeeze in phone calls with editors, dental appointments for the kids, and important dates such as birthdays and anniversaries. (If you've added those dates to any contacts in the Contacts app, however, you'll love that they're automatically added to the Calendar app!)

With iCloud, your Calendar app also synchronizes with any device running iOS or OS X. If you have an iPhone or a Mac laptop or desktop computer, you'll find it easy to access your calendar no matter which device you happen to have on hand at the moment.

Some of you might be concerned because you've gotten used to using a different calendar such as Google Calendar or the one in Microsoft's Outlook. Well, you'll be happy to know that it's super-easy to synchronize a variety of other calendars with the Calendar app, and I'll show you how to do so later in this chapter.

The Calendar app is only useful, however, if you actually use it. This means developing a habit of checking it in the morning to see what your day looks like or when you're speaking to someone on the phone who is offering up a day and time for a possible new event (such as a doctor's appointment). Before I developed a habit of using the Calendar app, I would frequently double-schedule myself, accepting a conference call invitation at the same time I was scheduled to meet with a client.

But that rarely happens anymore. The Calendar app is also able to give me pop-up reminders just like the Reminders app—I can even pick how early I want that alert, such as an hour, a day, or even a week in advance.

Let me show you the Calendar app now; you'll see that it's just as easy and intuitive to use as the other iOS apps, especially with the touch screen.

 NOTE   You'll find that the Calendar app is ideally designed to be used in Landscape view. It can be used in Portrait view, but any text on the screen (along with times) tends to get cramped. That said, there are no hidden buttons or features when in Portrait view, so what you see in Landscape you'll also see in Portrait.

Check Your Schedule

The Calendar app is pretty easy to spot. Figure 6.1 shows the icon you'll need to tap to open the Calendar app.

FIGURE 6.1

The Calendar app icon.

Tap the Calendar icon to open the app and you'll see a similar screen to the one shown in Figure 6.2—the only difference being the Month and Year views. I'm writing this sentence on November 5, 2012, and you can see in Figure 6.2 that the current date is labeled "Today" and highlighted in blue.

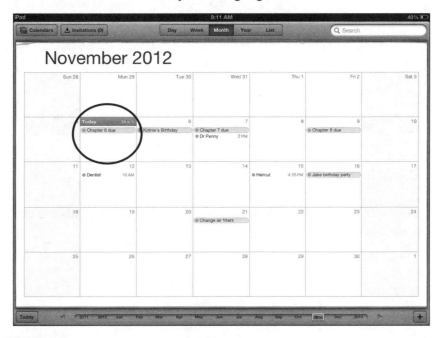

FIGURE 6.2

The opened Calendar app.

You'll also notice in Figure 6.2 a number of other items, including a birthday, some chapter due dates, and some appointments (doctor, dentist, and haircut). Some have times assigned to them (Dentist 10 a.m.) and others do not. Each of these is called an *event,* and they can have reminders set, or you can choose to have the event represented as only a bit of text on the calendar page.

At the top of the screen is a selection bar that allows you to change the view of the calendar. The options include Day, Week, Month, Year, and List. If I tap the Day button, for example, I get an hourly breakdown for the day, as shown in Figure 6.3.

FIGURE 6.3

The Day view displays events by hour.

A quick tap on the Week button changes the view to show only the current week's schedule of events, as shown in Figure 6.4.

FIGURE 6.4

A week's worth of scheduled events.

The default view is the Month view, but if you change to a different view and close down the Calendar app, the next time you open it the app will remember the last view you selected and use it.

Depending on the view you select, you'll also have some different options displayed along the bottom edge of the screen. For example, in Figure 6.4 where the Week view is displayed, you can tap any of the other weeks (such as Nov 11–17) to jump ahead or back to a different week of events.

If you tap the Year view that's shown in Figure 6.5, for example, you can view every month in the current year; scheduled events are represented as colored boxes on a particular month. But notice at the bottom of the screen that the viewing options have changed and now you can tap a previous year or a future year for viewing. If a previous or future year isn't available on the bar (or a previous week, month, or day), you can use the left- or right-pointing arrow to shift the displayed options ahead or back.

Tap here to jump back to today's schedule

Choose the calendar year here

Days with scheduled events are shown with shaded boxes

FIGURE 6.5

View an entire year on one page.

No matter how far or back you go in a calendar, you can always tap the Today button in the lower-left corner to jump right to the current day in whatever view you have selected. For example, if you're in the Day view and are looking a day from next month's schedule, you can tap the Today button and the Day view will show today's schedule. Just remember, the Today button doesn't change your selected view (Day, Week, Month, Year, List). Instead, it just moves the view to include the current day.

I've shown you four of the five views, so you're probably wondering about the List option. Tap it and you'll see a screen similar to the one in Figure 6.6.

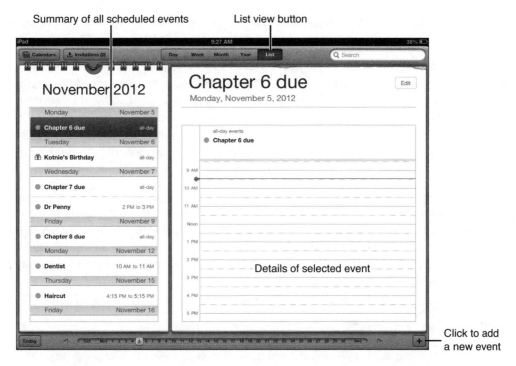

FIGURE 6.6

The List view is a good summary of upcoming events.

The List view summarizes all of your scheduled events on the left side of the screen. A single tap on any event in that list will display it's Day view on the right side of the screen.

The list is also scrollable. Figure 6.6 shows events up to November 16, but a quick swipe up with my finger and I can easily view more events.

The last two items I want to point out before we move to the next section are the two buttons in the upper-left corner of the screen: Calendars and Invitations.

Calendar—The Calendar app can display multiple types of events on a calendar. You can color-code your events so that those related to work are displayed in one color (orange, for example) and personal events are displayed in another color. You can pick the color, and you can turn a calendar on or off to hide its events from the current view. The events aren't deleted but are instead hidden until you turn them back on. You can even create new calendars (maybe one for each member of your family, for example). I'll explain these features and a few more later in this chapter.

Invitations—As for the Invitations button, you'll see later in this chapter how to invite others to an event you've created. When you invite someone to an event (such as a birthday party), those invitees will receive an email asking whether they can attend. The results of this poll will be displayed when you tap the Invitations button. More on the Invitation option shortly.

Create an Event

The Calendar app is all about events, so it makes sense that the key task you need to learn is how to create events. Creating an event is easy, and the Calendar app gives you two different ways to do so. The first and easiest is to tap on a day or time shown on the on-screen calendar. An Add Event window will appear like the one in Figure 6.7.

The first method is found in the lower-right corner of the screen. If you tap the plus sign previously shown in Figure 6.6, you get the Add Event window along with the onscreen keyboard, as shown in Figure 6.7.

FIGURE 6.7

Create a new event with the Add Event window.

You can tap the Cancel button in the upper-left corner of the Add Event window at any time to cancel any work you've done on creating a new event. Likewise, after you've entered a title and maybe selected some of the other options, you can tap the Done button in the upper-right corner to save your event.

Let's walk though the Add Event window now and look at the options available to you. To add an event, follow these steps:

1. Type in a short description of your event in the Title field, as shown in Figure 6.8. This step is required.

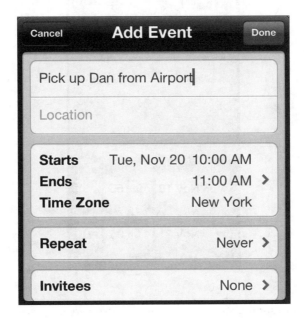

FIGURE 6.8

Give your event a description.

2. Add some text in the Location box if that will help you when viewing the event in the calendar. This could be useful, for example, if you live in a city with two airports (such as Houston, Texas) and need to remember which airport to pick up a friend from.

 CAUTION   Normally, the time zone doesn't need to be changed. Most of us make events that are in our current time zone, but if you know you'll be traveling to a different time zone for the new event, make certain to tap the Time Zone line and select the one that matches the event's time. Otherwise, you may find yourself being reminded of an event at 1 p.m. Central Time when you're in New York at 2 p.m. Eastern Time.

3. Tap on the Starts line and you'll see a screen like the one shown in Figure 6.9. It contains the familiar wheels at the bottom that let you dial in the day, month, and time (including a.m. or p.m.).

FIGURE 6.9

Use the wheels to set the start date and time for an event.

4. If you don't want to create an all-day event, skip to step 5. If you do want to create an all-day event, tap the Off button shown in Figure 6.9. It will change to On and the dials for setting the time (not the date) at the bottom will disappear.

5. Use your finger to dial in the start date and time.

 TIP   When setting a start time, remember that you need to account for your travel time and so on. In this example, I need to pick up Dan at the airport at 3 p.m., but it takes me an hour to get there, so I've set the start time accordingly.

6. You can tap the Ends option to use the dials to set the event's end time. If you've set the event as an all-day event, the Ends option only offers the ability to dial in the end date, not the time.

7. You need to finish setting the start and end times before you can gain access to additional options, so go ahead and tap the Done button to return to the Add Event window shown in Figure 6.10.

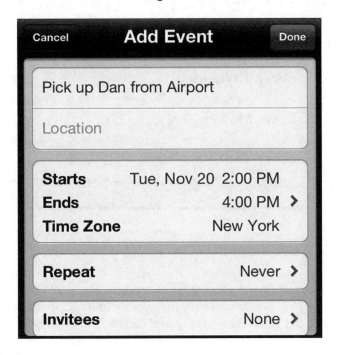

FIGURE 6.10

The title and start/end times are now set.

Create a Recurring Event

Earlier I mentioned that you can create a repeating event. Follow these steps to do so:

1. Tap the Repeat option shown in Figure 6.10 to display a list of repeat schedules, as shown in Figure 6.11.

FIGURE 6.11

You can choose to repeat an event.

2. You can select from Every Day, Every Week, Every 2 Weeks, Every Month, and Every Year. Let's assume I'll be picking my friend Dan up at the airport every month on the same date and time. Tap the Every Month option (a check mark will be placed next to this option) and tap the Done button.

3. When you select a repeating option other than None, you are also given the ability to select when to end the repeat action, as shown in Figure 6.12.

FIGURE 6.12

A repeated event can also have a date to end the repeat action.

4. The End Repeat option is automatically set to Never, but if you tap it, the familiar set of dials appears, which allows you to dial in the month, date, and year you wish to end the repeating event. As you can see in Figure 6.12, if I set the date to January 20, 2013, I will be reminded on February 20, 2013, March 20, 2013, and so on. Tap the Done button to return to the Add Event window.

5. Scroll down the Add Event window to view additional options. As you can see in Figure 6.13, these options include Invitees, Alert, Calendar, and Availability.

FIGURE 6.13

More options are available in the Add Event window.

6. Tap the Invitees button to select people from the Contacts app. For each person you want to add, tap the plus (+) button, as shown in Figure 6.14.

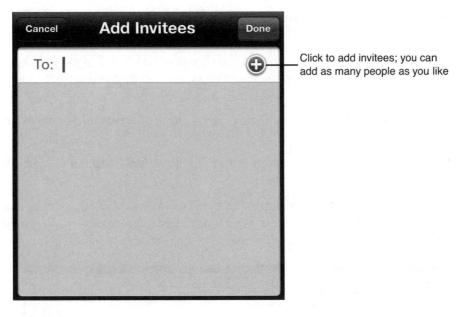

Click to add invitees; you can add as many people as you like

FIGURE 6.14

Add invitees to your new event.

7. Select those you wish to invite to your event, and they will be emailed an invitation to which they can respond Yes or No. A numbered counter will alert you to how many people have been invited. (Likewise, tap on an invitee's name to select it and then tap the Backspace key on the keyboard to delete that invitee.)

8. The Alert button lets you select how much time ahead of the event's start time you wish to have an alert pop up on the screen. The maximum amount of time is "2 days before" and the minimum is "At time of event."

 TIP For those of you who favor your alarm clock's snooze button, you can also tap the Second Alert option to configure a second reminder. But that's all you get! Note that some users may not have the ability to set a Second Alert—it depends on the type of calendar account you are using. I have a Google account for Gmail and Calendar, and the Google Calendar allows for two reminder alerts. Some services do not, so a Second Alert may not be available to you.

9. Below the Alert section, you'll find the Calendar option. This lets you assign your new event to a category such as Home or Work or other category. (I'll show you in a bit how to create new categories.)

10. Below the Calendar option is the Availability option. You can toggle between either Busy and Free.

11. Below the Availability option is the URL text field. Here, you can easily enter a web address for a company you'll be visiting or maybe the link to the online map.

12. Below the URL field is the Notes field. Add any kind of additional information you like here.

13. Now that we've completed the Add Events window, tap the Done button to add this event to your calendar.

14. After you tap the Done button, the new event is added to the calendar, along with a small window that contains the details so you can verify you entered everything correctly. You can see this small window in Figure 6.15.

FIGURE 6.15

A summary of the events you just added is displayed.

TIP Did you make a mistake? If you have set the start or end time improperly, or maybe forgot to configure an alert, you can tap the Edit button to return to the Add Event window to make the necessary changes. You can edit any event by tapping it and then tapping the Edit button on the small window that appears.

Add a New Calendar Category

I mentioned earlier that you can file events into specific categories that are color-coded. For example, I have my work-related items (Work) displayed with purple dots and my personal items (Home) shown with orange dots.

If you want to create a new category, simply tap the Calendars button and you get a pop-up window like the one shown in Figure 6.16.

FIGURE 6.16

The Calendars button lets you access calendar categories.

Notice in Figure 6.16 that I have the Home and Work calendars visible (they have check marks to the left of their names). I can tap on a calendar category to remove the check mark and those events will be hidden until I tap the calendar category again. I can also tap the small blue circle to the right of a category to change the color of the category or even rename it.

If you want to create a new category, tap the Edit button shown in Figure 6.16 and then tap the Add Calendar option shown in Figure 6.17. As you can see, I've created a new category named Books and given it the color green. I can now create events related to my writing (such as "Chapter 3 due") by assigning them to the Books category.

FIGURE 6.17

Add a new calendar category.

As for the Invitations button, you may have noticed in Figure 6.15 that I invited Laura to ride along when I pick up Dan from the airport. She received the email invite and declined. I can tap the Invitations button as shown in Figure 6.17 to see her response. Your invitees will always be listed here along with their response to any invites you've extended.

Importing Other Calendars

Although I use the Calendar app on my iPad quite often, I don't always have access to it. If I'm sitting at my laptop computer, I tend to favor using my Google Calendar, a free calendar tool that requires a Google ID. My wife, on the other hand, uses the calendar that comes with the Microsoft Outlook application. And many other calendar tools are out there. Fortunately, the Calendar app with iOS works with many other calendars, pulling in their events and even pushing out events you create using the Calendar app so they exist on your other calendar(s).

I cannot cover every calendar option available, so instead I'll point you in the direction you need to go to get your calendars synced with the iOS Calendar app.

If you use Google Calendar, be sure to visit the following link for instructions on synchronizing Google Calendar with the iOS Calendar app:

http://support.google.com/mail/bin/answer.py?hl=en&answer=139206

Here's another option for enabling your Google-related services (Gmail, Google Calendar, and so on) that also works for Microsoft Outlook calendar users, but it's a bit different:

1. Open up the Settings app and tap the Mail, Contacts, Calendars option.

2. On the right side of the screen, tap the Add Account button and you'll see a list of different services, such as Gmail, Hotmail, and Yahoo!, as shown in Figure 6.18.

FIGURE 6.18

Add different types of accounts in Settings.

3. Tap the appropriate option and then follow the onscreen instructions.

For example, if you're a Microsoft Outlook user, you'll want to tap the Microsoft Exchange option and follow the onscreen instructions to have your Outlook mail and calendars made available on your iPad. Tap the Gmail option and provide your Google ID username and password to have email and calendar information passed to the relevant app (Mail or Calendar, respectively).

For other calendar types, I suggest a simple Google search such as "Sync calendar X with iOS Calendar app" and see if any online instructions are available. Often, no answer is provided by Apple, but someone else has figured out a workaround or trick to make it happen. A Google search is your friend if you're using another calendar option you wish to sync with the iPad's Calendar app.

7

THE MAIL APP

Back in the early days, kings would send messengers to deliver communications to and from cities and even countries. These messengers moved by ship, by horse, and sometimes by the power of their own two legs. Communication was slow, especially if you wanted to deliver a message with the hand-painted portrait of the king congratulating the recipient on the purchase of their new castle and giving them something to hang over the fireplace.

Fortunately, those days are over. We have all sorts of methods for communicating with others, including phone, video conferencing, instant messaging, email, and, yes, the old reliable postal carriers.

Although I doubt you'll be giving your iPad to the mailman to deliver its saved messages and photos to your sister across the country, you can use it to make calls, do instant messaging, and send and receive email. And that's what this chapter is all about—email.

The app that comes with the iPad is called Mail. Not eMail or EMail, and definitely not iMail. Just Mail. And I'm going to show you how to set it up and use it in this chapter.

 NOTE Some email services have their own apps. Google's email service, Gmail, for example, has its own app that supports many of the special features that are built in to Gmail. If you use Gmail or another email service, be sure to read Chapter 12, "Apps for the iPad," where I cover using the App Store to search for apps. You'll want to search to see if there's a specialty app made just for your email service.

Configuring the Mail App

The icon for the Mail app is shown in Figure 7.1. Go ahead and tap it to open the Mail app.

FIGURE 7.1

The icon for the Mail app.

The first time you open the Mail app, you'll be given a list of email services that the Mail app supports, as shown in Figure 7.2.

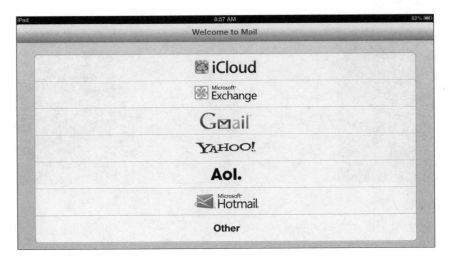

FIGURE 7.2

Email services supported by the Mail app.

If you don't see your email service in this list, don't worry—the Other option at the very bottom covers just about all other options.

 CAUTION If you use Outlook at work, there's a good chance you are using a Microsoft Exchange Server to handle email in your workplace; you may need to ask someone (an IT department employee or someone who just seems to know these kinds of things) because the Microsoft Exchange option requires some additional information, such as a domain name. The Microsoft Exchange option in Figure 7.2 is the only one I don't recommend trying to configure yourself, unless you understand the security risks posed by using an iPad that has access to a company email server. This is one of those times when it's best to ask your company its policy on using iPads for email access.

I'm going to set up the Mail app with my Hotmail email address, but the procedure is identical for just about every email service—you'll need to provide your email address and password, and the Mail app will handle the rest. Follow these steps:

1. Start by tapping the Hotmail option in the list shown in Figure 7.2. You'll see the screen shown in Figure 7.3.

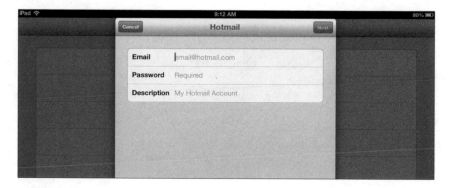

FIGURE 7.3

Setting up Mail with a Hotmail account.

 NOTE Hotmail has been replaced by Outlook.com, but the Mail setup still shows it as Hotmail. This may change down the road, but right now if you have an Outlook.com email address from Microsoft, it'll work just fine.

2. Enter your Hotmail email address, enter a password, and tap the Next button.

3. Select whether you want your contacts, calendars, and reminders from Hotmail to be imported. You can toggle these on and off by tapping the button to the right of each feature.

4. Tap the Save button.

5. Your account is added and you are taken to the Mail app's home screen.

Touring Mail

If you've just created a new email address, it's likely that the Mail app will be completely empty. Services such as Gmail and Hotmail, however, will often send you a welcome email. Regardless of whether you have a welcome email, let's review the various parts of the Mail app.

First, the left side of the screen displays the contents of whatever mailbox you have selected—these mailboxes include Inbox, Sent, Trash, Drafts, and more. When you first open Mail, it displays the Inbox, empty or not. Tap the Mailboxes button in the upper-left corner of the screen and you'll be given a list of all the mailboxes available. These are shown in Figure 7.4.

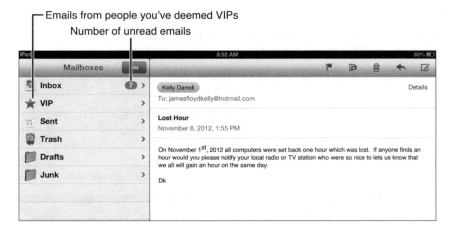

FIGURE 7.4

View the mailboxes available in Mail.

The number to the right of the Inbox indicates how many unread emails you have in that mailbox. The VIP mailbox, when tapped, displays only those emails you have starred. (I'll show you how to star an email shortly.)

The Sent mailbox contains an archive of all the email messages you've sent, the Trash mailbox contains deleted emails, the Drafts folder holds your email messages that you've begun but haven't yet sent out, and the Junk folder holds emails you receive that the Mail app determines are spam/junk. Occasionally a valid email will get sent here because the Subject line contains a word or phrase that the Mail app considers typical of spam, so you might check this mailbox if you're expecting an email and it never arrives. (Otherwise just do as I do and ignore the Junk mailbox altogether.)

Adding New Mailboxes

Tap the Edit button (shown in Figure 7.4) and at the bottom of the list of mailboxes you'll see a New Mailbox button. Perform these steps to add a new mailbox:

1. Tap the New Mailbox button.

2. Enter the name of your new Mailbox.

3. Tap the Save button to create your new Mailbox.

4. You can create sub-mailboxes (tucked into existing mailboxes) by tapping on the Mailbox Location button and choosing which existing Mailbox you wish to use to hold your new mailbox.

I'll show you in a moment how to move messages around, including into any new mailbox you might create. For example, I could create two new folders: Archive and Pearson. The Archive folder would be where I place messages I don't want kept in the Inbox but also don't want to send to the Trash. The Pearson folder would hold emails from my book publisher.

Tap the Inbox to return to your email messages. In Figure 7.5, you can see that new emails not yet opened have a small blue dot visible in the left column.

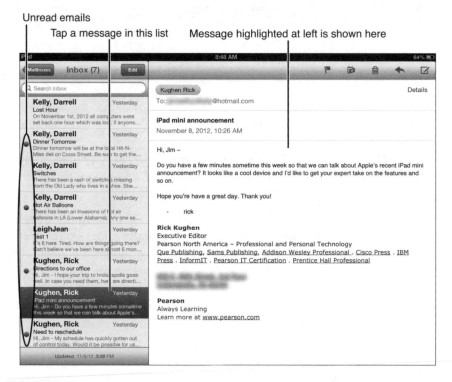

FIGURE 7.5

Unread emails have a blue dot.

Tap an email, and the contents of that email will appear on the right side of the screen.

Now let's focus on the right side of the screen. First, along the upper-right corner of the screen are five icons: Flag, Archive, Trash, Reply, and Compose.

Flagging Emails

If you tap the Flag icon, you'll get two options: Flag and Mark as Unread. Selecting the Flag option places a small flag to the left of the message in the mailbox column, as shown in Figure 7.6. (A flag is also placed at the top right of the opened email message itself.) The flag is meant to serve as a visual reminder to you—maybe you intend to respond to the email or maybe it contains important information such as a phone number that you need to quickly find later.

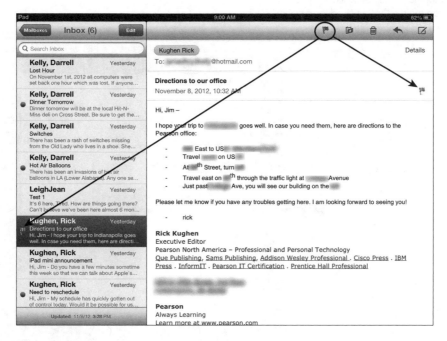

FIGURE 7.6

Flag an email to give yourself a visual reminder.

Marking an Email as Unread

When you tap an email to view its contents, the blue dot disappears. If you wish to reset the email to appear as if it hasn't been read, tap the Flag icon in the top-right corner of the open message and select the Mark as Unread option and the blue dot will reappear. I use this often when I find that an email's content is quite lengthy and I don't have time to read it at the moment—I mark it as unread and will return to it later. I could use the flag, but I use it to indicate messages I wish to respond to at a later time. You'll find your own uses for the Flag and Mark as Unread options.

Archiving and Trashing Email

The Archive button shrinks the message you are viewing and offers up a list of all the mailboxes, as shown in Figure 7.7. Tap a mailbox to move the current email to that location. This is useful for putting an email in the Junk folder should you discover it's actually spam or in a custom folder you created with the New Mailbox button.

Tapping a mailbox while an email is
open moves that email to the mailbox

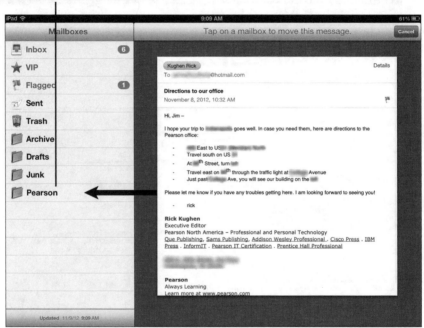

FIGURE 7.7

Move a message to a mailbox.

If I simply tap on the Pearson mailbox, this current message (from my editor, Rick) will be moved to there and disappear from my Inbox.

The Trash button is fairly self-explanatory—the current email you are viewing will be moved immediately to the Trash mailbox. When an email is sent to the Trash mailbox, that message disappears from the left side of the screen and the contents of the next message (below the one that was just deleted) are displayed on the right side.

Replying, Forwarding, and Printing

The Reply button offers three options: Reply, Forward, and Print. A fourth option, Reply to All, appears if there are two or more recipients who received the message.

If you tap the Reply button, the original message is appended to the end of the new email, as shown in Figure 7.8. Notice that the original sender's name is now in the To: box, and the original subject is retained. Use the onscreen keyboard to type your response and then tap the Send button to send the email on its way.

Original sender's name appears here

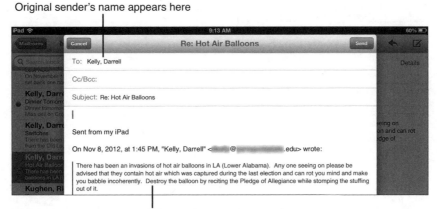

Original message is appended at the bottom of your reply

FIGURE 7.8

Reply to an email's original sender.

The Forward button opens a screen similar to the one in Figure 7.8, but the To: field is left blank, allowing you to type in an email address or select one from the Contact app by tapping the blue dot with the plus sign inside. Notice that the original message is appended to the end of the response you will send and the subject is retained; you can change the subject line if you wish and you can also completely delete the original message—tap and hold your finger anywhere in the message and then tap the Select All option that appears, as shown in Figure 7.9.

| Select | Select All | Paste | Insert Photo or Video | Quote Level |

FIGURE 7.9

Select the original message text.

After the text is completely selected, tap the Backspace/Delete key or the Cut option on the toolbar, and the text will disappear.

Finally, the Print option allows you to print the contents of an email if you have a printer that supports AirPrint.

Writing a New Email

The last icon in the upper-right corner of the screen is the Compose button. Tap it, and you'll be given a completely blank email message screen, as shown in Figure 7.10.

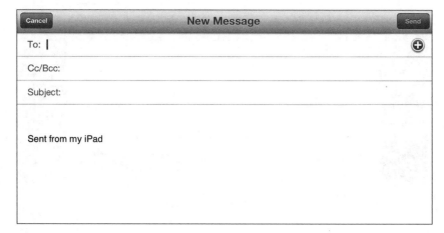

FIGURE 7.10

Use the Compose button to create a new email.

If you don't like the "Sent from my iPad" signature that gets added to every email you create, you can get rid of it easily enough. Go into the Settings app, tap on the Mail, Contacts, Calendars option in the left list, and then scroll down on the right side of the screen until you find the Signature option. Tap it and delete any text that appears in the text box or create a different signature. Return to the Mail app and tap the Send button when you're ready to send that message.

Extra Features

The Mail app is an extremely simple email tool, and that's why I like it—not a lot of bells and whistles to get in the way. Still, Mail has a variety of other features that aren't so obvious, so let's look at how they work.

First, at any time you can force the Mail app to check for new email messages. Normally email is pushed out to the Mail app from the email provider (such as Hotmail). This seems to happen about every 5 minutes or so, but some services may do so every 15 minutes or maybe even just once an hour. If you wish, you can manually check for new messages by changing to the Inbox mailbox and then tapping and holding on the left side of the screen as you pull down. As you can see in Figure 7.11, a small spinning wheel appears at the top of the list to let you know the Mail app is checking for new email.

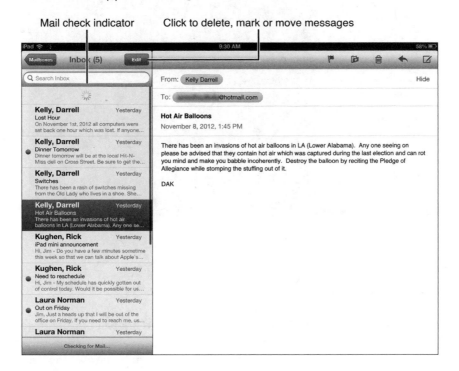

FIGURE 7.11

Check for new email messages manually.

You might have also noticed the Edit button just above the current mailbox (and to the right of the Mailboxes button). If you tap it, the list of emails shifts slightly to the right and a small circle appears next to each message, as shown in Figure 7.12. Three buttons also appear at the bottom of the list: Delete, Move, and Mark.

After tapping the edit button, a circle appears to the left of each message...

If you decide not to delete, move, or mark a message, click Cancel

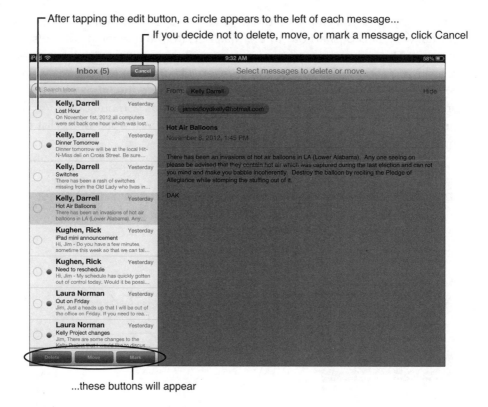

...these buttons will appear

FIGURE 7.12

Use the Edit button to perform tasks on multiple messages.

Tap the circle to the left of an email, and a check mark will appear inside, as shown in Figure 7.13. Selecting multiple messages is allowed, and this is indicated by the small stack of messages that appear on the right side of the screen.

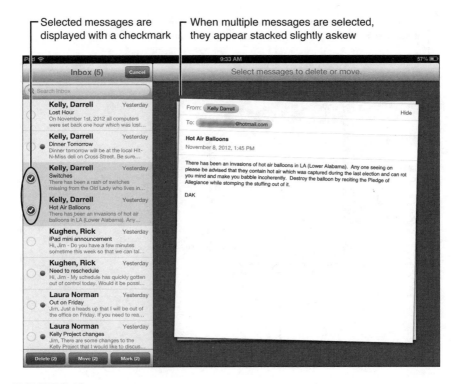

FIGURE 7.13

Select multiple email messages.

After you've placed a check mark in the box next to one or more email messages, you can perform the same task on all selected emails by tapping the Delete, Move, or Mark button:

- **Delete**—Tapping the Delete button moves all emails with a check mark to the Trash mailbox immediately.

- **Move**—Tapping the Move button displays all existing mailboxes; tap a mailbox to move the emails with check marks to the selected mailbox.

- **Mark**—Tap the Mark button either to add the Flag icon described earlier or to mark the selected messages as Unread.

Finally, tap an email in the list on the left and view its contents on the right. Notice that the sender's name is highlighted in blue. If you tap the blue button containing the sender's name, you'll see a window appear like the one in Figure 7.14 (if that person is not already in the Contacts app).

Select a message here and it appears at the right

Tap a name in the message and if that person is not already in your Contacts list...

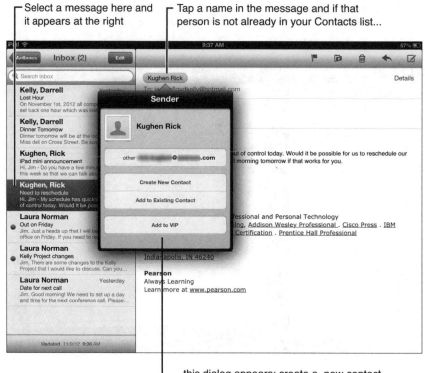

...this dialog appears; create a new contact or add information to an existing contact

FIGURE 7.14

Tap a sender's name to view details.

First, you'll see the sender's email address below his or her name. Because the sender is not already in your Contacts app, you may tap the Create New Contact button to add him or her, along with any other information you wish to include. (Refer to Chapter 4, "Contacts," for details on adding new contacts.)

If this person's name is already in the Contacts app but you know that the email address is not part of that contact's information, tap the Add to Existing Contact button and you can select that person from the scrollable list that appears. Tap the contact's name in the list, and that email address will be added to the contact information page.

If the sender is already in your Contacts app when you tap his or her name in an email, you'll see a different window that offers the following options:

- **Send Message**—Tap the Send Message button and a blank message box will open with this person's name in the To: box. Fill in a subject, type the body of your email, and click Send.

- **FaceTime**—If you'd like to have a video chat with this person, tap the FaceTime button.

- **Share Contact**—If you'd like to send this person's contact information to someone else, click Share Contact.

- **Add to Favorites**—Choosing Add to Favorites will place this person in the FaceTime Favorites list so you can always contact him or her with FaceTime by just opening that app.

- **Add to VIP**—Tap the Add to VIP button to add someone to your list of VIPs. When you open the VIP mailbox only emails from those you've added as VIPs will be displayed.

 TIP Don't use the Add to VIP button too often. I suggest flagging less than 10 people with the VIP status so you can quickly view messages in the Inbox folder by filtering out everyone else. Tap the sender's name again to get the Sender info box back so you can tap the Remove from VIP if you wish to remove a contact from the VIP mailbox.

The ability to add someone to the Contacts app or to the VIP mailbox isn't limited to the sender of the email either. Take a look at Figure 7.14 and you'll see to the right of the sender's name an option called Details. Tap the Details item and any recipients in the message will have their name also highlighted in a blue button. Tap the blue button, and you can add recipients to the Contacts app and make them VIPs, just as you did with the sender.

When you tap the Details item, it changes to Hide. Tap the Hide item to hide the recipients to an email message.

Sending Attachments

If you're familiar with email, you're probably familiar with attachments. Attachments are files you send along with an email message for the recipient to open. Attachments can include music files, photos, documents, and much more.

Notice in Figure 7.15 that I've attached an image to this email.

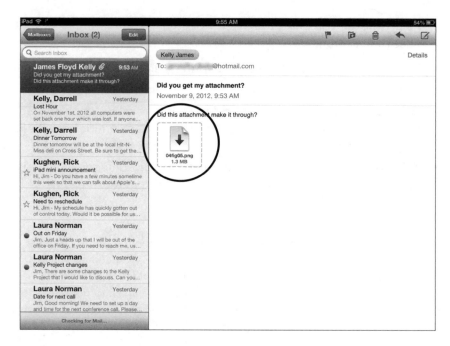

FIGURE 7.15

An attachment included with an email message.

To open an attachment that someone has sent to you, simply tap it. If the attachment can be opened with any of the iPad's apps, the contents of the attachment will be displayed, as shown in Figure 7.16.

FIGURE 7.16

Tap an attachment to view it.

It's important to note that not every attachment can be opened on the iPad until you download the proper application. Sometimes, however, no app will be available to open the attachment, meaning that you will be forced to open it on a computer running the proper app.

Typically if an app is installed on your iPad that can open a special attachment, that app will launch automatically when you tap the attachment to view it—but not always.

As for sending your own attachments, unfortunately the Mail app limits you to sending only photos and videos. Photos and videos are stored in the Photos app, which I cover in Chapter 9, "Apps for Photos and Videos." Once you have some photos or videos stored on your iPad, it's quite easy to send them to others in an email message.

First, tap the Compose button or Reply/Reply to All and type up your message. Then, when you're ready to add your attachment, simply tap and hold your finger on any blank space in the message until the toolbar shown in Figure 7.17 appears.

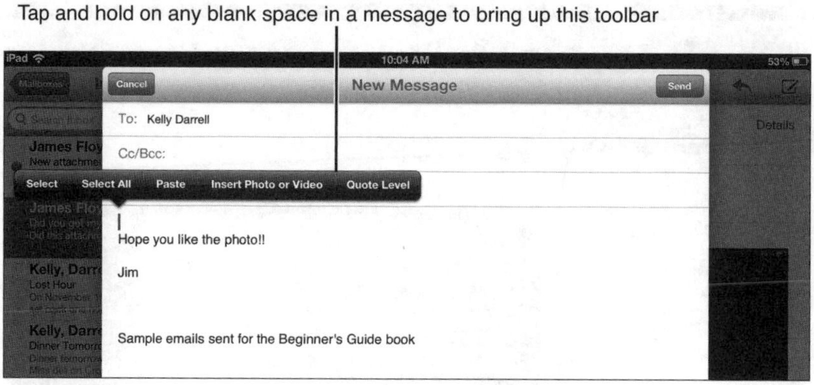

Tap and hold on any blank space in a message to bring up this toolbar

FIGURE 7.17

Tap and hold in a message for this toolbar to appear.

Tap the Insert Photo or Video button and then select the image or video from the pop-up window that appears. The photo or video will be inserted as shown in Figure 7.18. Tap the Send button to get the message and attachment moving on their way.

FIGURE 7.18

Emailing a photo.

Other Email Apps

I told you earlier in the chapter that some email services have their own apps. You'll learn about the App Store in Chapter 12 and how you can use it to search for other types of apps to install on your iPad.

One of these apps, for example, is the Gmail app shown in Figure 7.19. Although the Mail app can send and receive email from a Gmail account, it doesn't support some of the power features that Gmail offers, such as labels and filtering support. (If you're not familiar with these features, visit Gmail.com to learn all about Gmail.)

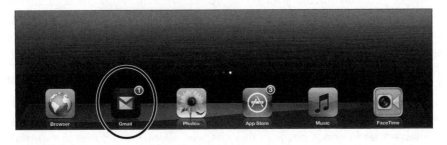

FIGURE 7.19

The Gmail app is a specialty email app for the iPad.

Other services may have their own app for the iPad, but the only way to know for certain is to visit their website or email them and ask.

 CAUTION A search in the App Store might find you something that sounds like it will work with your email service, but these apps aren't the "official" ones and are instead created by a third party. Although I think you can usually trust these apps, I tend to stick with the official ones released by the service I wish to use.

One reason that Gmail users might wish to use the Gmail app instead of the Mail app is if they've enabled Gmail's 2-Step Verification process. This process prevents someone from obtaining your password and using it to access your email account. When you use the Gmail app, every 30 days or so, you'll get a pop-up window that asks you to type in a verification code that is sent to your mobile phone. The thinking is that if someone steals your email password, they probably don't have your mobile phone. Only someone with the phone number on file can obtain the text message that contains the code required to access the Gmail app.

NOTE Not all services offer two-step verification, and it's not required by Google for Gmail users. Still, it's a nice security feature if you want it. Just be aware that it does require using the Gmail app and not the Mail app if you enable 2-Step Verification. For more information on this process, visit http://support.google.com/accounts/bin/answer.py?hl=en&answer=180744.

Email Access with a Web Browser

Some of you may access your email from a web browser. Users of Gmail and Hotmail/Outlook.com are already familiar with opening a web browser to Gmail.com or Outlook.com and logging in. Email is visible onscreen and stored by the service provider and not on the user's computer.

The iPad does support this, especially for Gmail and Hotmail/Outlook.com users.

Using the web browser to access my Hotmail account is a lot different from using it with the Mail app. Additional menu items, buttons, and features are available that I cannot cover in this chapter. If you want to learn more about either the Gmail.com or Hotmail/Outlook.com web email service, visit Gmail.com or Outlook.com to get all the details.

Mail Settings

Closing out this chapter, I want to give you some thoughts on the various settings available for the Mail app. Go ahead and open the Settings app and tap the Mail, Contacts, and Calendars option.

Scroll down the right side of the screen until you see the Mail category, which allows you to alter a number of settings:

- **Show**—Modify this option to increase or decrease the maximum number of email messages displayed in the Mail app. Any messages not displayed aren't gone—they're just hidden until you scroll further up to view them.

- **Preview**—This option lets you pick how many lines of text from the email you wish to display under the email in the Mailbox list. The more you choose, the fewer emails will be visible on the iPad screen (more lines equals more space). Options run from zero to five lines.

- **Show To/Cc Label**—Turn this on or off to hide the To: and CC: fields in a message you are composing.

- **Ask Before Deleting**—Turn this on if you wish to get a pop-up window asking you to confirm the deletion of an email.

- **Load Remote Images**—Turn this on if you want any embedded images that are referenced using a web link displayed in an email.

- **Organize by Thread**—Turn this on or off, depending on whether you wish to see any previous back-and-forth conversations in an email you are viewing. This option will also display the number of conversations (emails) in parenthesis for the current discussion.

- **Always Bcc Myself**—Only turn this on if you want to receive an email every time you send a message out. It's annoying and time consuming to get a copied email, so use this option only if you absolutely must.

- **Increase Quote Level**—Leave this on if you want the original text of a message included in a reply to be slightly pushed to the right for ease of reading.

- **Signature**—Mentioned previously, you can modify the text in this option, and that text will always be added to your emails (replies included).

- **Default Account**—If you have multiple email addresses, you can add them in Settings by tapping the Add Account option. Even with multiple email addresses configured, only one will be used when you send outgoing emails. Select that email account as the default account. If you only have one account, this option can be ignored.

8

THE SAFARI APP

These days, having an Internet connection provides a lot of distractions—movies, games, and socializing (via Facebook, for example), are just a few things I can think of where I've used my Internet connection. But if I tracked my time spent with the iPad and monitored carefully what I use its connection to the Internet for the most, it would be a tie between email and web browsing.

When the iPad was released in 2010, it was promoted as a content-providing device; that is, it was designed to download and present information (content) to its user. Since the iPad's release, however, the device has proven itself to be much more than a simple device for watching video, browsing the Web, and checking email. iPad owners now use the tablet to create content and send it out in the world—videos, artwork, games, and much more.

But, ultimately, the iPad still is a content-providing device. Most of the apps that iPad owners use (including those apps downloaded from the App Store) are still primarily focused on delivering something to the iPad user—a video, a game, an email, a reminder, and so on.

Although the iPad isn't as small or lightweight as a mobile phone, it's still fairly easy to carry with you. And it has one advantage over its mobile phone cousin when it comes to checking email, viewing a website, and playing a game (to name a few tasks). What is it? It's the larger viewing area.

Whether you have the 9.7" iPad or the 7.9" iPad mini, reading an email, scanning a favorite blog or website, and playing a game are much easier on the eyes due to the larger displays. You can certainly use a mobile phone to do most of the same tasks you'd perform on an iPad (assuming you have an Internet connection and/or data plan), but I've found that most tasks that involve typing more than a sentence or two (such as typing a fast reply email or sending a text message) are easier on the iPad.

I do a lot of technology research via the Web, and I can tell you that browsing a website, reading technical specifications, and trying to click on links using my mobile phone is frustrating. The text is small, so I have to enlarge the screen, thus reducing the amount of information that can be displayed at one time. Tapping a link is a cross-your-fingers event, especially if there are a lot of links on the page (my fingers just aren't that accurate when I'm trying to tap a link that is the size of a rice grain).

Nope, when it comes to web browsing on a mobile device, I reach for my iPad. (I'll use my laptop when it's available, but I love the iPad because it frees me from carrying my laptop everywhere I go.)

And the iPad is ready to go for web browsing the moment you turn it on and have an Internet connection established. It has a great built-in app called Safari, and I'm going to show you how to use it in this chapter.

 NOTE There are a ton of web browsers available for the iPad, and many of them have added features that are missing in Safari. You may choose later to investigate a new browser or two, but the Safari app actually benefits from the simplicity of its design—fewer features mean a more streamlined, less cluttered app. You'll also find that the iPad is designed to open the Safari app by default whenever you click a web link embedded in an email or text message, for example. Apple isn't offering a way to change the default browser at the moment, so it'll benefit you to learn how Safari works and how to use its basic features.

Opening Safari

Figure 8.1 shows the Safari app icon—tap it to open Safari.

FIGURE 8.1

The Safari app icon.

When Safari opens, you'll see a blank screen. What I like best about Safari is how simple it looks. But don't let the uncluttered screen fool you—it has plenty of features tucked away. You'll notice that some of the buttons on the toolbar along the top edge of the screen are grayed out (disabled). That's because there isn't a web page displayed. Let's go ahead and change that before I explain all the various toolbar items.

Tap your finger in the large text box that reads "Go to this address" and enter any web address you like. Figure 8.2 shows the onscreen keyboard that appears when I tap in the text box.

TIP   I love the .COM button that appears at the bottom of the onscreen keyboard. Yes, it saves you only four keystrokes, but when you're doing a lot of browsing from site to site, that little shortcut can really add up in saved typing time. Type in the first part of your address (and remember, you don't have to type **www**) and, assuming the address ends in .com, you can save yourself four keystrokes by tapping the .COM button to add the period and COM. Obviously, if the address ends in .net, .edu, .mil, or anything else, you'll have to type it longhand.

Enter the website address here

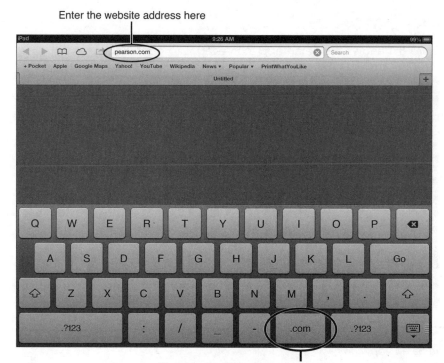

Pressing this button automatically types ".com" with one tap

FIGURE 8.2

Enter the web address using the onscreen keyboard.

Tap the Go button on the keyboard, and the website will be loaded. Figure 8.3 shows Pearson.com's website. Notice also that some of the toolbar buttons that were previously disabled are now available.

 NOTE If the website you typed in doesn't load, check the spelling and try to load the page one more time. If it still doesn't load, type in a different web address. If you're unable to load any web page, be certain to check the Settings app to confirm you have a valid Internet connection. Refer to Chapter 3, "iCloud and Settings," for steps on joining a Wi-Fi network or your provider's data network.

Unavailable buttons

Available buttons

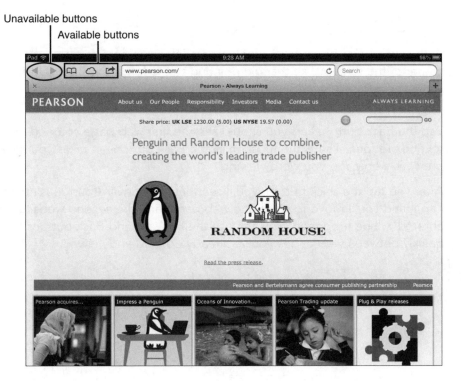

FIGURE 8.3

The website loads in Safari.

As with any app you use on your iPad, the Safari app supports gestures, so you'll find that swiping up or down will move the web page up or down, allowing you to view all its content. (Some websites do not have scrollable home pages, so swiping may not work because the entire home page is visible on the iPad's screen.)

Before we move on, go ahead and tap in the web address box again. A small gray circle with an X inside will appear to the right of the address.

Tap the X and the web address will disappear. Go ahead and type in a new address and tap the Go key to load the new page. I'm having you load a second web page so we can demonstrate one of the tools on the Safari toolbar shortly.

Now that you have a new web page open, let's take a look at Safari's toolbar and some of its tucked-away features.

Touring Safari

With a web page open, take a look at the Safari toolbar, starting in the upper-left corner of the screen. The triangle pointing to the left is the Back button, and if you've never used Safari on your iPad before, the triangle pointing to the right (the Forward button) is grayed out.

Tap the Back button, and you should see the first web page you entered in the text box reopen. That's the function of the Back button—it takes you back to the previous web page you were viewing.

After you tap the Back button, you'll see that the Forward button is now available. Tap it and you'll move forward one web page, and the second website you entered will be reopened. You can use the Forward and Back buttons to move quickly between web pages you've already opened and viewed.

 TIP If you tend to open a lot of web pages like I do, there's a better way to move between pages you need to switch between often—it involves using tabs, which I'll introduce to you shortly. The Back and Forward buttons are best used for one or two jumps at most. Anything more and you'll quickly start forgetting where a website is in the queue—is it ahead or behind of the currently viewed page?

Notice in Figure 8.4 that a small plus sign (+) appears to the right of the gray bar displaying the web page's name.

Click the + button
to open a new tab

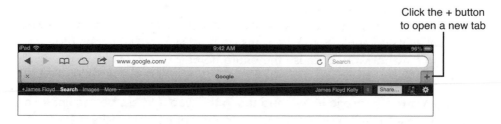

FIGURE 8.4

The plus button opens a new tab.

Go ahead and tap the plus button, and you'll see an interesting visual effect happen. First, the web page you were previously viewing is shrunk and its name is pushed to the left side of the screen. Second, the onscreen keyboard appears again and a blank web address text box is provided to you. All of this is shown in Figure 8.5.

FIGURE 8.5

Entering a new web address to be displayed on a tab.

Enter a new web address (I'm going to enter **bing.com**) and tap the Go button. Now you can see in Figure 8.6 that I have two tabs—one showing Google.com and the other showing Bing.com.

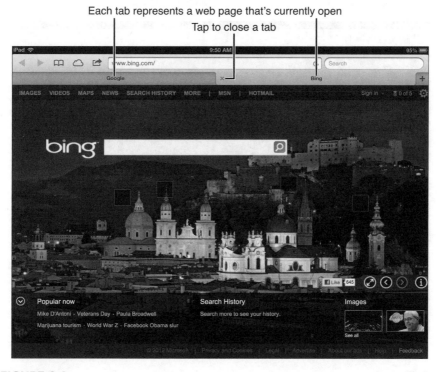

FIGURE 8.6

Two web pages are open and can be displayed with a single tap.

Each of these web pages is being stored on a tab, and all it takes to move between the two web pages is a single tap on either of the tabs. Rather than using the Back and Forward buttons, you can now keep multiple web pages open simultaneously. (When I say open, I mean they are available by tapping the tabs rather than retyping in a web address—any information on those screens is not visible on the iPad's screen but the website is sitting idle, ready for you to view again with a single tap of the tab.)

Notice also in Figure 8.6 that the currently viewed page has its tab displayed in a lighter shade of gray and has a small X on the left of the tab. Tapping this X will close the currently viewed tab.

What happens if you tap on the plus sign again to the right of the new tab? Not surprisingly—a third tab opens. The two current tabs are squeezed to the left to allow the third tab to fit onscreen (and the keyboard appears as well).

You may continue opening tabs, though eventually, you will run out of room on screen. The tabs are still there, though you will need to swipe the tab bar to the right in order to see them.

As you saw in Figure 8.6, a small box is labeled Search. Clicking it opens the keyboard as shown in Figure 8.7.

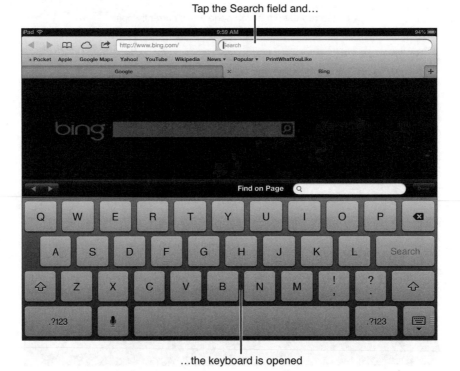

FIGURE 8.7

The Search feature in Safari.

When you tap in the Search box, two things happen. First, the onscreen keyboard allows you to type in one or more keywords to use in your web search. Second, just above the keyboard you'll see another Search box that allows you to search only on the currently viewed page. This is useful if you're looking for a specific word or maybe a part number or some other unique piece of information that exists on a dense, text-filled web page.

Figure 8.8 shows the results I get for my search on "iPad Mini" after tapping the Search button on the keyboard.

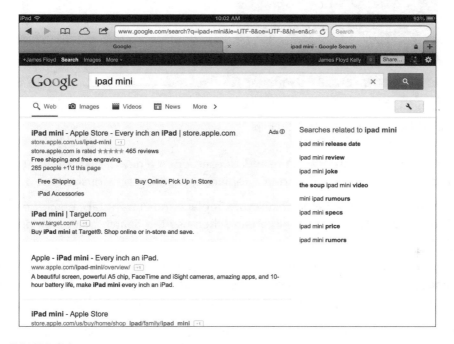

FIGURE 8.8

Use the top Search box to perform a web search.

 NOTE Did you happen to notice that the web page I was viewing was Bing.com? And did you also notice in Figure 8.8 that the search results for "iPad Mini" were returned using Google.com? You can configure the default search engine used in Safari by opening the Settings app, tapping the Safari option in the left column, and selecting your preferred search engine on the right side by tapping the Search Engine option—your options are Google, Yahoo!, and Bing.

I can swipe up or down to view the search results and then tap a link if I wish to open it. Figure 8.9 shows that the Search tool will provide you with the number of matches found for the text typed into the Search bar.

FIGURE 8.9

Searching using keywords "iPad mini."

Tapping a link in the search results doesn't open a new tab—instead, the link you tap is opened in the existing tab, replacing anything previously viewed.

If you'd rather not have search results replace the current tab, be certain to tap the plus sign to open a blank tab and then use the Search box provided on that tab.

If you chose to use the Search box that searches only the currently displayed web page, type in your search term. Safari will automatically move the web page to the first occurrence of your search term, as shown in Figure 8.10.

Scroll forward and backward through the matches   The first instance of the search term is highlighted.   The total number of matches is shown here.

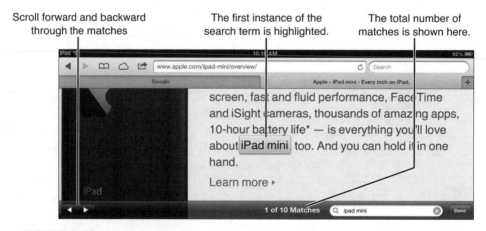

FIGURE 8.10

Search for keywords on a web page.

Take a look again at Figure 8.10, and you'll see a few other bits of information. You can see that there are ten instances (matches) of the term "iPad mini" on the current page. You use the left/right arrow buttons to move forward and backward through the instances. Each instance where the search term is found will be slightly enlarged and highlighted in yellow.

Using the Share Feature

Now let's return to the left side of Safari's toolbar. Tap the Share button and you'll see a small window open with a number of options inside, as shown in Figure 8.11.

Tap the Share button to make this window open.

FIGURE 8.11

The Share button has many options for you to use.

If you tap the Mail icon, a blank email message will open with the web page included as an attachment. You can then type in a recipient's email address to share that website with him. (When he receives it, if he taps on the attachment, the web page will open in his default web browser.)

The Message, Twitter, and Facebook buttons allow you to share the website using these three social tools. I cover the Messages app in Chapter 10, "Apps for Instant Communication" and Twitter and Facebook apps in Chapter 11, "Social Apps."

If you tap the Add to Home Screen button, you'll be asked to give the shortcut a name (using the onscreen keyboard), as shown in Figure 8.12.

FIGURE 8.12

Create a web page shortcut.

Tap the Add button (in Figure 8.12), and the shortcut will be added to the home screen, as shown in Figure 8.13. Note that although the shortcut looks like an app icon, when it's tapped it will simply open the Safari app and display the web page you added as a shortcut.

A shortcut added to your iPad's desktop

FIGURE 8.13

The web page shortcut appears on the home screen.

Returning to the Share button's options, if you tap the Print button, you can print the web page to any printer that supports AirPlay.

The Copy button copies the web page address to the iPad's clipboard so you can use the Paste command in any app that supports it.

The next two buttons, Bookmark and Add to Reading List, perform two interesting actions. The Bookmark button adds the web page address to a saved list of web pages called *Bookmarks*. The Add to Reading List adds the web page to a list you can view at any time—this list holds web pages you wish to view (and read) at a later time, not necessarily right now. Tap the Add to Reading List button when you find a web page you want to come back to later, but you don't necessarily want to bookmark and keep indefinitely.

Tap the Bookmark button and you'll see a screen like the one in Figure 8.14.

FIGURE 8.14

Use the Bookmark button to save the web page.

You can use the onscreen keyboard to change the title assigned to the bookmark—I suggest you shorten it as best you can. Also, the Bookmark tool can organize your saved web pages in categories (folders) that you create. I'll show you how to do this in the next section, but if you have created new categories, you can tap the button at the bottom of Figure 8.14 and select the category where you wish to file away the bookmarked web page. Tap the Save button when you're done, and the web page will be stored.

As for the Add to Reading List, go ahead and tap the Share button again and then tap the Add to Reading List button. Unlike adding a bookmark, no window appears; instead, the web page is filed away to the Reading List.

Now that you've added a bookmark and a web page to the Reading List, let's take a quick look at how you use those two features.

Bookmarks and Reading List

Tap the button on the Safari toolbar that looks like an open book, and you'll see the Bookmarks menu appear, as shown in Figure 8.15.

FIGURE 8.15

The Bookmarks menu.

The Bookmarks menu has a number of features that aren't always obvious. First, tap the Edit button at any time to delete a folder or saved bookmark. Folders look like, well, folders (in Figure 8.15, Jim is a folder), and bookmarks have a small book icon to the left of their title. When you tap the Edit button, you can delete any item (except for the Bookmarks Bar and Bookmarks Menu folders) by tapping the small red circle with the minus sign inside, as shown in Figure 8.16. You can also tap the New Folder button (also shown in Figure 8.16) to add a new folder, which is useful for filing away bookmarks by category such as Home or Work. Tap the Done button to close the Edit feature.

FIGURE 8.16

The Edit button allows you to manage folders and bookmarks.

Tap on a folder to open it and view any saved bookmarks inside, or tap a bookmark not filed away in a folder to immediately open that web page in Safari.

At the bottom of the Bookmarks menu, you'll see three icons. Left to right, they are Bookmarks, History, and Reading List. Tapping the History button will show you a list of recently viewed web pages.

The History tab is useful because it also saves a week's worth of browsing history.

TIP If you don't want someone viewing your browsing history, you can use the Clear History button at the top of the History window. Keep in mind that any web pages you haven't bookmarked are gone for good when you use the Clear History option.

Tap the Reading List button (it looks like a pair of eyeglasses) and you'll now be given a list of all the web pages you've saved using the Add to Reading List button. Notice that two buttons are shown in Figure 8.17—the All button and the Unread button.

FIGURE 8.17

The Reading List saves your web pages for later viewing.

Tap the Unread button and then tap a web page to view it. Once you've viewed a web page stored in the Reading List, it is marked as Read and moved to the All list. When you're viewing the All list, a left swipe on any web page in the Reading List box will offer up a Delete button so you can remove the web page from the Reading List.

There's also a fast way to add a web page to the Reading List. While the Reading List is open, tap the plus sign in the upper-right corner and the web page that is currently displayed in Safari will automatically be added to the Unread list.

 TIP   The Unread button is a great way to track those web pages you've saved for later reading but haven't yet had time to read. Just be sure to occasionally purge the All list; otherwise, it will be time consuming to search through it. If you find a web page that you absolutely must keep, consider adding it as a bookmark and then remove it from the Reading List.

iCloud Tabs

The last button on the Safari toolbar is the iCloud Tabs button, shown in Figure 8.18. As you can see, I've not yet synced my web browsing between my iPad and my other iOS devices.

FIGURE 8.18

iCloud Tabs lets you continue viewing web pages from other devices.

The way iCloud Tabs works is simple. If you have an iPhone, iPod touch, or any other device running iOS that is also configured to use iCloud with your Apple ID (refer to Chapter 3 for more details), any open tabs you have in Safari can be shared between devices.

Put simply, if I'm viewing the Peachpit.com web page on my iPhone while standing in line for a movie and I've configured iCloud to sync with Safari, then when I get home and pick up my iPad I can immediately pick up where I left off on my iPhone by tapping the iCloud Tabs button. The page I was viewing while standing in line will be visible.

APPS FOR PHOTOS AND VIDEOS

I'll admit it—I'm not so fond of holding my iPad or iPad mini up in front of me to take a photo or shoot a video. But I must admit, there are times when I don't have my mobile phone handy or a real camera in hand and an opportunity presents itself that just screams to be documented. Most of the time this need for impromptu photos and videos is related to my kids doing funny or cute things. However, I did have an opportunity recently where I used my iPad after witnessing a fender bender—I shot some photos and a quick video because the driver who was rear-ended lacked the ability.

The iPad comes preinstalled with three apps that are photo/video related: Camera, Photo Booth, and Photos. The Camera app is used to shoot photos and videos. Photo Booth lets you take fun, quirky snapshots just like you'd do in those little novelty photo booths that spit out four small images of anyone in the seat in front of the camera. And the Photos app is where you view your photos and videos and apply some editing techniques.

I cover all three of these apps in this chapter; when you're done reading, you'll be ready to take photos, shoot videos, perform some edits, and even share your little works of art with friends and family.

Using Camera

Let me start by having you tap the icon for the Camera app, shown in Figure 9.1.

FIGURE 9.1

The icon for the Camera app.

Remember, the primary camera is on the back of the iPad (as opposed to the front-mounted webcam used for FaceTime—see Chapter 10, "Apps for Instant Communication"), so you'll want to make certain you're holding the iPad in such a way that the rear camera lens is not obstructed. Figure 9.2 shows that I'm pointing the iPad at my favorite two-year-old.

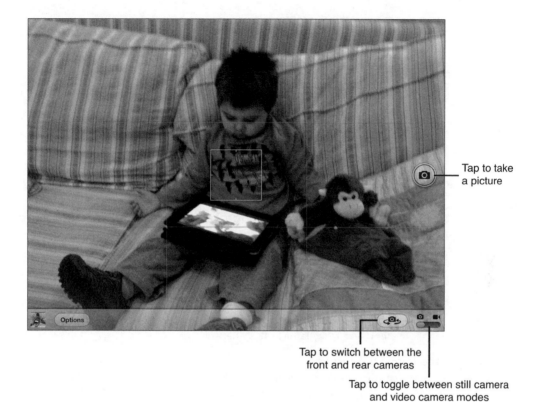

Tap to take
a picture

Tap to switch between the
front and rear cameras

Tap to toggle between still camera
and video camera modes

FIGURE 9.2

The view when using the iPad's rear camera.

Now for a quick tour. Starting on the right side of the screen about halfway down is the Shutter button. Press that button and you'll take a picture. Easy! Notice in Figure 9.2 that there's even a small icon on the button that looks like a camera. There's a good reason for this, and it has to do with the next item of interest.

Continue down the right edge of the screen, and you'll run into a toggle button that changes the Camera app from camera mode to video mode. Every time you touch the toggle button, it moves to the other position. Notice in Figure 9.3 that the toggle button is now underneath the small video camera icon.

 NOTE Sorry, lefties, but if you rotate the iPad in hopes that the Shutter button will be on the left side and easier for you to press with your left thumb, you're going to be disappointed. The Shutter button will always be on the right side, no matter if the iPad is in Portrait or Landscape view.

FIGURE 9.3

The toggle button is now set to video mode.

When the Camera app is set to video mode, notice that the Shutter button icon changes from the small camera to a red Record button. Tap the Record button, and your iPad will now begin to record video.

 TIP Go ahead and shoot some video (maybe 30 to 45 seconds worth) and take some photos. I want you to have some photos and videos stored on your iPad so you'll be able to do some hands-on tasks later in this chapter.

Look to the left of the toggle button and you'll see a small button with an icon of a camera with rotation arrows surrounding it. Tap the Camera Swap button and the iPad will switch from using the rear-mounted camera to the front-mounted webcam. Figure 9.4 shows my iPad ready to take a self-portrait at my favorite coffee shop in Atlanta using the webcam.

Thumbnail image   Front/Rear camera toggle

FIGURE 9.4

Taking a self-portrait with the webcam.

 NOTE Did you notice anything funny about Figure 9.4? This is actually a screen capture I took by pressing the Home button and the Sleep/Power button simultaneously. Notice that when I'm looking at the iPad with the webcam, the image is reversed! Don't worry—when I take the actual photo by tapping the Shutter button, the actual photo will not be reversed.

One thing you'll notice right away with the webcam photos and videos is that they are much grainier. The quality of the webcam is much lower than the rear-mounted lens, so always make certain to use the rear-mounted camera when you want to take higher-quality photos and video.

Now look in the lower-left corner of the Camera app and you'll see two items. The first is a small thumbnail image that, when tapped, will open the most recent photo or video you have taken with the Camera app. If you tap the small square, the Camera Roll is opened; I'll introduce you to the Camera Roll later in this chapter, but for now just know that it's part of the Photos app and is where you go to view all the photos and videos you take with the iPad. Figure 9.5 shows the Camera Roll open and displaying a picture of my son—tap anywhere on the screen and you'll see a blue Done button in the upper-right corner of the screen; tap it to return to the Camera app.

Click Done to go back to the Camera app

Choose a thumbnail here and that picture will fill the screen

FIGURE 9.5

View the most recent photo or video.

To the right of the thumbnail is the Options button. (If you don't see the Options button, tap the toggle button to change the Camera app back to photo mode—the Options button isn't available in video mode.)

It's a bit funny to me, but the Options button only has one actual option—Grid—as you can see in Figure 9.6. When you tap it, it changes to a Done button. When you click Done, it toggles back to Options.

The Option button toggles to the Done button

FIGURE 9.6

The Options button in camera mode.

If you turn on the Grid by tapping the toggle button shown in Figure 9.6, you'll see the screen divided up into nine sections, as shown in Figure 9.7.

Tap to toggle Grid view on and off

FIGURE 9.7

The Grid button divides the screen into nine sections.

The Grid doesn't show up in any photos or videos you take while it is displayed on the screen. Instead, the Grid is a useful tool for photographers who like to use the Rule of Thirds when shooting photos.

TIP If you've never heard of the Rule of Thirds in a photography class, visit http://en.wikipedia.org/wiki/Rule_of_ thirds to learn more. Believe it or not, I've been using the Rule of Thirds for a few years now to take photos and I've gotten quite a few compliments on them. It's worth learning and implementing, especially with the Grid turned on.

Tap the Grid button again to toggle the Grid to the Off position, if you prefer to not have it displayed.

Believe it or not, that's it for the Camera app! Pretty simple app, isn't it? One of the reasons I like the Camera app so much is because it's so simple to use. It doesn't even have a section in the Settings app for you to tweak.

NOTE For those of you who want some more options when it comes to taking photos and videos, you'll want to investigate the Photo & Video category in the App Store. See Chapter 12, "Apps for the iPad," for more information on the App Store as well as how to use categories to filter down and find specific types of apps. The App Store has hundreds (yes, hundreds!) of apps that use the built-in camera and webcam on your iPad and iPad mini.

Using Photo Booth

Tap the Photo Booth app icon shown in Figure 9.8.

FIGURE 9.8

The icon for the Photo Booth app.

Unlike the Camera app, the Photo Booth app is only for taking photos—it does not offer a video mode. Figure 9.9 shows the Photo Booth screen before you take any photos.

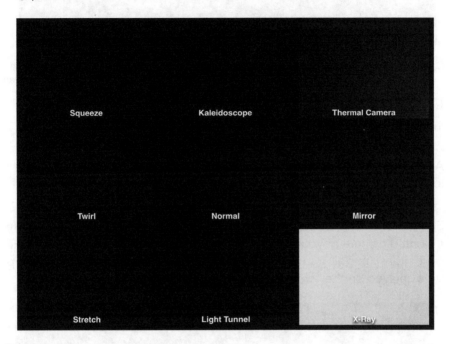

FIGURE 9.9

Nine options are available for taking photos with Photo Booth.

As you can see in Figure 9.9, you're offered nine image variations of whatever the camera lens is pointed at, with most of them being somewhat comical.

In the center is the Normal option. If you want to take a normal, unaltered image, you can always switch to the actual Camera app. It's the other eight options that offer some fun with the iPad's built-in camera and webcam.

Yes, both cameras are supported, but first you'll need to tap an option to change the camera mode. I'm going to tap the Squeeze option, which takes me to the screen shown in Figure 9.10.

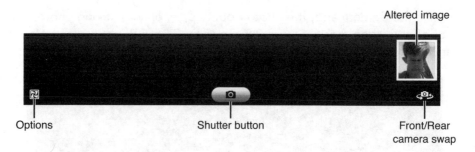

FIGURE 9.10

The Squeeze option applies a funny format to the subject.

All nine options provide the same toolbar along the bottom of the screen. In the lower-right corner is the Camera Swap button, which changes the view from the rear-mounted camera to the webcam.

The button at the center of the toolbar is the Shutter button. Point the rear-mounted camera at your subject (or tap the Camera Swap button to take a self-portrait, as I'm going to do here) and tap the Shutter button. Your new photo will be displayed on the screen, as shown in Figure 9.11.

FIGURE 9.11

Take your funny picture by tapping the Shutter button.

Tap the small box in the lower-left corner of the toolbar to return to the nine photo options shown back in Figure 9.9.

My kids love Photo Booth; I do believe they'd sit for hours just taking silly photos of themselves with the webcam. Thankfully, the photos taken with Photo Booth don't take up a lot of my iPad's storage space. But once they're done with the app, I usually find myself having to open up the Photos app to delete a lot of photos while saving a few key ones for use during their teenage years.

And speaking of deleting and saving photos, those two tasks and more are done using the Photos app.

The Photos App

The icon for the Photos app is shown in Figure 9.12—go ahead and tap it to open up the app.

FIGURE 9.12

The icon for the Photos app.

The Photos app offers three views when you first open it: Photos, Photo Stream, and Albums.

The Albums view allows you to organize your photos and videos into folders that you can create by tapping the plus sign button in the upper-left corner of the screen. Figure 9.13 also shows that I'm creating a new album titled "Chapter 9."

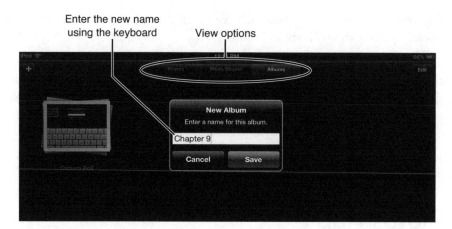

FIGURE 9.13

Create a new album for storing photos and videos.

After typing the album title, I tap Save and then a new screen appears like the one in Figure 9.14.

FIGURE 9.14

Selection screen for the new album.

After creating a new album, you simply tap on the photos you wish to have placed inside your new album. You can select multiple photos and videos from the screen by scrolling up and down and then tapping on the selections—a blue circle with a check mark will appear on the thumbnails, as shown in Figure 9.15.

Tap a photo to select it;
tap again to de-select

Check-marked items will be placed into the new album

FIGURE 9.15

Select photos and videos by tapping on them.

After you've selected all the photos and videos you wish to move into your new album, tap the Done button. You'll be returned to the Album screen and your new album will appear along with the Camera Roll album, as shown in Figure 9.16.

New album

FIGURE 9.16

The new album is added to the Albums view.

Tap an album to open and view its contents.

When viewing the contents of an album, you can distinguish between photos and videos easily—videos appear with a small video camera icon in the lower-left portion of the thumbnail, along with the length of the video in minutes and seconds, as shown in Figure 9.17.

Tap the Albums button in the top-left corner to return to the Album view, or tap the Slideshow button to immediately start displaying all photos and videos inside the album as a slideshow.

Now tap the Edit button. Additional options will appear, as shown in Figure 9.17.

Tap the Edit button and these options appear

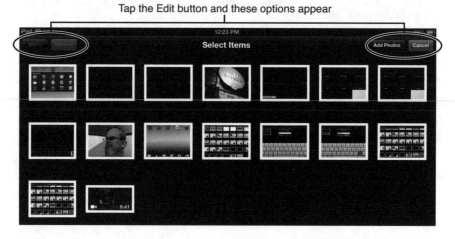

FIGURE 9.17

Options are available when viewing contents in an album.

If you tap the Add Photos button, you'll once again open the Camera Roll album, where you can select additional photos and videos to add to the current album.

While you can delete photos and videos from any album you have created, you can only permanently delete photos and videos from the Camera Roll album. (Think of photos and videos you add to an album you've created as copies.) Tap on any photos or videos in one of your custom albums and then tap the Remove button to remove the selected items. A message will appear telling you the photo will be removed from this album, but will remain in the Photo Library. Click Remove from Album to take the picture out of the album.

Also while in Edit mode, you can tap and hold any photo and drag it to a new position. All other photos will shift positions, allowing the photo you are dragging to be dropped in place when you remove your finger.

 NOTE Consider photos and videos stored in your own custom albums as nothing more than shortcuts to the original photos and videos that are stored in the Camera Roll. This saves on space (so you don't have two copies of every photo and video, one in Camera Roll and one in your custom albums) and allows for easier sharing of only selected images rather than making your entire Camera Roll album visible.

To the left of the Remove button is the Share button. If you select a video from your album and tap the Share button, three options will appear: Mail, Message, and YouTube. Tapping on any one of these three apps will open that app and let you upload the selected video(s) using it. (Mail is covered in Chapter 7, "The Mail App," and the Message app is covered in Chapter 10.)

The YouTube button will open a window that allows you to use a YouTube username and password to upload the video along with setting some options such as the quality of the video and whether it is public or private. The YouTube app was removed from iOS 6, so if you wish to use this feature, you'll need to visit YouTube.com and create a user account.

If you only select photos to share, you'll get many more options when you tap the Share button, as shown in Figure 9.18.

FIGURE 9.18

Share options for photos.

I covered some of these options in earlier chapters (such as Mail, Print, Assign to Contact, and Copy) and others will make more sense when you read their respective chapters (such as Chapter 11, "Social Apps," for Facebook and Twitter or Chapter 10 for Messages). A simple option I can show you now is the Use as Wallpaper option. Tap it, and your home screens will use the selected image as the wallpaper.

Notice also in Figure 9.18 that there's a Photo Stream option, which I'll explain shortly. It involves adding a photo to an album that you can make visible to your friends and family or the entire world.

By the way, if you choose a mix of photos and videos and tap the Share button, you'll only have four options available—Twitter, Facebook, Print, and Copy.

Go ahead and tap the Cancel button to exit the Edit screen and return to your custom album. Then tap the Albums button to return to the Albums view. Now I want to talk to you about the Photos button. Tapping the Photos button is the same as opening the Camera Roll album—you will see a scrollable screen (up and down) that displays all of your photos.

Once again, you can tap the Edit button, but this time the options are different, as shown in Figure 9.19.

Tap Edit and these options appear

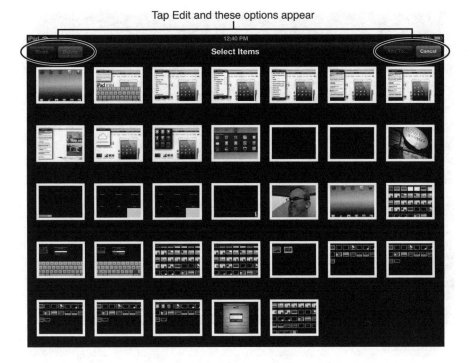

FIGURE 9.19

The Edit screen for Camera Roll offers different options.

Now, when you select one or more photos or videos, instead of the Remove button you can tap the Delete button to permanently remove those items from your iPad. You cannot undo a deletion, so be certain you want a photo or video deleted before you tap the Delete button—once it's gone, it's gone.

You'll also notice in Figure 9.19 that where the Slideshow button was located for your custom albums, there is now an Add To button. Tapping this button after selecting photos and videos in the list will allow you to move those selections to an existing album or to a new album, as shown in Figure 9.20.

FIGURE 9.20

Place selections in a new or existing album.

Remember, you're not really moving a photo or video to a new or existing album. The photos and videos stay in the Camera Roll, and a shortcut thumbnail is placed in the custom album you specify. If you tap the Add to Existing Album option, you will be shown all of your current custom albums (plus the Camera Roll for some reason); tap a custom album and the shortcuts will be created.

Likewise, if you tap the Add to New Album button in Figure 9.20, you'll see a screen similar to the one shown previously in Figure 9.13 so that you can type the name of your new album. When you're done, tap the Save button and your selected images and videos will have shortcuts placed in the new album. Easy!

Before exiting the Edit screen for the Photos view, you'll also notice there's a Share button in the upper-left corner of the screen. Just as you saw earlier for custom albums, the options for sharing change depending on whether you have selected photos or videos. Tap the Cancel button to return to the Photos view.

Finally, before I show you how to edit photos and videos, let me cover the last view option, Photo Stream.

NOTE Photo streams require iOS, so this feature is only available to those with iPads, iPhones, and other devices running iOS.

The first thing you'll need to do is to create a photo stream. Think of photo streams as albums or folders; you can have more than one, and you can specify who has access to particular photo streams. Start by tapping the plus sign in the upper-left corner and type the email address in the To: text box shown in Figure 9.21. You can also tap the blue circle with the plus sign to select from your Contacts app.

FIGURE 9.21

Create a new photo stream.

In addition to entering the name or names of any people you wish to give permission to view your new photo stream, you must also give the photo stream a name and select whether you want the photo stream to be public (anyone can view the photos by visiting iCloud.com) or private (which is the default setting—Public Website is turned to Off, as shown in Figure 9.21).

Make your selections and then tap the Create button. Your new photo stream will now be visible, and it works just like a custom album.

When I tap the new photo stream, it opens and is empty at first. I can tap the Add Photos button to add videos and photos.

Once you've created a photo stream and set its permissions, you can't change it. If you wish to make a photo stream visible to anyone, you'll need to create a new photo stream and turn the Public Website option shown in Figure 9.21 from Off to On.

Editing Photos

Before I end this chapter, I want to give you a very brief overview of editing photos.

 CAUTION The editing capabilities built in to your iPad are extremely limited, so if you want more advanced color editing for your photos, you're going to have to do some research on the various editing apps available from the App Store. You'll also find there are no editing options for videos, so once again you'll need to hunt down an app with video-editing features. Refer to Chapter 12, where I cover the App Store. Remember, you'll want to examine the Photo & Video category.

Open either the Camera Roll album or one of your custom albums and then tap on a single photo to open it as shown in Figure 9.22.

FIGURE 9.22

A photo ready for some editing.

In Figure 9.22, you'll see a thin band of images running along the lower edge of the screen. You can tap one of those tiny images to jump to that photo, or you can swipe your finger on the screen (left or right) to move forward and back through an album.

You'll also see in Figure 9.22 the Share button and the Slideshow button; tap either of these to see options appear for the photo you are currently viewing. Tap the trashcan button to delete the current image.

 TIP   Also visible in Figure 9.22 is the AirPlay button. If you have an Apple TV hooked up to your television, you can set it to display anything shown on your iPad, including a slideshow, an individual photo, a video, and much more. Visit Apple.com/appletv for more details.

It's the Edit button shown in Figure 9.22 that you need to tap now. When you tap the Edit button, you'll see a new toolbar at the bottom of the screen and some options in the upper-left corner of the screen, as shown in Figure 9.23.

Edit options

FIGURE 9.23

Edit options for the current photo you are viewing.

The Rotate button rotates the image 90 degrees counterclockwise for every tap. The Enhance button attempts to brighten or sharpen the image; you have no control over the change it makes, so that's where the Undo button in the top-left corner comes into play. Tap the Undo button if you don't like the changes the Enhance button makes to your photo.

The Red-Eye button allows you to tap any fiery eyeballs that appear in a photo. The app attempts to detect the red and remove it. Again, you can tap the Undo button if you're not happy with the results.

And finally, the Crop button will shrink the image slightly and put a draggable frame around it, as shown in Figure 9.24.

FIGURE 9.24

Use the Crop button to crop the photo if needed.

Tap your finger on any of the four corners and move the gridded frame that is over the photo. As you can see in Figure 9.25, by adjusting each of the four corners, you can select the part of a photo you wish to keep; anything outside the gridded area will be removed.

FIGURE 9.25

Drag the grid's four corners to crop out unwanted parts of the photo.

When you're done, tap the Crop button in the upper-right corner of the screen and your edited photo will be saved as a new photo when you tap the Save button. The original will be kept safe in your Camera Roll.

 TIP   If you make a bunch of changes to the photo at once (for example, cropping, followed by red-eye removal, and then maybe using the Enhance button) and are unhappy with the results, tap the Revert to Original button at any time, and the original photo will be reloaded.

10

APPS FOR INSTANT COMMUNICATION

Email is great; it's fast, easy to use, and you don't have to pay a small fee every time you send a message. I use it every day. You just can't beat email when it comes to sending off a fast message. Or can you?

Your iPad comes with two preinstalled apps that are outstanding for what I call instant communication: Messages and FaceTime. Why isn't the Mail app on that list? Well, Mail is instant when it comes to sending a message, but it's not so instant when you're waiting for a reply. You may send a fast message to your friend asking him to meet you for lunch in 15 minutes, but if he isn't sitting in front of his computer when the message arrives, you may be dining alone. And even those people with smartphones that offer email access might not be able to reply if they're in a meeting or in the dentist's chair, for example. Nope, email can be fast, but it's by no means instant.

For instant communication, what you need is instant messaging or video chat. Both offer you the ability to communicate with other iOS users in real time. Just like a face-to-face conversation, instant messaging allows you to communicate as fast as you can type (and it's not the same as text messaging on your phone). And video chatting is even faster, but this time you can see the person with whom you're chatting.

 NOTE Text messaging and instant messaging are completely different animals, even though they can often behave the same and even use the same app. If you and a friend are sending text messages back and forth, it can often seem like you're using instant messaging, but what if your friend has left his phone in the car or is in a meeting? Yep, you've got to wait for a response. Instant messaging, on the other hand, implies that both you and the other participant have the instant messaging app open and have no distractions.

In previous chapters, I have mentioned these two apps that allow you to have instant communication across long (or short) distances. Now it's time to see how the Messages and FaceTime apps work.

The Messages App

Take a look at Figure 10.1, and you'll see the icon for the Messages app.

FIGURE 10.1

The icon for the Messages app.

When you first open the Messages app, you're going to see a mostly blank screen. Assuming that you have not yet used it for any text messaging, you won't have any previous discussions visible.

Communication between you and another person with the Messages app can take the form of text messaging or instant messaging, but that person's contact information must be stored in the Contacts app. Type the name or number of the person you wish to chat with (using Messages) in the To: text box with the onscreen keyboard, as shown in Figure 10.2.

 CAUTION The Messages app on the iPad can be used for text messaging and instant messaging with any person who is using a device that runs iOS 5 or greater; this communication is done using Wi-Fi or a cellular data connection.

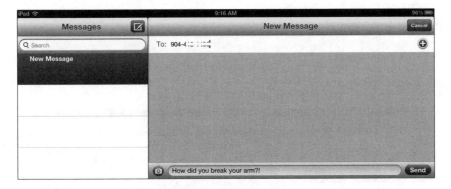

FIGURE 10.2

Typing in a phone number in the Messages app. The recipient's number has been intentionally obscured.

Next, tap in the message text box (to the right of the small camera icon), type your message, as shown in Figure 10.3, and then tap the Send button.

Type recipient's name or number here

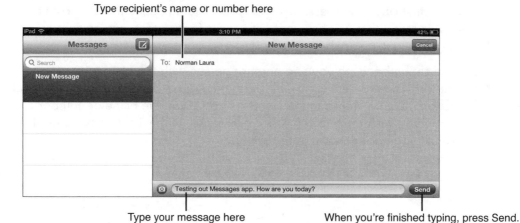

Type your message here   When you're finished typing, press Send.

FIGURE 10.3

Type your message in the text box.

Notice in Figure 10.4 that your message is placed into a text balloon in the conversation window.

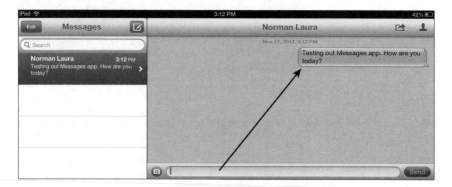

FIGURE 10.4

Your message is added to the conversation window.

As you and your contact trade messages, they will be stacked in the conversation window, with the oldest message moving toward the top and then eventually off the screen. Your messages will be along the right side of the conversation window and your contact's replies will be to the left. Each side of the chat will also have a different color, thus making it easy for both of you to follow the conversation. Figure 10.5 shows a back-and-forth I'm having with one of my Pearson editors, Laura.

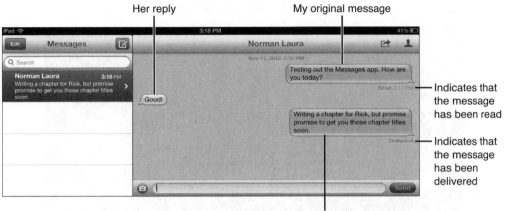

Her reply

My original message

Indicates that the message has been read

Indicates that the message has been delivered

Another message to the recipient; you can send multiple messages, long or short regardless of whether your recipient replies.

FIGURE 10.5

A chat with my editor using the Messages app.

Notice underneath my original message in Figure 10.5 that the word "Read" appears. This lets me know that my message was received and read. In my follow-up, you see the word "Delivered." This lets me know that the message successfully arrived, but was not read. If I don't get an immediate response, I at least know the message will be waiting for Laura. Figure 10.6 shows how the Messages app alerts you to a new message. The number (called a badge) lets you know that you have a message waiting to be read.

 NOTE You can set configure the Messages app to alert you when a message has been read. Open Settings, select Messages, and view the various options available (including the ability to turn on a Subject line).

FIGURE 10.6

The Messages app tells me a message is waiting.

See the little ellipsis icon that appears in Figure 10.7? That icon lets you know that the other person is typing. This is helpful in controlling the pace of a conversation. Just as a face-to-face conversation usually has one person speaking at a time, this icon reminds you to wait for the other person to finish their response.

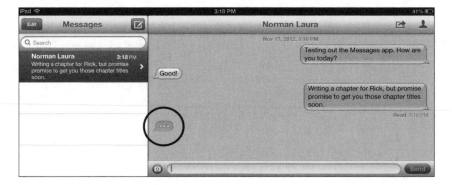

FIGURE 10.7

Someone is responding...be patient.

To the left you can see that the conversation I just had with my editor is being saved as a message. As more text chats occur with other people, each conversation will be saved in this list. At any time, you can tap the right-pointing chevron, and that conversation will be displayed to the right, allowing you to revisit any chat you've had in the past.

If you wish to delete a conversation, simply tap on the message in the left column and swipe to the left. A Delete button will appear. Tap the Delete button to permanently remove the conversation, or tap on the left side of the screen on any white area to cancel and return to the Messages window.

At any time, you can open an old conversation and type in a response, and the conversation will start up again. But this is not always desired, especially if the subject of your conversation has changed. In that case, you'll need to delete the existing message and start a new message by clicking the New Message button. A new, blank message window will appear to the right.

As you can see in Figure 10.8, the new conversation is added to the list on the left and the conversation is visible on the right.

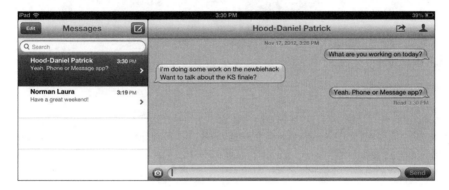

FIGURE 10.8

Another conversation added to the Message list.

While you're in a conversation, you can tap the small button in the upper-right corner (looks like a person's shoulders and head) to view that person's contact information and even update it by tapping the Edit button, as shown in Figure 10.9. Tap anywhere on the screen to close the Info box.

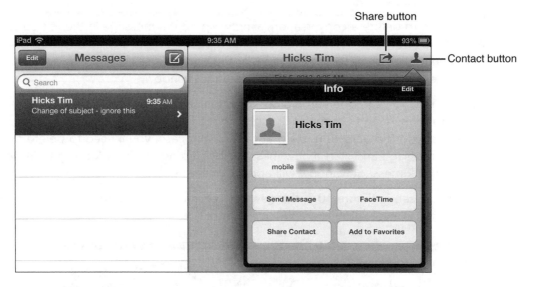

FIGURE 10.9

View a contact's information screen and update it.

As shown in Figure 10.9, a Share button appears to the left of the Contact button. Tap it, and each of the pieces of a conversation will have a small circle placed to their left, as shown in Figure 10.10. Tap a circle and a check mark will appear inside.

Select a message by tapping the circle next to it

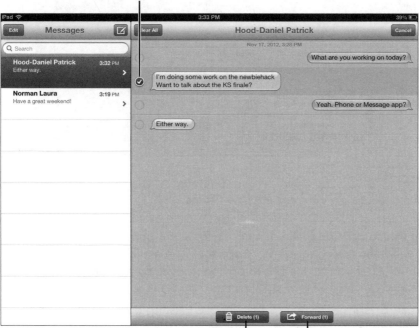

Tap delete the selected message ┘   └ Tap forward the selected message

FIGURE 10.10

Select a piece of a conversation to share.

After you select one or more responses, you can tap the Delete button at the bottom to remove them from the conversation. Alternatively, you can tap the Forward button to create a new message containing the selected responses (in their entirety) for forwarding to someone else in a different message. (This is useful if someone provides a phone number or address that might be useful to another one of your contacts.)

Finally, you might have noticed the small camera icon to the left of the text box. Tap it, and you'll see these two options (also shown in Figure 10.11):

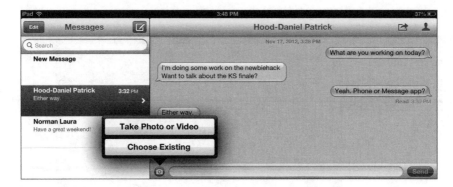

FIGURE 10.11

Take a photo/video or choose one from the Photos app.

- **Take Photo or Video**—If you choose to take a photo or video, the Camera app will open (see Chapter 9, "Apps for Photos and Videos," for details on using it). After you take a photo or video, it will be sent to your contact using the Messages app—he or she can tap the photo or video to view it.

- **Choose Existing**—If you tap the Choose Existing button, you can browse the Photos app (also covered in Chapter 9) and pick a photo or video to send to the other person in a message. Figure 10.12 shows that I've done the email equivalent of sending an attachment by embedding a photo in the text window—and I can also add a message!

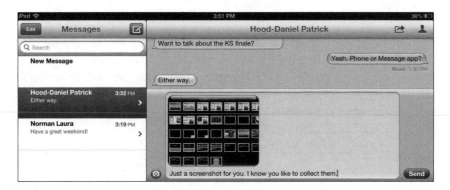

FIGURE 10.12

Embed a photo or video and include a message.

That's it for the Messages app. As you can see, it's a great way to have a back-and-forth conversation with a contact. And just like text messaging and email, you can include a photo or video with a message.

Messages is a great app, but I find it does have limitations. For example, I can definitely talk faster than I can type, and I imagine you can, too. Sometimes my replies have spelling errors, and if I insert a little sarcasm into a text message, sometimes my recipient doesn't read the way I intended and might be offended.

For those moments when the Messages app just doesn't cut it, you'll want to open the FaceTime app for face-to-face voice chat.

Using FaceTime

FaceTime is awesome. Any contacts who are running iOS 5 or greater on a device with a front-facing camera can be "dialed up" with the FaceTime app, and you'll see their shiny, happy face onscreen. The icon for the FaceTime app is shown in Figure 10.13, but don't tap to open it just yet.

FIGURE 10.13

The icon for the FaceTime app.

Before opening FaceTime, you need to open the Settings app and add one or more email addresses that will be used to communicate between devices running the FaceTime app. Figure 10.14 shows the Settings app open and the FaceTime option selected. Notice on the right side that FaceTime uses a combination of your Apple ID email address and any additional email addresses you wish to add that other FaceTime users can use to contact you.

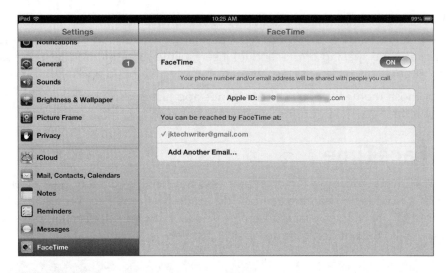

FIGURE 10.14

Your Apple ID and your FaceTime email address.

CAUTION Although you can use the email address associated with your Apple ID to run FaceTime, I highly recommend that you use a separate email address that you can provide to other FaceTime users. This email address must be added to the other user's FaceTime Contacts (you'll learn how to do this in a moment); otherwise, FaceTime calls between you and the other person will not work.

You can tap the Add Another Email link and add as many email addresses to be associated with FaceTime as you like. I have multiple email addresses that I use for personal and work-related activities, but for FaceTime I only use one (not my Apple ID email address) and provide that to any of my friends or colleagues running FaceTime so they can call me. The flip side to this requirement is that I must also have my friends and colleagues provide me with their FaceTime email address so I can add it to the FaceTime Contact list.

After you've added an email address in the "You Can Be Reached by FaceTime At:" field, close down the Settings app and tap the icon for the FaceTime app to open FaceTime. You'll see a screen like the one in Figure 10.15. The camera shows your image (or whatever your camera is pointed at when FaceTime opens).

FIGURE 10.15

Opening up FaceTime.

You haven't made a FaceTime call yet, so you'll see your face on the screen along with some buttons. In the bottom-right corner, you'll see these three buttons:

- **Favorites**—Tap the Favorites button. Any contacts you've added to your Contacts app and made a "Favorite" (refer to Chapter 4, "Contacts," for instructions on how to do this) will be listed here. The Favorite button is simply a faster method for locating people you wish to FaceTime—if someone isn't in the Favorite listing, you'll have to hunt them down using the Contacts button.

- **Recents**—As you will see later in this chapter, a complete list of all FaceTime calls is provided, including the date and which email address was used (home or work, for example).

- **Contacts**—Tap this button, and you'll see a screen similar to the one in Figure 10.16 (your list of contacts will obviously look different). This is nothing more than a list of all your contacts from the Contacts app. The difference is that anyone listed here who does not have a device that runs FaceTime or does not have an email address associated with their FaceTime app cannot be contacted.

FIGURE 10.16

The Contacts list. Full names and email addresses are blurred intentionally.

CAUTION Remember, to place a video call to someone in your Contacts list, two conditions must be met:

- The person you want to call must have your FaceTime email address saved in his or her Contacts app (meaning you have been added to their Contacts app and have an information page containing your FaceTime email address).

- You must have that person's FaceTime email address saved in your Contacts app. If both of these conditions are met, you can make a FaceTime call!

TIP As with a standard phone, using FaceTime requires you to simply tap one of your FaceTime contacts to make the call. The problem is that the person you're calling may not be ready to take that call. It's always best to send a quick text message or email to set up a FaceTime call. If the person's device isn't set to vibrate or the volume isn't turned down, the FaceTime app will ring a tune that can be disruptive if the recipient of the FaceTime call isn't ready for it.

To make a FaceTime call, tap a contact's name and a screen will appear, like the one in Figure 10.17.

FIGURE 10.17

A contact who can receive FaceTime calls.

How do I know this person can make and receive FaceTime calls with me? Easy! See that little video icon to the right of the person's email address? That means Ashley has my FaceTime email address in her Contacts app—and obviously I have *her* FaceTime email address. All that's required to make the FaceTime call is to tap the email address (or tap one if multiple email addresses are listed).

Figure 10.18 shows what the person you're trying to call sees. If the call recipient chooses to answer, a FaceTime call is started. As you can see in Figure 10.19, you see the person you're talking to in the larger portion of the screen, while you see yourself in a smaller window. The person you're talking to sees your video in the main screen and theirs in the smaller window. If the person you try to call doesn't answer within 30–45 seconds, the call will cancel.

FIGURE 10.18

What your incoming call looks like to the recipient.

If the person you're calling answers the phone, you'll be greeted by that person's face as shown in Figure 10.19.

You see the person you're talking to here

The person you're talking to sees your video in the smaller window

FIGURE 10.19

A call that has been accepted with FaceTime.

A few things are going on here. You can tap and hold the small windows showing your video and move it to any of the four corners of the screen.

At the bottom of the screen, you'll see three buttons: Mute, End, and Swap Camera.

Mute—If you tap the Mute button, the microphone on the iPad will stop transmitting your voice to the other caller. This can be useful, for example, if you're in a noisy area and wish to find a quieter spot—tap the Mute button to spare the other person the noise until you're in a place where you can be heard and then tap it again to turn the Mute option off.

End—The End button is easy—tap it once and the FaceTime call ends. There is no confirmation screen that pops up asking, "Are you sure?" When you tap the End button, the call is over immediately.

Camera Swap—Finally, the Camera Swap button is useful when you're making a FaceTime call and maybe want to share something you're looking at with the other person. When my wife travels, we use FaceTime and I'm able to swap to the rear camera so she can see our two boys playing well together (not always). This feature also came in handy when a friend swapped the camera so he could show me a piece of furniture he'd just built in his workshop.

 NOTE Swapping the camera allows you to keep your eyes on the small box so you can make certain the other FaceTime user is seeing what you want them to see. Without the rear-facing camera, you'd have to turn the iPad around and away from you, and it'd be a bit difficult to tell where you were pointing the camera.

You can use the volume control buttons on the side of the iPad to increase or decrease the sound volume. Turning the volume all the way down is the same as tapping the Mute button.

When you're done with your call, tap the End button, and FaceTime once again will show your own face onscreen.

As mentioned earlier, you can see a list of your recent calls by tapping the Recents button.

The most recent FaceTime call will be listed at the top, and the list will scroll down if you need to view older calls that are not on the screen. At any time you can tap the small circle with the arrow pointing to the right to view more details about the call. Figure 10.20 shows information on my most recent call—I can see that a few calls were cancelled (not answered) and that the actual FaceTime call lasted 17 seconds.

FIGURE 10.20

View details about a FaceTime call.

Other options shown in Figure 10.20 include sending a message to the person (using the Messages app), sharing the contact information, and adding this person to the Favorites list. I can also tap the email address again to make another FaceTime call. The Edit button allows you to make similar changes to a contact without actually opening the Contacts app. Refer to Chapter 4 for details on adding new fields, setting ringtones, and more.

And that's it for FaceTime. Remember, FaceTime requires an email address to be added in the Settings app. You must provide this email address to other people who wish to call you using FaceTime, and you must have their FaceTime email address added in your own Contacts app.

 CAUTION   FaceTime calls can be made using Wi-Fi or your cellular data service, but long calls will definitely eat up your data plan and can cost you some serious money. I always try to do my FaceTime calls when I have a Wi-Fi connection, either at home or away (such as at my favorite coffee shop).

11

SOCIAL APPS

There are a lot of social apps and services out there, but the two you've most likely heard of (even if you don't use them) are Facebook and Twitter. These two services have taken the world by storm. Entire books have been written on both Facebook and Twitter, and there's simply no way I could do either service justice by attempting to cover every aspect of how it is used in a single chapter.

Instead, I'm going to point you to some online resources that can provide you with help and guidance on using these two services to their full potential and just focus on showing you how to install and use their built-in integration.

If you've already tried both services and they're just not your cup of tea, feel free to jump to the next chapter. Facebook and Twitter have fans and non-fans, and what's interesting about the iOS versions of these apps is that they're not automatically installed on your iPad—you'll have to make the decision to install them (and if you want them, it's extremely simple to install the apps, as you'll see shortly).

Facebook and Twitter are ideally suited for iPad and iPad mini users, however. Both services typically don't involve lengthy paragraphs, so the onscreen keyboard is really all you need to take advantage of these two apps. What's more, the touchscreen makes it easy to attach photos, post responses and comments, and perform many other Facebook and Twitter tasks. As you'll see, the apps are simple to install and simple to use.

 TIP To learn more about Facebook, check out *Easy Facebook* by Michael Miller (Que Publishing).

Installing Facebook and Twitter

Open the Settings app and scroll down the left column until you see the Twitter and Facebook options shown in Figure 11.1.

If you've already installed the app, and created an account, you can just log in

Click Install if you haven't already downloaded and installed it

Click to create a new account

FIGURE 11.1

The Facebook and Twitter options in the Settings app.

Figure 11.1 shows the Twitter app settings selected. Notice the Install button in the upper-right corner of the screen. You'll tap that button and enter your Apple ID password to install the app. If you already have a Twitter account created, you can enter your Twitter username and password into the fields, as shown in Figure 11.1, prior to installing the app. Tap the Sign In button below the username and password fields and a window will appear asking if you'd like to go ahead and install the Twitter app. Choose Later if you want to delay installing Twitter.

 NOTE You do not have to provide the login credentials until after the Twitter app is installed. I provided my login information so that after the Twitter app is installed, I won't have to return to the Settings app. If you do not already have a Twitter account, when you open the Twitter app for the first time, you'll be given a chance to create an account.

After Twitter finishes installing, tap its icon to open it, and you'll see buttons for Signing Up and Signing In to Twitter. Tap the Sign Up button if you do not already have a Twitter account, or tap the Sign In button to provide your existing username and password.

If you tap the Sign Up button, you'll see a screen like the one in Figure 11.2. Fill in your name, your email address, and provide a Twitter username and password. All Twitter usernames start with the @ symbol, so don't let that disturb you—leave the @ symbol in place and type a username. If the name appears in red, that means the username is already taken, so you'll need to try something else.

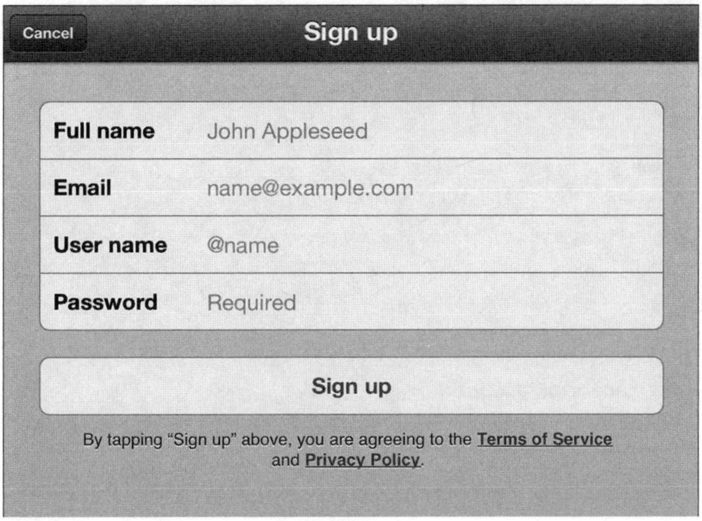

Cancel	Sign up	
Full name	John Appleseed	
Email	name@example.com	
User name	@name	
Password	Required	
	Sign up	

By tapping "Sign up" above, you are agreeing to the **Terms of Service** and **Privacy Policy**.

FIGURE 11.2

A new Twitter user will see this signup screen.

After you provide the required information, tap the Sign Up button and the Twitter app will open. If you're using a new account, the screen will be mostly empty. Existing Twitter users will see a screen full of their Twitter friends and contacts.

To install Facebook, open the Settings app, scroll down to Facebook, and tap it. Enter your Facebook username and password.

Once again, if you provide your login credentials and tap the Sign In button, a window will appear asking if you'd like to install the Facebook app. Install it or tap Later to postpone the install.

If you don't have a Facebook account, tap the Install button, provide your Apple ID password, and you'll see the new app installed.

Tap the Facebook icon to open the app—you'll see a login screen, where you can log in with your existing Facebook account or tap the Sign Up for Facebook button at the bottom of the screen.

If you tap the Sign Up for Facebook button, Safari will open to an account creation website, shown in Figure 11.3. Fill in the required information and tap the Sign Up button. Then, when the account is created, tap the Home button and tap the Facebook app to log in.

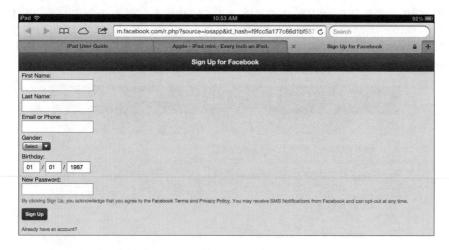

FIGURE 11.3

Create a new Facebook account.

Built-in Integration

Once you have installed Twitter and Facebook, you can open them by tapping the icon on the home screen, as shown in Figure 11.4. As I stated earlier, you can find a lot of help online for both of these apps, and I'll point you to some great websites later in this chapter as well as a couple of books that you're sure to find useful.

FIGURE 11.4

Icons for the Twitter and Facebook apps.

We'll now discuss how the Facebook and Twitter apps, once installed, are integrated into other tasks you perform on your iPad. Find an interesting website you'd like to share with your Facebook friends? It's easy to do so and doesn't require closing down the web browser and opening up Facebook. Take a great photo you want to tweet? You can tweet the photo along with a comment from inside the Photos app—you don't have to open up the Twitter app and then browse the photos to find the one you wish to share.

Yep, you'll find Facebook and Twitter integration in a number of apps. For example, take a look at Figure 11.5, which shows a photo in the Photos app we can share with Facebook friends.

Click to share this photo

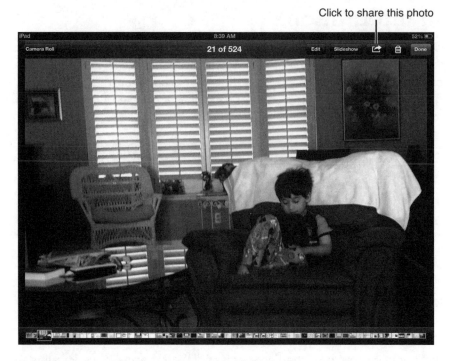

FIGURE 11.5

Share a photo on Facebook.

If you tap the Share button in the upper-right corner, you see that two of the options are Facebook and Twitter, as shown in Figure 11.6.

FIGURE 11.6

Choose Facebook to share with friends.

When you tap the Facebook option, a window pops up, like the one in Figure 11.7.

FIGURE 11.7

Posting a status update in Facebook.

This is called posting a status update. Although most status updates are just text (such as "I just finished writing a book—taking a week off!"), this one also includes a photo.

As you can see, I've typed in a comment to go along with the photo. Now, if I tap the Post button, the update is added to my Facebook page. Notice in Figure 11.7 that I can choose to add the location where the photo was taken by tapping the Add Location link in the lower-left corner of the pop-up window. I don't normally like to advertise where my photos are taken, so we won't use that feature.

In the lower-right corner of the pop-up window, you can see the security setting that defines who can read the status update and view the photo. Right now, it's set to Friends, but if you tap that button, you get a menu like the one in Figure 11.8.

FIGURE 11.8

Choose who can view your new status post.

This menu allows you to specify other options such as Public (anyone in the world can view—not recommended) and Only Me (totally private and only viewable while logged in to your Facebook account). Other options that might appear include any schools you've attended and added to your Facebook account, your place of work (if they have a Facebook page that you've joined), and the loosely defined "Acquaintances," which means friends-of-friends.

Tapping the Post button in the upper-right corner of the pop-up window will add these updates to my Facebook page for all my friends to view.

Now, refer back to Figure 11.6 and the Twitter option. If you tap the Twitter option, you get a similar pop-up window like the one shown in Figure 11.9.

FIGURE 11.9

Tweeting a photo is as easy as posting an update to Facebook.

With Facebook, you can type quite a lengthy post, but with Twitter, you're limited to a certain number of characters. For a blank tweet with no photo or link, that limit is 140 characters. But when you attach a link or photo, that reduces the number of characters. Look in the lower-right corner of Figure 11.7 and you'll see the number 119. This means only 119 characters are left to type a message in the text box—21 of those have been taken up by the link that will point to the photo we're attaching.

 CAUTION   As with the Facebook pop-up window, you can choose to tag the tweet with a location by tapping the Add Location button in the lower-left corner. This would be useful, for example, if I were tweeting a photo I just shot of the Grand Canyon or maybe if I wanted to include the location of a new restaurant I'd discovered while walking around downtown Atlanta. But for personal photos, be careful when using this option.

Let's take another look at Facebook and Twitter integration. Figure 11.10 shows the Safari app with a nice article on the iPad mini and how it's poised to become the de facto iPad for most users.

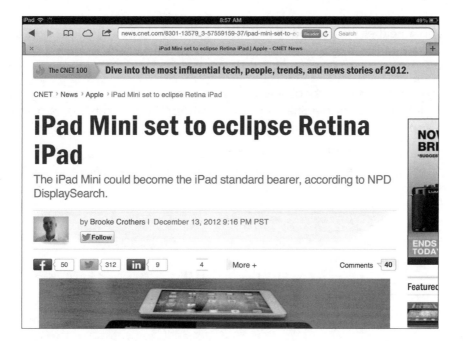

FIGURE 11.10

An article viewed in the Safari web browser.

After reading this article, I'd like to share it with my Twitter followers. To do this, I tap the Share button in the upper-left corner and there they are—Facebook and Twitter, as shown in Figure 11.11.

FIGURE 11.11

Tweet or post an update with a link to a website.

Tapping either the Facebook or Twitter option will open the basic pop-up window you saw earlier in this section—tweet a link to the website or post a status update to your Facebook page. Easy!

I use Twitter and Facebook integration to occasionally recommend apps to friends and followers. With the Share option in the App Store, I can easily share a link to an app in a tweet or a status update.

Look at Figure 11.12, and you'll see that I've tapped the Share button in the upper-right corner of an app's information page. There's Facebook and Twitter, ready for me to tap and share a link to this app with my friends and followers.

FIGURE 11.12

Share an app's information page with friends and followers.

Not every service on an app will have Facebook and Twitter integration; about the only way you'll know for certain is to find the Share button, tap it, and see if Facebook and Twitter are available options. As far as I can tell, the current Facebook and Twitter integration only works with the native apps provided by Apple that come preinstalled on your iPad when you purchase it. But maybe this will change down the road.

Twitter and Facebook Resources

I didn't want to leave this chapter without first pointing you to some excellent sources on Facebook and Twitter. Obviously, you can always visit Facebook.com or Twitter.com and search through the sites' help files and FAQs. But if you're looking for some online resources or books, here's a list of some places to start.

Facebook

- **Official Facebook help page:** https://www.facebook.com/help/382987495087424/

- **Mashable.com online guidebook:** http://mashable.com/guidebook/facebook/

- **GCFLearnFree.com resource:** http://www.gcflearnfree.org/facebook101

- **Que/Pearson book(s):** http://www.facebook.com/groups/23806107424/

Twitter

- **Official Twitter help page:** https://support.twitter.com

- **Mashable.com online guidebook:** http://mashable.com/guidebook/twitter/

- **GCFLearnFree.com resource:** http://www.gcflearnfree.org/twitter101

- **Que/Pearson book(s):** https://twitter.com/QuePublishing

12

APPS FOR THE iPAD

When the iPad was released in 2010, it was promoted as a device for downloading and presenting content. But what is *content*? The general definition for content (in relation to the iPad tablet) is anything that is obtained online, either via a download or a web browser. This includes email, music, video, games, digital books (called eBooks), how-to articles, weather reports, news, and so much more. Content is king, as they say, and the iPad's original (and still current) mission is to give users access to all the digital content they can handle.

You've already seen how easy it is to access email, Facebook, Twitter, websites, and digital photos and videos, and now it's time to see how your iPad offers up additional content—new apps.

Your iPad came preloaded with 20 apps, but currently over 250,000 apps are available from Apple via its App Store. The App Store offers apps from a variety of software developers, not just Apple. Most of these apps are free or extremely cheap (most apps are less than a dollar), and a smaller subgroup can be had for much less than you typically pay for software for a computer. And access to all of these apps comes via the App Store app, which you'll learn how to use shortly.

 NOTE Before you go and use the App Store app, I need to remind you that downloading content will require an Apple ID, a password, and a saved credit card on file with Apple. Refer to Chapter 3, "iCloud and Settings," for information on setting up an Apple ID.

Exploring the App Store

Tap the App Store icon to look for new apps.

After you open the App Store app, you'll see a screen similar to the one in Figure 12.1.

FIGURE 12.1

The App Store opens to the Featured page.

When you open the App Store, the Featured screen will look different from the one in Figure 12.1. That's because the App Store is constantly changing in appearance. Think of the Featured screen like the display window outside a clothing store—it's always changing to show you the latest arrivals. The App Store works the same way—popular apps are shuffled to the Featured screen in the hopes that you find something you like.

Along the bottom of the screen you'll see five buttons: Featured, Top Charts, Genius, Purchased, and Updates. Let me explain what each of these are and then I'll show you how each one works:

- **Featured**—First, the Featured button will always bring you back to the Featured screen, where you can see the latest recommendations. It will usually consist of a mix of new, popular apps that are selling well along with an occasional category (such as the Halloween category during the month of October, which offers up Halloween-related apps). This screen scrolls down to reveal much more. You'll see sections such as New to iPad?, Great Games for iPad with Retina Display, and New and Noteworthy (although these may not appear every time you access the App Store). The categories change, but if you scroll all the way to the bottom, you'll see the Quick Links section, as shown in Figure 12.2.

FIGURE 12.2

The Quick Links section.

The Quick Links section sometimes changes, but not often. You'll find collection buttons (such as Education Collections) that take you to additional screens that show only apps related to the collection topic. You'll also find a useful button called Apps Starter Kit, which always contains a good mix of free and paid apps that Apple considers beneficial to most iPad users.

You'll also see your Apple ID listed along with any credit you currently have (from Apple gift cards, for example). To the right of the Apple ID is a Redeem button—if you ever obtain an Apple gift card (such as an iTunes gift card for music), you'll click the Redeem button and enter the long code found on the back of the card. This will add the gift card amount to your account so you may purchase apps, eBooks, music, and much more.

 NOTE   Your Apple ID isn't just for the App Store. Other apps such as iBooks, Newsstand, and iTunes (all covered later in this book) have access to any funds credited to your account. Whether you buy an eBook, a movie, a song, or an app, if you have credit available, the purchase price will first be applied to the credit before any additional charge is made to your credit card on file.

- **Top Charts**—Tap the Top Charts button and you'll see three columns of apps listed—Paid, Free, and Top Grossing—as shown in Figure 12.3.

FIGURE 12.3

Top Charts shows a mix of free and paid apps.

Top Charts is a great place to visit occasionally because you'll always find one or more interesting apps you might not have found otherwise. Using the App Store is often like looking for a needle in a haystack if you're just hoping to happen upon something interesting. Top Charts does the job of presenting you with some of the most popular apps that other iPad users are downloading. I show you in the next section how to download an app to your iPad, but for now I want to point out the small button to the right of each app's image. This button contains one of five things: a price, the word *Free*, the word *Install*, the word *Update*, or the word *Open*.

If the button has the word *Open* on it, that means you already have the app installed on your iPad. The Update option simply means the app developer has modified the app with some improvements or bug fixes—tap the Update button to update the app on your iPad. The word *Install* means you've purchased the app already (or downloaded it previously and then deleted it). The word *Free* means it won't cost you anything to install the app on your iPad, and the price… well, that's how much it costs if you want to download the app to your iPad. (Again, I'll show you how to do this in the next section.)

- **Genius**—Tap the Genius button next. To use the Genius for Apps service, tap the Turn on Genius button, enter your Apple ID password, and then agree to the terms of service. If you turn on the Genius service, Apple will examine the apps you use the most (or the ones you tend to purchase most often) and then offer up recommendations.

  The Genius for Apps service is just another option for finding apps that you might find fun or useful; you'll still need to pay for any paid apps, but free apps can be downloaded at no charge.

- **Purchased**—Next, tap the Purchased button. If you've not yet purchased any apps, this list will be empty. (Please note that free apps will show up here; think of them as purchased for $0.00.) You'll click on the small cloud icon to the right of any app to download and install it again on your iPad. (This allows you to delete apps that you're not using anymore, but they're always available for reinstallation should you change your mind!)

- **Updates**—The last button along the bottom is the Updates button. App developers are constantly adding new features to their apps…and fixing bugs. Whenever an update to an app you have downloaded is made available, you'll see a small number appear on this button, as shown in Figure 12.4.

FIGURE 12.4

The small number tells you that there are updates to be installed.

Tap the Updates button, and you'll see a list of the apps offering updates, as shown in Figure 12.5. To the right of each app is an Update button you can tap to update a specific app, or you can tap the Update All button in the upper-left corner. The latest version of iOS will automatically begin updating the apps for you, and a progress bar on each app's icon will show you how far along the update has proceeded.

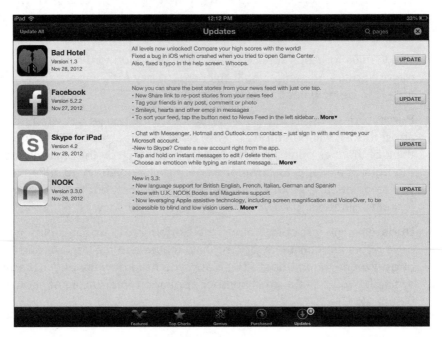

FIGURE 12.5

Update one or more apps with a single button tap.

NOTE If you tap the Update or Update All button and are asked to provide your Apple ID password, you are running an older version of iOS. When iOS 6 was released, Apple changed the update process so that a password wasn't required to update the apps.

Searching the App Store

At the top-right corner of the App Store screen you'll see a Search text box. Type in a keyword or the actual name of an app, and you'll get a small list of matches, as shown in Figure 12.6.

FIGURE 12.6

Search for words or the name of an app.

Tap one of the results, and another screen will appear that lists the best matches for your keyword. If you typed in the actual name of an app, that app should be shown first, as shown in Figure 12.7.

FIGURE 12.7

Suggested matches for your search term(s).

Tap an app's icon, and that app's information page will appear, as shown in Figure 12.8. This page contains a lot of information, so you'll need to swipe down to view it all.

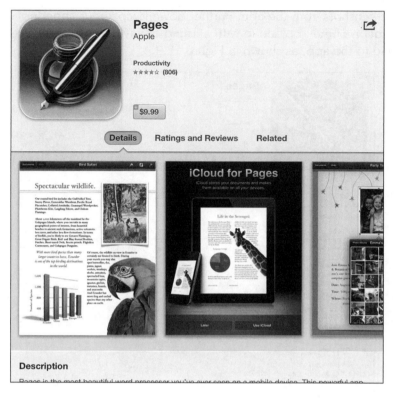

FIGURE 12.8

An app's information page.

No matter where you tap an app (on the Featured screen or the Genius for Apps screen, for example), you'll be shown the app's information page.

Now it's time to actually install an app from the App Store. Keep reading to see how a purchase is made (for paid apps) and how the installation occurs.

Purchasing an App

When you're viewing an app's information page, you'll see that familiar button listing the app's price or the word *Free*, *Install*, or *Open*. The Install option only appears if you've previously purchased an app, and the Open option appears if the app is already installed on your iPad. For this section, we're only concerned with free apps or paid apps that you do not already own.

Back in Figure 12.8, you can see information about the Pages app from Apple. Its price is $9.99. If you wish to read more about the app or view some screenshots, you can use the Details button. Swipe your finger right or left to view up to five screenshots from the app. Further down (swipe your finger up) you'll find a description of the app, along with a listing of any updates that have recently been applied to the app, as shown in Figure 12.9.

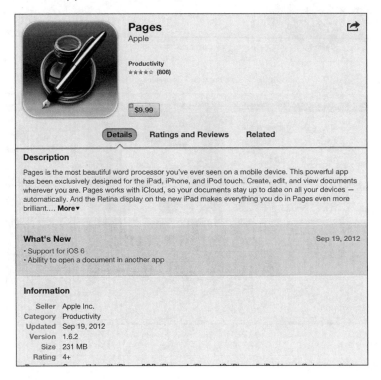

FIGURE 12.9

Read details to find out about app updates.

Further down the Details page is information on the app's developer (in this case, Apple Inc.), the size of the app (231 megabytes), an age recommendation (not sure if four-year-olds are really ready for Pages, but okay), and a list of devices on which the app will work.

CAUTION Always check the Requires section of the Information screen to make certain the app is compatible with your version of the iPad as well as the iOS version. Don't risk spending money or wasting time on an app that your iPad cannot run!

You can tap the Ratings and Reviews button to read what other users are saying about the app.

In addition to reading reviews, you can award the app between one and five stars (if you have purchased the app). You can also write your own review by tapping the Write a Review button.

Tap the Related button to see apps from the same app developer and, in some instances, apps that might have similar features.

Once you have decided on an app to purchase (or simply download if it's free), you'll want to tap the price/Free button. It will turn into either a green Buy App button or simply an Install App button (for free apps).

When you tap the Buy App button (or the Install App button), you'll be asked for your Apple ID password.

 TIP Don't worry about accidentally tapping the Buy App button—all app downloads, whether free or paid, require you to type in your Apple ID password.

After you enter your password, the app will begin to install. You can watch the progress on the app's information page, as shown in Figure 12.10 or you can tap the Home button to leave the App Store and watch the app install on your iPad's home screen. You don't even have to watch it download at all; you can do something else and come back to it. When the app is done installing, simply tap the newly installed icon to open the app.

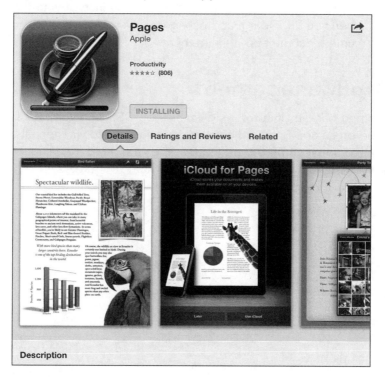

FIGURE 12.10

The installation of the app begins.

Again, the process is the same whether the app has a price, is free, or if you've purchased it previously (and deleted it) and wish to install it again.

Speaking of deleting an app, if you decide you want to remove an app from your iPad, the process is extremely easy. On the home screen, hold your finger on the app's icon until you see all the icons dancing, or wiggling side to side.

Any app that can be deleted from your iPad will have a small X in the upper-left corner of its icon. Tap that X, and a box will appear confirming you want to delete the app. Tap Delete, and the app is deleted. Tap the Home button, and the app icons will stop dancing.

 NOTE A deleted app is simply removed from your iPad; you still own the app (if you paid for it) and can reinstall it at any time. To do so, open the App Store, tap the Purchased button, and find the app in the list. Tap the Install button (no price is listed because you already bought it once before), provide your Apple ID password, and the app will (once again) be installed.

Installing new apps on your iPad isn't difficult at all. Because it's so easy, you'll quickly find that apps are taking over every square inch of your iPad's home screen. When you find your iPad hosting dozens and dozens (or hundreds) of apps, it's time for some app management.

Good App Management

You learned back in Chapter 2, "Overview of iOS," how to make folders. You tap and hold on an app until you get the dancing app icons. Then all you need to do is drag one app icon on top of another app icon, hold for a second, and the two icons will merge into a new folder you can name. Figure 12.11 shows that I've created a new folder called Games where I'm storing all my game apps.

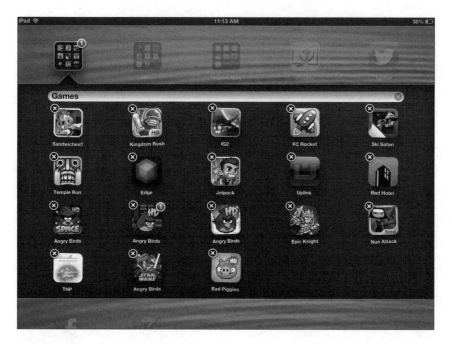

FIGURE 12.11

Create folders for storing apps.

Although you can create folders to hold any mix of apps you like, I highly recommend you try to create folders with themes—games, productivity, personal, and so on. This makes it faster and easier for you to find the app that you need.

In addition to organizing apps using folders, you'll also find the occasional app purge helpful. Every three or four months I'll sit down and go through all my apps, looking for those I just haven't opened or used for some time. When I find an app that's just taking up space, I go ahead and delete it. I can reinstall that app if I ever find I really need it back. By deleting unused apps, you'll free up valuable storage space on your iPad.

 TIP Apps are getting larger in size! When the iPad was upgraded to the Retina Display, users suddenly noticed that apps that were under 500MB in size were now well over 1GB in size! That high-resolution display really adds to the size of apps. Therefore, you should delete apps you're not using so you don't run out of space.

Go into the Settings app and tap the General option on the left, as shown in Figure 12.12.

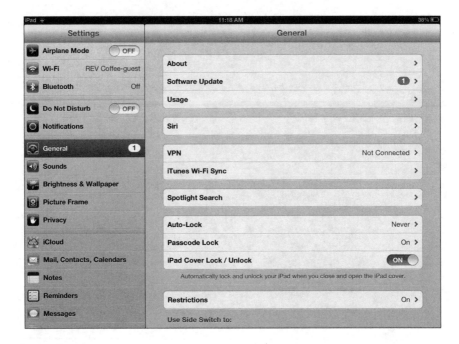

FIGURE 12.12

The Settings app and the General option.

On the right side of the screen, tap the About option and you'll see an information page like the one in Figure 12.13. Below the Capacity listing, you'll see the Available listing, which tells you how much free space you have left. Keep an eye on it, because the iPad's internal memory cannot be upgraded—you'll need to delete apps to free up more space.

FIGURE 12.13

Check your iPad's free space occasionally.

And that's about it for the App Store. It's your go-to place for finding new and interesting apps for your iPad. Over time, you'll build a library of apps that will give your iPad additional functionality and provide you with plenty more ways to use your iPad.

13

iBOOKS AND THE iBOOKS STORE

If you like to read books, you're going to love what your iPad brings to the table. I love books. My home office's shelves are full of a variety of topics, but the problems I've always had with my books are that they take up a lot of space and it's not easy to tote more than one or two around at a time.

That's why over the last few years, I've slowly been moving over to eBooks. Digital versions of books have no weight (well, other than the device you're carrying them on), and with your iPad you could easily carry thousands and thousands of books in one place without ever hurting your back.

The typical eBook is a little less in price than its print version. And reading an eBook on your iPad or iPad mini is pretty much the same experience as reading a physical book.

CAUTION The only complaint I have about eBooks is that you can't give away or donate an eBook when you're done reading it. That's why I typically buy my fiction books in print. If it's a book I expect to keep for a long time and not give away, I buy it in digital format. Yes, you can delete an eBook from your iPad and download it again at any time, but I'd much prefer some sort of option that lets me pass on the eBook at least once, but so far there's no technical solution for doing so.

Exploring iBooks

The iBooks app is not automatically installed on your iPad, so you're going to have to browse the App Store (refer to Chapter 12, "Apps for the iPad") and install it. The iBooks app is free, so just tap the Free button followed by the Install App button and provide your Apple ID password to finish up the install. Once it's installed, locate the icon for the iBooks app, shown in Figure 13.1, and tap it to open iBooks.

FIGURE 13.1

The iBooks app.

If you've never purchased a book from the iBook Store, you'll see an empty bookshelf. I've made some purchases over the last year or two, and you can see that my bookshelf has 13 books on it, as shown in Figure 13.2.

Store ─ Collections

FIGURE 13.2

The iBooks app displays your eBooks on a shelf.

Each eBook appears on the shelf with its full-color cover displayed. A single tap on a newly downloaded book will open that book to the first page, letting you begin reading immediately. (Otherwise, you're taken to the page you stopped reading—iBooks remembers where you left off.)

NOTE I've purchased many more books than you see here, so why is my bookshelf so sparse? Easy—I've deleted a lot more books to free up storage space on my iPad. Any book I've purchased from the Apple iBook Store can always be added back to the shelf at no additional cost, so keep that in mind as your eBook collection begins to grow.

Take a look around the iBooks app screen for a moment. In the upper-left corner you'll see two buttons: Store and Collections.

The Store button will immediately open the Apple iBook Store where you can browse for books and make purchases. I'll show you how this works in the next section.

If you tap the Collections button, you'll see a menu appear, like the one in Figure 13.3.

FIGURE 13.3

The Collections button offers different shelf views.

As you can see in Figure 13.3, a check mark appears next to the Books option. This means the shelf will show all books you have currently installed on your iPad. The Purchased Books option will display all books you've ever purchased from the iBooks Store, including those you've deleted from the shelf. This is an easy way to find a deleted book and restore it to your shelf. Figure 13.4 shows a small cloud icon in the upper-right corner of a book that is deleted, but a simple tap on the icon will immediately download the book again.

Note the tiny cloud icon in the upper-right corner of this book cover; the cloud icon indicates that the book has been deleted, but that it can be downloaded from the cloud.

FIGURE 13.4

A deleted book with the cloud icon for downloading again.

Tap the PDFs option shown in Figure 13.3, and you'll see any PDFs that you've downloaded to iBooks stored here. How do you get PDFs into the iBooks app? Glad you asked. If you find a PDF file while browsing the Internet, a single tap on it will open it in the Safari web browser. But if you'd like to store that PDF on your iPad, tap the page and you'll see an option appear in the upper-right corner of the display that says "Open in iBooks." Tap that button and the PDF opens in iBooks.

 TIP If you want to create custom shelves (maybe a shelf for a science fiction genre and another shelf for history books), tap the New button shown in Figure 13.3 and type in the name of a new shelf.

If you go back to the PDF collection, you'll see three more buttons: Shelf View, Details View, and Edit.

The Shelf View does just that—it displays your eBook or PDF collection on the shelf with a color cover. This is the default view, but the Details View is useful for viewing the actual titles of books and PDFs as well as their categories, as shown in Figure 13.5.

FIGURE 13.5

The Details View provides more information on your collections.

At the bottom of the Details View, you can see four buttons—Bookshelf, Titles, Authors, and Categories—that organize the list based on the button you press. Bookshelf lists items in the order that they have been downloaded, Titles displays them alphabetically, Authors shows all collections grouped by author, and Categories breaks up your collections into genre sections.

Depending on whether you're in Shelf View or Details View, the Edit button works a little differently. In Shelf View, tapping the Edit button lets you tap one or more books to place a check mark on them, as shown in Figure 13.6.

FIGURE 13.6

Select books by tapping them to put a check mark on the cover.

Tap the Delete button, and all books with a check mark will be removed from the shelf. You can also tap the Move button to move selected books to any custom shelves you might have created.

If you are in Details View, the Edit button will put a small circle to the left of each book or PDF. Tap the circle to place a check mark in it.

Once again, you can use the Delete or Move button to delete PDFs or eBooks or move them to other shelves.

Visiting the iBooks Store

To open the iBooks Store, tap the Store button in the upper-left corner of the iBooks app when you're viewing any shelf.

What you'll see on the iBooks Store home page changes constantly, just like the App Store. New books and recommended titles are displayed on this scrolling screen. You'll want to swipe up and down and look at all the categories available—New in Fiction, New in Non-Fiction, Buzz Books, and Popular

Pre-Orders are just a few of the sections that the iBooks Store uses to help you narrow down what you're looking for. And a single tap on any book cover you see will open that book's information page, as shown in Figure 13.7.

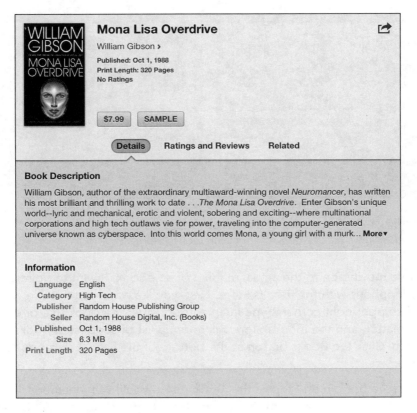

FIGURE 13.7

The information page for an eBook.

The iBooks Store offers up information pages very similar to the App Store. You'll see the familiar Details, Ratings and Reviews, and Related buttons that allow you read book summaries, see what other readers think, and find others books from the author, respectively.

Unlike the App Store, however, most eBooks have the option to buy the book for the listed price plus a Sample button that you can click to download the first 30 to 40 pages. If you'd rather just purchase the book, tap the button with the price in it and then click the Buy Book button—the book will begin downloading to iBooks, as shown in Figure 13.8. To delete a Sample, tap the Edit button in the upper-right corner, tap the Sample so a blue check mark is placed on it, and then tap the Delete button in the upper-left corner.

NOTE As with the App Store, purchasing books from the iBooks Store requires an Apple ID and password and a credit card on file.

FIGURE 13.8

Downloading a purchased book from the iBooks Store.

Before moving on to the actual reading of an eBook, I want to point out a few more options with the iBooks Store. First, you'll always find the Search Store bar in the upper-right corner. Type in an author name or a book title or even a subject matter, and the iBooks Store will return a list of suggested books that fit your search. Click the Books button at the bottom of the screen to return to the iBooks Store.

Along the bottom and top of the iBooks Store you'll see a number of buttons that help narrow your search. At the top are the category buttons—All Categories, Fiction, Nonfiction, and More. The More button offers up more genres that you can use to filter what is displayed in the Store.

Along the bottom are buttons related to current best sellers, such as those listed on the *New York Times* Best Sellers list, as well as the Top Charts and Top Authors buttons, which show you which books and authors are currently popular purchases. The Purchased button will, obviously, show you all eBooks you've purchased so you can immediately download them again if they're not still on a shelf.

Reading an eBook in the iBooks App

After you've downloaded a new eBook, it appears on the shelf with the New banner on it, as shown in Figure 13.9.

FIGURE 13.9

New eBooks are easy to spot with the New banner.

Tap the book's cover or title (if you're in Details View) and iBooks will immediately open the book to the first chapter and first page of text, as shown in Figure 13.10.

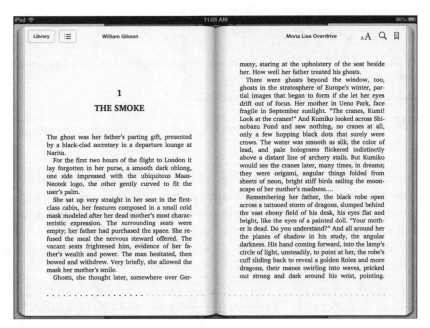

FIGURE 13.10

The new eBook opens.

As you can see, I'm holding my iPad in Landscape view so two pages of the book are displayed at once. But I prefer to read my books in Portrait view, so I'll rotate the iPad and the page changes slightly, as shown in Figure 13.11.

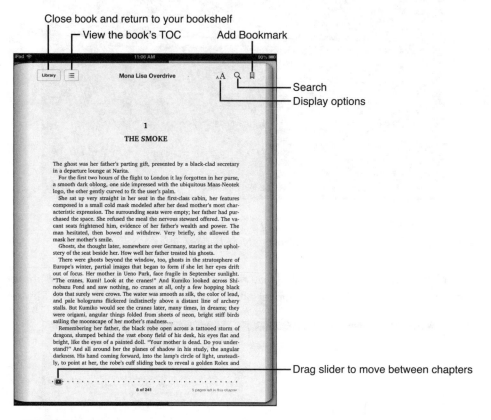

FIGURE 13.11

My eBook in Portrait view.

At the bottom of the page is a series of dots and below that is the current page number I'm on and the total number of pages. I'm on page 8 of 241, and I can even see a small bit of text that tells me I've got five pages left in this chapter. I can also place my finger on the small brown square and drag left or right to move from one chapter to the next. Feel free to experiment with a book of your own so you'll see how this works.

In the top-left corner is the Library button—tapping it will close the book and return you to the shelf. The button to the right of the Library button is the Table of Contents button. If you tap it, you will immediately be taken to the Table of Contents, as shown in Figure 13.12, and a tap on any chapter will immediately jump you to that position in the book.

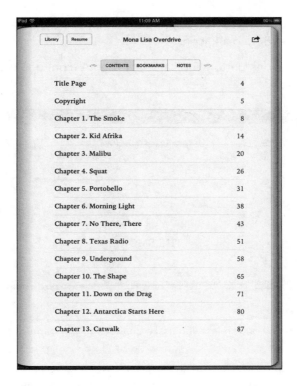

FIGURE 13.12

The Table of Contents.

While viewing the Table of Contents, if you tap the Resume button in the upper-left corner, you'll return to your book, but before you do that, let me explain a few more options shown in Figure 13.12. You should still be on the Contents page, so the Contents button is selected.

As you read your eBook, you can place multiple bookmarks (not just one) on pages by tapping the small bookmark icon found in the upper-right corner of every page—more on that in a minute. The Bookmarks button shown in Figure 13.12 will show you a listing of all bookmarks, and a tap on one will move you to that place in the book.

Also while you're reading, you can jot notes in the eBook, but it doesn't require an actual pen or pencil. I'll show you how to add notes shortly, but tapping on the Notes button in Figure 13.12 will show you all the notes you've entered for an eBook and tapping on one moves you to that page in the book.

Finally, in the upper-right corner of the Table of Contents page is the Share button. Tap it, and you can post a little link to the book on Facebook or Twitter, or send it via a message or email to a contact.

As you can see in Figure 13.13, there are three more items—Display options, Search, and the Bookmark icon.

The Display options button (indicated by the AA icon) opens a menu like the one in Figure 13.13.

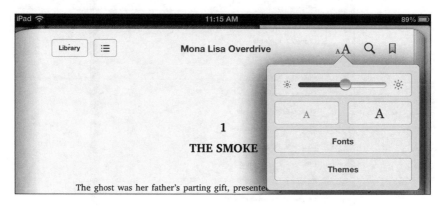

FIGURE 13.13

The Display options button lets you make changes to the page display.

Tap and drag the slider bar at the top to lower the screen's brightness or increase it. When you're reading at night, drag it almost all the way to the left—it's much easier on your eyes and they'll adjust quickly to the lower light.

You can tap the larger A button to increase the size of the font or the smaller A button to decrease it. You'll have to experiment with this to find the font size that works best for you.

Additionally, the Fonts and Themes buttons allow you to change the font style and the background color of the page, as shown in Figure 13.14.

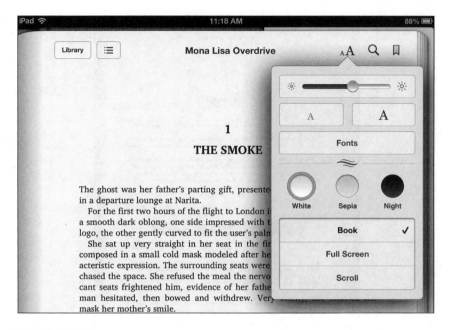

FIGURE 13.14

Change font style and page color.

For example, you can change the color of the page from White to Sepia for a less-glaring page color. The Night option turns the page black and the text white, which is supposed to be easier on your eyes. You can also change the display from Book to Full Screen or Scroll if you prefer not to have the text look like an actual page from a physical book.

Turning the page of your eBook requires nothing more than a swipe right to left like you're turning the page of a real book. Likewise, a single tap of your finger anywhere near the middle-right side of the page will also turn the page. Swipe left to right and you'll see the previous page come back into view.

Finally, I mentioned earlier that you can type your own notes into an eBook. Well, you can do that plus a few more special things. Tap anywhere on a bit of text in your eBook and you'll see a small menu appear like the one in Figure 13.15.

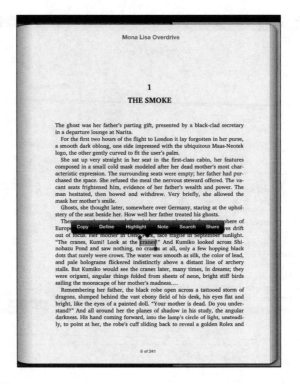

FIGURE 13.15

Options are available for selected words or paragraphs.

You can use your fingers to drag the small dots left and right to expand the selected text from a single word to an entire paragraph or two. Once you've selected a word or paragraph, you can tap the Copy button to save the text to the clipboard for pasting into an email or other app that supports the clipboard.

Tap the Define button while a single word is selected, and a definition will appear, as shown in Figure 13.16—you'll remain on the page while the word is defined but you can tap the Search Web or Search Wikipedia button, which will close the iBooks app and open up Safari.

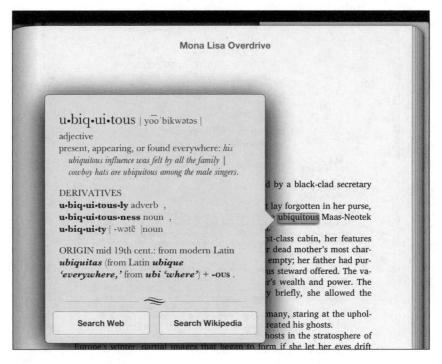

FIGURE 13.16

Have a selected word defined for you.

If you've selected a sentence or paragraph that you wish to highlight, tap the Highlight button and the selected text will be highlighted in yellow.

You can change the color of the highlight using the small menu that appears above the highlighted text. Tap the yellow circle at the left end of this small menu to select from five colors or to underline the text.

Other options include the Clear highlight button, the Note button, and the Share button. The arrow button pointing to the right simply allows you to copy, define, or search on a selected word or phrase.

Finally, tap the Note option (shown in Figure 13.15) and you can type in your own note, as shown in Figure 13.17.

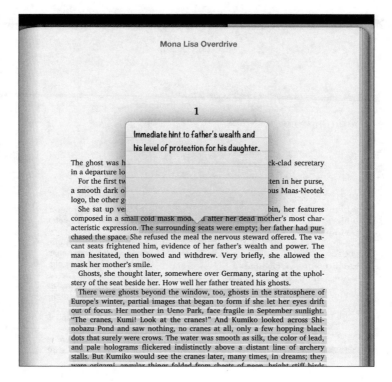

FIGURE 13.17

Add your notes to a selected bit of text.

When you are finished typing your note, tap anywhere on the screen to close your note. Notice in Figure 13.18 that a small sticky note appears in the right column; tap a sticky note to view the comments you provided.

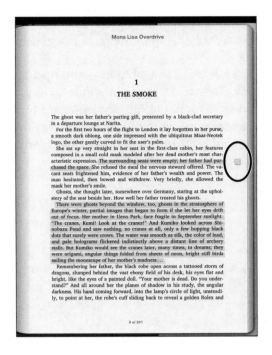

FIGURE 13.18

Notes are indicated by a small sticky note.

Remember, closing down a book or the iBooks app itself won't make you lose your place in an eBook. iBooks remembers the last page displayed when an eBook is closed, so you'll always be returned to the page where you left off.

Alternatives to iBooks

Before I close out this chapter, I want to briefly mention other options to the iBooks app. If you're an Amazon customer (or a Kindle owner) or a Barnes & Noble customer (or a Nook owner) and prefer to purchase your books from either of those sellers, you'll find two apps in the App Store if you search for them:

- **Kindle app**—This free app will let you view any eBooks you've purchased from Amazon.com for your Kindle. If you don't own a Kindle, you can still purchase books from Amazon.com and have them sent to your iPad's Kindle app. For more information, download the free Kindle app from the App Store and read the documentation and instructions it provides.

- **Nook app**—This app is also free and allows you to download eBooks you've purchased from Barnesandnoble.com, either for your Nook or simply as eBooks for reading on your iPad. Again, download the free Nook app from the App Store and read its documentation for assistance.

Many more eBook readers are available from the App Store—way too many to cover in this book. That said, most of them require your eBooks to be downloaded in a specific format (ePub and mobi are two examples). Make certain whichever eBook reader you use is capable of displaying eBooks you purchase online. Because this can be frustrating to manage, I tend to stick with the iBooks, Kindle, and Nook apps for all my reading needs.

14

MOVIES, MUSIC, AND MORE

If you're not familiar with iTunes, this is the chapter for you. iTunes on your iPad gives you access to movies, television shows, music, and much more.

At this point in the book, you've learned how to use your iPad for so many things—email, web browsing, eBooks, video chat and messaging, social media (Facebook and Twitter), and taking photos and videos. Well, now it's time to add the ability to watch movies and television shows and listen to music and podcasts. For me, iBooks, the App Store, and iTunes truly turn an iPad into an all-in-one entertainment device.

NOTE If you're not familiar with podcasts, think of them as prerecorded radio shows that you can listen to at any time. They are available for every possible topic you can imagine, including comedy, news, sports, and much more. Podcasts are to your iPad what books on tape were for your car, but the difference being you can listen to podcasts anywhere you can carry your iPad.

Exploring iTunes

One of the first things you have to learn about iTunes is that to get to it on your iPad, you must first go through the Music app. Figure 14.1 shows the Music app icon you'll need to tap to open iTunes.

FIGURE 14.1

The icon for the Music app.

Tap the icon to open up the Music app. If you've never purchased any music from iTunes before, it will say "No Music."

Because you probably don't have any music yet, tap the Store button to open the iTunes store.

 NOTE You can download music to play on your iPad from music CDs you currently own. For instructions on doing this, visit http://www.ehow.com/how_6199240_transfer-cds-ipad.html and read the instructions provided.

You'll see an animated menu appear like the one in Figure 14.2. These are new albums and singers that Apple is currently promoting.

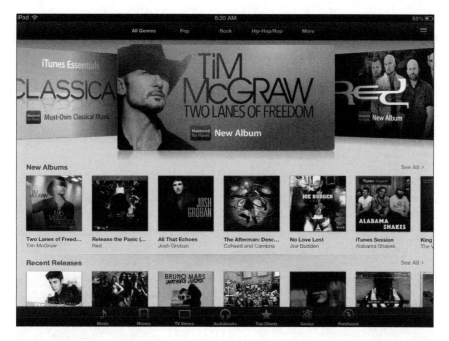

FIGURE 14.2

The iTunes music store is open for business.

If this screen looks a bit familiar, you're right—it follows a format similar to the iBooks Store and the App Store. Along the top are various category buttons that you can click to filter out other styles to display what you are interested in. (Click the More button to see more categories.)

Along the bottom are the buttons that let you change the type of media you wish to search—Music, Movies, TV Shows, Audiobooks, and the Top Chart sellers—as well as Genius suggestions (based on your previous listening/viewing purchases) and a button to view all previously purchased content from iTunes.

Because I'm currently viewing the Music library offered by iTunes, let me show you how to search, listen, and buy a song. The steps are the same whether you're searching for a song, an album, a TV show, a movie, or any other type of media that iTunes sells, such as audiobooks or podcasts.

Along the top is a rotating number of featured artists or albums—this will frequently show you newly released albums or artists that iTunes is currently promoting. At the time I write this, one of the albums that Apple is promoting is from Tim McGraw.

I can tap the Tim McGraw banner at the top of the screen to immediately visit a page dedicated to this singer and his albums and music. Likewise, you'll notice that in the upper-right corner of the screen is the familiar Search Store box—type in a keyword, a song, the name of an album, or an artist's name, and you can view songs related to your search term.

NOTE   Remember, the Search feature is specific to the type of media you are currently searching. Use the Movies, TV Shows, and other buttons at the bottom to first change the type of media you wish to search and then use the Search box to find what you need.

As you can see in Figure 14.3, I can tap on an album cover to view (and listen to) all the songs contained in that album, or I can tap individual songs. Most songs on iTunes can be purchased individually, with the average price being $1.29 per song. Other songs can only be purchased as part of a digital album, and these are usually around $9.99 to $14.99.

FIGURE 14.3

Tap on albums or individual songs for more details.

Right now, I'd just like to listen to a single song before I consider a purchase. If I tap on a song ("One of Those Nights"), a small circle appears to the left of the song title, as shown in Figure 14.4.

FIGURE 14.4

Tap a song to hear a snippet.

If you have your iPad's volume turned up (and not muted), you'll immediately begin to hear the song play. Apple lets you listen to about 60 seconds of a song (it used to be 30 seconds) to help you decide if you'd like to make the purchase. If you don't want to hear the entire snippet, then tap on the song and it will stop.

If I click on an artist's name, I'm provided with an information page similar to the one you find with the iBooks app. I can review all the songs, read listener reviews, and view related music from the artist or band, or I can click on an album cover to view songs specific to that album (a pop-up window will appear similar to the one shown in Figure 14.3).

After I've found an album or song I wish to purchase, I tap the price button, provide my Apple ID password, and the song is downloaded to my iPad's music library. Easy!

Tap the Movies button at the bottom, and you'll see a familiar layout, shown in Figure 14.5, with scrolling (left-to-right) movie banners at the top, a Search Store box in the upper-right corner, and movie categories as you swipe down the page.

FIGURE 14.5

View movies for purchase or rent.

 TIP If you want to preorder movies not yet released so they are immediately downloaded to your iPad on the day they become available, scroll all the way to the bottom and tap the Pre-Order Movies button and follow the instructions.

Now, here's the great thing about movies on your iPad—you can buy them or… you can rent them! Not every movie is available for rent, and the only way you'll know for sure is to tap the image for a movie to view its information page, as shown in Figure 14.6.

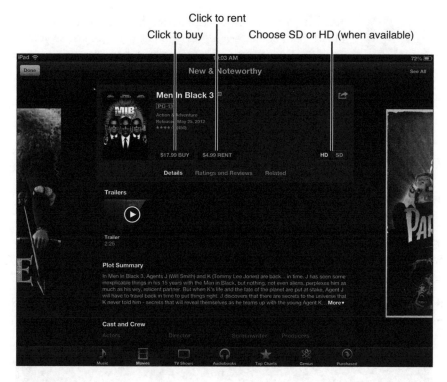

FIGURE 14.6

A movie's information page.

Once again, you'll see the price button to buy the movie as well as some buttons that let you read summaries of the film, read reviews, and view similar movies that other customers have purchased. Notice in Figure 14.6 that this movie also has a Rent button—tapping the Rent Movie button or the price button will require an Apple ID and password to purchase, but the difference is that a movie you buy can be kept on your iPad for as long as you like, whereas a rented movie is only available for 24 hours after you first tap the Play button. (You've got 30 days to press Play, so don't dawdle!)

NOTE You can delete purchased movies off your iPad and reload them at a later time as often as you like, just as you can with eBooks and apps. A rented movie, however, will disappear forever 24 hours after you tap the Play button, so be sure to watch it all before it's gone!

Also, if you plan on watching the movie on your iPad, leave the HD (High Definition) button selected, as shown in Figure 14.6. If you think you might watch it on a computer screen or your iPhone, you might want to download the SD (Standard Definition, as in pre-HD) version because it will take up less space and will download faster. (By the way, with iCloud enabled, you can also view your movies on any other device you own that has iCloud running!)

If you choose to rent or buy a movie or television show, it will appear in the Movies app on your iPad. I will show you how to use the Movies app in Chapter 15, "Magazine, Newspaper, or Movie?"

If you tap the TV Shows button while in iTunes, you'll see a screen like the one in Figure 14.7.

FIGURE 14.7

Purchase television shows by season or episode.

You can use the Search Store box to find what you are looking for or swipe down the page to see what iTunes is currently recommending. As with music or movies, tapping on a TV show's Season icon will display that season's worth of episodes, as shown in Figure 14.8.

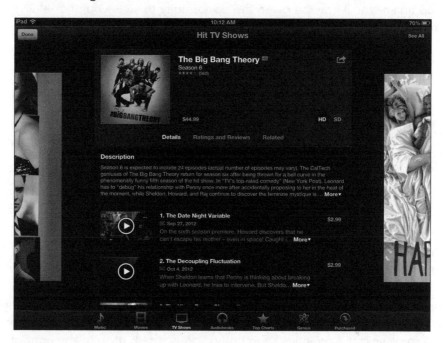

FIGURE 14.8

Purchase an entire season or just an episode.

As you can see, you can tap the full season's price button to download all episodes, or you can scroll down and tap the price button for a single episode. Downloaded episodes are stored on your iPad and can be viewed using the Movies app. (You should also be aware that you cannot rent television show episodes; you can only purchase them.)

Purchasing music, TV shows, movies, and audiobooks is easy with iTunes. In fact, that's probably one of the reasons Apple has been so successful with it—users have the ability to immediately grab a song or TV show and can watch or listen to it on their iPad. And because you've purchased these items from the iTunes store, they're also available on any other devices you have that are running iTunes or have iCloud configured. One added benefit of iCloud is that it will even remember where you left off with a movie or TV show! Start watching a movie on your iPad, and finish it later by watching it on your iPhone!

I'll show you in Chapter 15 how to watch movies and TV shows, but before I end this chapter, let me show you how easy it is to listen to music on your iPad.

Listening to Music

You'll need to tap the Home button to exit iTunes, and then re-tap the Music button to open up your iPad's music library for a listen. When you tap the Music app again, you'll now be given the opportunity to view your (hopefully growing) music library. Figure 14.9 shows the basic controls of the Music app.

FIGURE 14.9

The Music app lists your music and offers up controls.

In the top-left corner, you'll see the traditional Play button—it's the triangle pointing to the right. To the left of the Play button is the Back button that will begin playing the previous song in the library; the button to the right of the Play button is the Forward button that will jump you to the next song.

In the top-right corner is the volume controller—while you can use the iPad's Up/Down volume buttons, this draggable volume controller is a fast way to adjust the volume manually and in small increments as opposed to the Up/Down buttons that affect the volume in larger incremental changes.

 NOTE If you've got an Apple TV, you can also tap on the AirPlay button to the right of the Volume slider control to play your music through the Apple TV. The sound will be provided by your television's speakers or sound system.

As a song plays, you can see the name of the song scrolling across the top of the screen and a small orange bar that shows you how far along the song has progressed.

The progress bar is draggable, so you can easily drag it back a bit to replay a bit of a song (or all the way to the left to start at the beginning). There are two small icons I'd like to point out to you—one is to the left of the song's progress bar and one is to the right.

The icon to the left is the Repeat button; tap it once to hear a song play over and over…tap it again to have it repeat just once (a small numeral 1 will appear), and tap it once more to turn it off.

The icon to the right is the Shuffle button; tap it and all the songs in the library you are viewing will be played in a random order.

You might also notice the small Genius icon; tap it and the song you are listening to will be added to the list of songs used by the Genius feature to help you find music with a similar sound that you might enjoy. You'll need to access the Genius button in iTunes to see what iTunes offers up, but it's a nice way to tag a song that you like and wish to use to help iTunes find new music you might not know about.

As you begin to collect music in your iPad's library, you're going to want to start organizing it so you can more easily find what you want to listen to at any given time. While you can manually swipe up and down to find a song, a better method is to organize your music into what are called playlists, and I'd like to show you how to use them.

Using Playlists

Imagine you have a large music CD collection. You could stack them alphabetically by artist or band name, or you could make a bunch of smaller stacks by organizing your CD collection by the music genre—Classical, Rock, Country, and more.

With physical stacks, however, a CD can only be one stack. If you have a stack for Rock Music and a stack for '80s Music, your Def Leppard CD is going to be found in only one of those, not both.

But playlists are different. Think of playlists as labels that you could print, peel, and stick to all of your music CDs, allowing you to give them multiple categories such as Rock and '80s Rock. The difference being that with physical CDs, if you want to listen to '80s Music (not just Rock), you've got to sift through all your CDs to pull out only those that have an '80s Music label.

Playlists allow you to quickly and easily view only songs, but first you've got to assign a song to a playlist. And even though the Music app comes with some pre-made playlists, you're going to want to create your own (especially if you have a category such as '60s Country Duets).

After you've opened the Music app and are viewing your music library, tap the Playlists button at the bottom as shown in Figure 14.10.

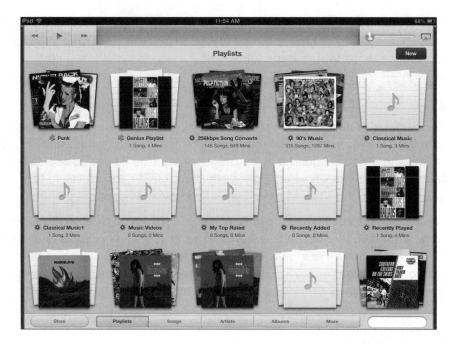

FIGURE 14.10

The Playlists button is selected.

As you can see, there are playlists such as My Top Rated, Recently Played, and more. Some of the ones you see in Figure 14.10 were created for me, and others I had to create myself.

To create a playlist, tap the New button in the upper-right corner. A small window will open where you can type the name of your playlist. Tap the Save button to create it.

Now you need to assign some of your music library to your new playlist. After you create a playlist, you're immediately taken back to your music library, but this time notice that every song has a circle with a plus sign at the far right as shown in Figure 14.11.

Tap the plus sign to the right of every song you wish to add to a playlist. As you tap each song, the song's title will appear in a lighter color to indicate it's been added. Tap the Done button to assign the playlist to the selected songs. (Or you can tap the Add All Songs button, but that's not a good idea as you're basically creating a new playlist that is the same as the complete music library.)

After you tap the Done button you'll see a list of all the songs you selected displayed as shown in Figure 14.11.

FIGURE 14.11

Confirm your playlist songs.

If you're happy with the selections, tap the Done button. You can also tap the Add Songs button if you want to add more. If you'd like to remove a song, tap the red circle with the minus sign to the left of the song's name, and then tap the Delete button that appears. Remember—you're not deleting the song from your iPad, only from the playlist. The song will still exist in your main music library!

 TIP At the bottom of th list of songs you'll find a small Cloud button. I don't have room to go into it here, but Apple offers a yearly subscription service called iTunes Match that basically stores your entire music collection in iCloud (see Chapter 3, " iCloud and Settings") until you choose to download them to your iPad by tapping the small Cloud button. This is beneficial because you can choose to only download certain playlists and leave the rest of the songs off your iPad to save memory. For more information, visit http://www.apple.com/itunes/itunes-match/.

After you've created your playlist and stored some songs in it, tap the Playlists button again, and you'll see your new playlist along with any others you've created.

The great thing about assigning songs to playlists is that you can play the same song in multiple playlists. By creating playlists for specific types of music, you can easily tap a playlist to listen to music that you're in the mood for and nothing else. Putting a song in a playlist doesn't create a duplicate of that song, so you can store a song in one, ten, or even a hundred playlists without any penalties.

 TIP The software version of iTunes that you run on a computer has many more features than the iPad's Music app, including the ability to burn CDs from playlists.

The Music app is a great way to take your music with you. Any music you play can be heard through the iPad's speakers, or you can listen privately with a set of headphones plugged into the iPad's headphone jack.

Keep in mind that the version of iTunes that you install on a computer will have many more special features (such as tracking the number of times a song is played or making changes to the sound quality of a track). If you have iTunes running on a home computer and can synch your iPad with that computer, you'll find many more tools available for managing your music collection as well as backing up your music.

15

MAGAZINE, NEWSPAPER, OR MOVIE?

The previous two chapters introduced you to iBooks and iTunes, two apps that allow you to download a variety of content—books, songs, movies, and more. But these two apps aren't the only ones that offer you the ability to purchase or view content (or download and watch free content).

Your iPad comes with two additional apps, one for purchasing content and the other for viewing it. The first is the Newsstand app, which allows you to purchase magazines and newspapers as well as subscriptions. And while you can download movies and TV shows from iTunes, it's the Movies app that is required to actually view them.

Exploring Newsstand

Tap on the icon shown in Figure 15.1 to open up the Newsstand app.

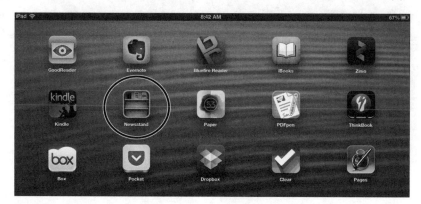

FIGURE 15.1

The icon for the Newsstand app.

The Newsstand app looks similar to the iBooks app, with the only difference being that instead of a bookshelf, you'll be greeted by the magazine rack shown in Figure 15.2 (notice that it doesn't fill the entire screen).

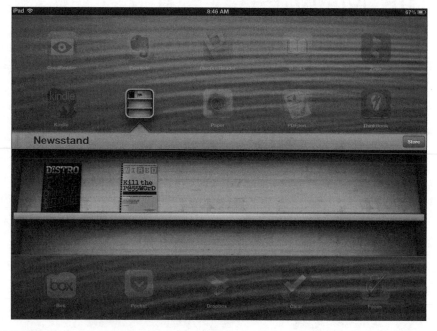

FIGURE 15.2

The Newsstand app offers up a magazine rack.

I have a couple magazine subscriptions (one paid, one free), as you can see, but your magazine rack will most likely be empty if you haven't purchased a newspaper or magazine subscription from the Newsstand Store.

In the upper-right corner of the magazine rack, you'll see the familiar Store button—tap it to open up the Newsstand Store, as shown in Figure 15.3.

 NOTE As with any purchase made from iBooks or the App Store or iTunes, you'll need an Apple ID and password to make purchases in the Newsstand Store.

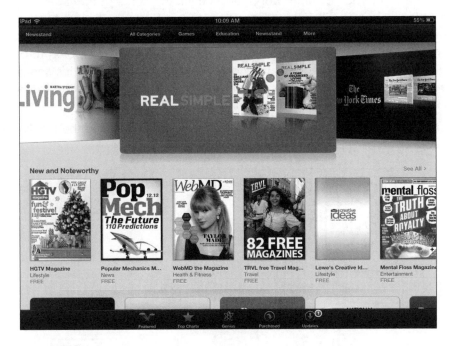

FIGURE 15.3

The Newsstand Store offers up magazines and newspapers.

In my opinion, the Newsstand Store is a confusing mess, so let me explain. Notice along the top of the screen that you have various categories, such as All Categories, Games, Education, Newsstand, and More. If you tap on any of those buttons, except for the Newsstand button, you'll essentially be back in the App Store browsing for apps such as games or recipe apps.

The same goes for the buttons along the bottom of the screen—Featured, Top Charts, Genius, Purchased, and Updates. These buttons all are App Store buttons, not Newsstand features. If you're interested in buying a single magazine issue, a newspaper, or a subscription, you'll want to make certain you tap nothing but the Newsstand button at the top—anything else will take you away from the Newsstand. It's annoying, and I'm not quite sure why Apple doesn't have a Newsstand-only app. However, this is what we've got for now.

That said, while you're viewing the Newsstand options, you'll find a scrollable screen (swipe up and down) with a number of magazines available for purchase.

Don't get too excited about all the FREE listings—these aren't free magazines (usually). Instead, the "free" part is simply an app that installs on your iPad and alerts you when new issues are available for purchase. Yes, it's misleading—and, no, I don't think Apple's going to change it.

Let me show you how it all works, and I think the concept of magazine purchases and subscriptions will make a little more sense. First, you'll want to find a magazine for which you might consider purchasing an issue. Unfortunately, there is no Search bar, so you'll need to do a lot of swiping and tapping to burrow down into various categories to find what you might like. Yes, it's annoying. And again, I'm not expecting a fix for this issue. (Like I said earlier, the Newsstand app is a mess and not even close to being as useful as it could be.)

Once you've found a magazine, tap the cover and you'll see the familiar information page, as shown in Figure 15.4.

FIGURE 15.4

A magazine's information page.

I've always liked the print version of *Popular Mechanics*, but I can always check out reviews and read a description of any magazine I might not be familiar with. In order to get pricing details, you can examine the information found in the Description section or you can tap the FREE button to install the magazine's app and then tap the Install App button that appears.

 TIP By installing the free app, you'll be able to browse older issues that you can purchase individually as well as see if there are any subscription specials available—these aren't always listed in the Description section, so it's often a good idea to install the free app to see if there are any special prices being offered.

After you provide an Apple ID password, the magazine begins to download, as shown in Figure 15.5.

FIGURE 15.5

The magazine app begins to download.

 TIP If you'd like to see some pages from the magazine before downloading the app, swipe left or right through the five page samples—you can tap on a page sample to get a larger image that will give you a better idea of the font used by the magazine and whether it looks nice (to you) on your iPad's screen.

After the app is installed, you can tap the Open button or you can tap the Home button and then relaunch the Newsstand app.

When you return to the magazine rack, you'll see your new magazine app appear on the magazine rack, as shown in Figure 15.6.

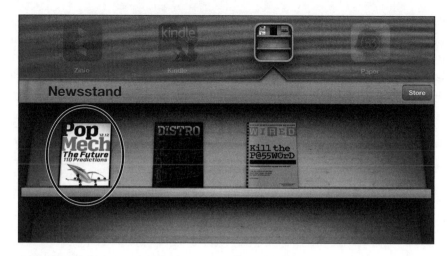

FIGURE 15.6

The magazine app is added to the magazine rack.

Whether you tap the Open button or tap the magazine app that just appeared on the magazine rack (in Figure 15.6), you'll start a process that walks you through purchasing an issue or a subscription.

Every magazine I've ever considered subscribing to on my iPad behaves a little differently when I first open the magazine's app, but the goal is ultimately the same—to get you to purchase an individual issue or a subscription. As you can see in Figure 15.7, the *Popular Mechanics* magazine app opens and asks whether you're already a subscriber. After you read a magazine issue, you can always delete it to free up space. But if you decide at a later time you want to reinstall an issue (that you've already purchased), you can do so by tapping the Restore button. The Newsstand Store records will be checked to verify any previous purchases; if they are found, you'll be given a chance to reinstall one or more issues you've deleted.

If you're not an existing subscriber, tap the Cancel button, shown in Figure 15.7.

FIGURE 15.7

You can reinstall issues if you're a subscriber.

Now you can swipe left or right to view the current issue and older issues. Notice the big red Buy Issue button, just below the Contents button in Figure 15.8.

FIGURE 15.8

You can view a magazine's contents or purchase an issue.

At the bottom of the screen is a free sample of the magazine; not all magazines offer a full issue for sampling, so the number of pages may vary. Also, not every magazine will have all of its past issues available for download.

Along the top of the screen, you'll see a banner offering a full subscription. Sometimes there's a discount advertised, but there will always be a button that allows you to purchase a subscription. If you tap that button, a window appears offering you a monthly subscription (basically buying the current issue one month at a time for a year) or a yearly subscription (usually at a discount) at a listed price, as shown in Figure 15.9.

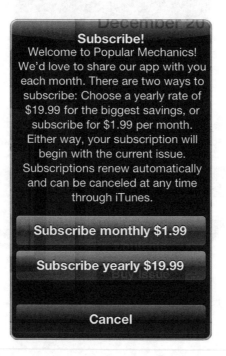

FIGURE 15.9

Select your magazine purchase option.

No matter which selection you choose, you have to confirm the purchase.

Some magazines request personal information, such as your name, email, and zip code. You can choose Don't Allow or Allow, but after tapping one of these buttons, the current issue will begin to download.

 NOTE Downloading a magazine issue will often take some time. This is a large document and even with a high speed Internet connection, it can take some time to download the full issue. Be patient.

Again, not all magazine subscriptions behave the same, but the basic idea is that after a magazine issue finishes downloading, it will be available in the magazine app's library, as shown in Figure 15.10.

FIGURE 15.10

Tap the cover of a purchased issue to open and begin reading.

You might not want a magazine issue to download automatically. If that's the case, open the Settings app and tap the Newsstand option on the left. Every magazine you subscribe to will have the option to automatically download content. You can turn the toggle button to On or Off, as shown in Figure 15.11.

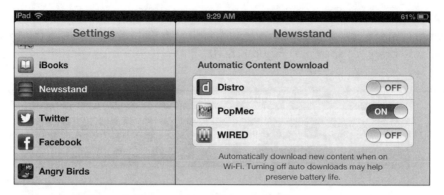

FIGURE 15.11

Choose whether or not to download magazines automatically.

If you don't have your magazine downloading automatically, you'll need to open the magazine app again and browse to the issue you purchased. Instead of a Buy Issue button, you'll see a Download button; tap it to start the download of the magazine.

To open a magazine for reading, just tap the cover. Most magazines are taking advantage of the iPad's full-color screen and fast processor, so don't be surprised to see some animation or maybe even a video about the current issue's contents!

Although the Newsstand app is a buggy mess, actually reading magazines on the iPad is amazing. First, some magazine covers are actually touch sensitive—if you see a headline that interests you, tap it and you'll jump immediately to the start of that article. Not all magazines do this, however, and those that do offer it don't always have every headline working as a fast-jump to the article.

Reading a digital magazine works just like reading an eBook—a swipe from right to left turns the page, and a swipe left to right returns you to the previous page. Every magazine I've ever read on my iPad offers a slightly different toolbar, but most of them offer you the toolbar if you tap somewhere near the center of the screen. As you can see in Figure 15.12, when you tap the center of the page, you get some buttons at the bottom and near the top.

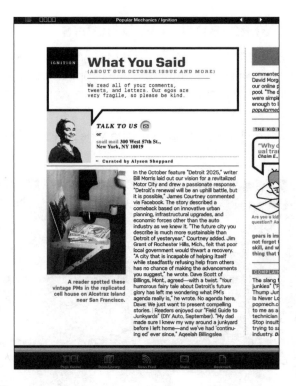

FIGURE 15.12

Most magazines have a toolbar.

You'll have to experiment with these buttons because they'll almost always differ from magazine to magazine, but some fairly common buttons provide the ability to return to the magazine's Table of Contents and a quick listing of all the articles. There is also usually some method for bookmarking a page and maybe even sharing a link to an article with a friend.

Everything I've described so far about buying issues or subscriptions to magazines also applies to newspapers. You won't find a lot of newspapers available in digital format, but those that are available will typically offer up the ability to buy a single day's worth of news or a longer subscription. And again, every newspaper will work a little different in terms of navigation and downloading, but it always starts with downloading the app from the Newsstand Store.

Watching Movies and TV Shows

Back in Chapter 14, "Movies, Music, and More," you learned how to purchase movies and television shows with the iTunes app. Once you have a TV show or movie purchased (or rented) and downloaded to your iPad, you'll probably want to watch it, right?

Well, to do that you'll want to open up the Videos app, whose icon is shown in Figure 15.13.

FIGURE 15.13

The icon for the Videos app.

If you open up the Videos app and have no movies or TV shows installed on your iPad, you'll see a video screen.

What I love best about the Videos app is its simplicity! All you have to do to watch a movie or TV show is tap the icon. The movie or show will open its information page so you can read a synopsis. When you're ready to start watching, tap the Play button shown in Figure 15.14.

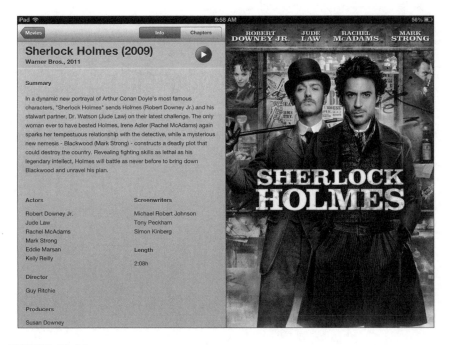

FIGURE 15.14

Read details of the movie or tap the Play button to start watching it.

The only choice you need to make now is whether to watch in Portrait or Landscape view. I prefer Landscape because you get a larger image, but some prefer Portrait (especially on airplanes) because it offers up a bit more privacy and doesn't feel like you're sharing your movie with those around you. (Plug in some headphones and nosy neighbors might be able to watch the action, but the lack of sound will eventually run them off.)

The Videos app offers the most basic of controls—Play, Pause, and buttons to jump to various locations. You can also tap and drag the progress button at the top of the screen left or right to move forward or backward through a show. These buttons will disappear as the show plays, but you can get them back at any time by tapping in the center of the iPad's screen, as shown in Figure 15.15. (Tap the Done button to close the movie or TV show—your location will be saved so you can start watching from where you left off the next time.)

FIGURE 15.15

Simple controls for playing and pausing shows.

And that's it for the Videos app! Well, almost. To delete a movie, tap and hold your finger on a movie or TV show, and then tap the X that appears in the upper-left corner. Or, if you want to buy more movies or shows, tap the Store button, and you will be taken to the iTunes Store.

 TIP You can get movies onto your iPad without buying or renting them from iTunes. This involves ripping a DVD movie to your computer first (save it as an mp4 or m4v), so you'll need to Google some instructions for doing this based on the operating system you're using on your computer. After the movie is ripped and stored on your computer, you use the iTunes software installed on your computer to synchronize with your iPad. You can then browse to the movie on your computer and use iTunes to move it over to your iPad's Movies folder. Again, instructions vary from computer to computer. I documented my particular method, and you can read it by visiting http://www. quepublishing.com/articles/article.aspx?p=1655237.

16

FINDING THINGS

It may seem like a bit of a stretch, but your iPad can provide three capabilities when it comes to finding things. The first is finding things on the device itself, such as songs, movies, and addresses. The second is finding the way to a physical location. And, the third is using a built-in voice-activated tool called Siri. I've lumped these three features together in this chapter for two reasons:

- They're extremely easy to use.
- They're all about finding something.

Your iPad has a simple Search feature built in to it that can often help you hunt down something that might be buried in a folder or in an app. It also allows you to jump to the Internet if you can't find what you need on your tablet. Your iPad also has the Maps app, which allows you to enter an address and have it displayed on the iPad's screen. Furthermore, you can enter a starting address (such as your home) and get driving directions to the destination. And finally, the Siri service allows you to ask a question ("I need directions to the Atlanta Zoo."), and then the service goes and retrieves what it can find for you. The Siri service does have some limitations, but what it can do, it does well.

I'll start our discussion with the Search tool and show you how it works.

Using Search

The Search tool doesn't have an icon like the standard apps you've been using. Instead, you'll start on your primary home screen and swipe to the right until you see the screen shown in Figure 16.1. (From any home screen, you can swipe to the right until you see the Search screen.)

FIGURE 16.1

The Search tool.

The Search tool will initially be blank. You haven't attempted to search for anything yet. Use the onscreen keyboard to type a keyword, a song title, a contact name, or anything you care to hunt for (see Figure 16.2). In this example, I'm hunting for a particular contact's phone number, so I've entered his first name in the Search box.

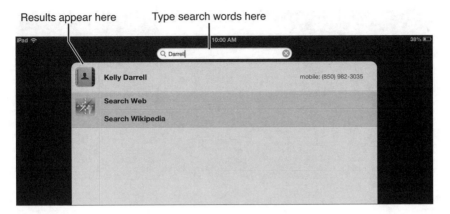

FIGURE 16.2

Type in a word or phrase to search.

As you type letters in, the Search tool immediately begins offering up possible matches for your search. Suppose you want to enter **catalog**. When you have entered **cat**, you might find a picture of a cat or the phone number for Catalina Restaurant. Only when you type the next letter (**cata**) will the photo of the cat disappear, but Catalina Restaurant will still appear. Next, entering **catal** will still show Catalina Restaurant, but when you type in the next letter, **o**, the Catalina Restaurant listing will disappear. Only when you finish typing in **catalog** will the search list finish updating and offer any possible matches.

Tapping any of the search results opens that item.

 TIP I frequently use the Search feature instead of opening up the Contacts app when I need a phone number quickly. I also use it when I obtain a new piece of information for that contact (such as an email address change or a new phone number); I simply type in the name of the contact in Search, tap the search result, and then tap the Edit button to make the change.

You can also use the Search tool to find files on your iPad. Notice in Figure 16.3 that you can immediately jump to watching a movie downloaded to your iPad from iTunes. Tapping the movie listing opens the movie immediately (skipping the information page) and starts playing from the beginning or the spot where you last closed down the Video app.

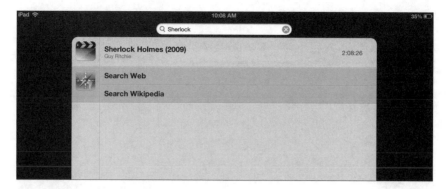

FIGURE 16.3

Search for movies on your iPad.

The Search tool also works for music. If you type in the name of a song, it shows up in the listing; a single tap on the song will open up iTunes and begin playing the song. Even better, you can type in the name of a band, as shown in Figure 16.4, and a complete list of all the songs on your device is displayed, allowing you to pick one to start playing.

FIGURE 16.4

Find a song or a band/artist's complete listing.

Finally, one of my favorite uses for the Search tool is for quick Internet search. For instance, let's say I want to find a good recipe for making molasses cookies. As you can see in Figure 16.5, I searched but no results were provided because I lack a recipe stored on my iPad.

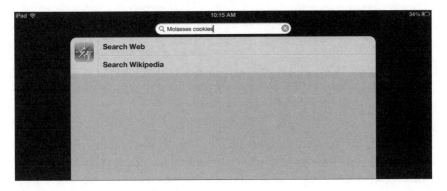

FIGURE 16.5

Not all searches provide results.

Fortunately, the Search tool allows me to continue my search either on the Internet or on Wikipedia.org.

If I tap the Search Web button as shown in Figure 16.6, I find that there's no shortage of recipes for molasses cookies on the Web.

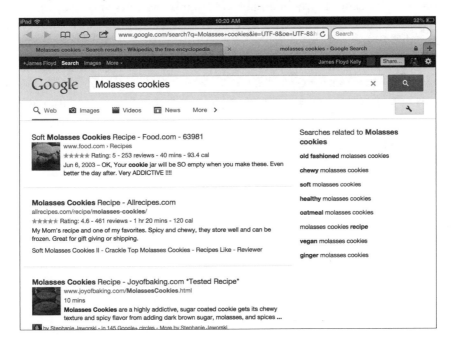

FIGURE 16.6

Sending a search to the Internet.

NOTE Keep in mind that your search results will be provided using the search engine you specify in the Settings app. Your choices are Bing, Google, and Yahoo!, with Google being the default. If you want to change search engines, open the Settings app, scroll down to the Safari option in the left column, and then tap the Search Engine option in the right side of the screen—tap on one of the three search engines to select it.

At this point, it's in my hands to search through the results provided to find the best recipe. At any time I can return to the Search tool and refine my search using additional keywords (such as "molasses cookies quick recipe").

What else can the Search tool do for you? Well, it can search the Reminders and Calendar apps, and you can even type in the name of an app to open it directly from the Search tool. It also searches the Messages app and hunts down keywords found in any conversations you've saved. It will also sift through the Notes app.

What won't the Search tool do for you? Unfortunately, the Search feature does not provide search results for eBooks stored on your iPad. I have absolutely no idea why you cannot type in an author's name and have it display any eBooks you have in the iBooks app. Maybe this will be updated later, but for now you have to open the iBooks app to search for a particular eBook or author.

Also, the Search tool won't search the Maps app for street addresses or the location for the nearest Greek diner. For that, you'll actually need to open the Maps app. And speaking of the Maps app, it's now time to see it in action.

Explore the Maps App

The Maps app icon is shown in Figure 16.7. Go ahead and tap it to open up the Maps app.

FIGURE 16.7

Tap this icon to open the Maps app.

I don't know where you're currently located, but the easiest way to show you how to use Maps is to start at the world map displayed and type in an address in the upper-right corner, as shown in Figure 16.8.

FIGURE 16.8

Enter an address to find it on the map.

As you type a keyword (or street name) in the search box, Maps attempts to figure out what you're looking for and offers up some options. Notice in Figure 16.8 that some of the locations have a small red pin to the left of their name—this lets you know that these are actual physical addresses you can find using Maps and not just a general area (such as a park). All you need to do is tap one (such as the

Hartsfield Jackson Airport result in this example) and the map zooms in to give you a bird's-eye view, as shown in Figure 16.9.

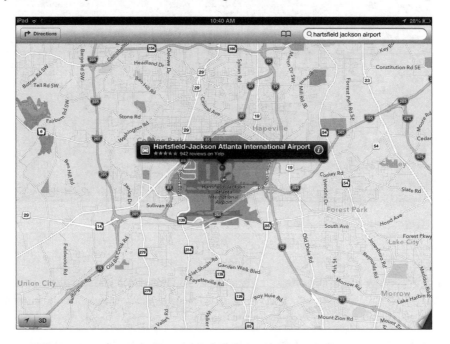

FIGURE 16.9

Maps zooms in and displays the location you specified.

If you tap the small blue dot with the *i* inside (for Information), a much more detailed information page opens, as shown in Figure 16.10.

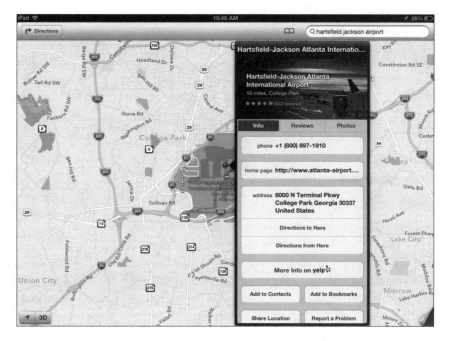

FIGURE 16.10

A location's information is displayed.

This information page isn't available for every address you'll ever type into the Maps app, but it's usually found for businesses (such as restaurants and shops) and public sites (such as parks and libraries). You'll often find a phone number, a website, and even reviews for businesses.

Now, let's say you'd like to get driving directions to the address you've just found. Notice in Figure 16.10 the Directions to Here button. Tap it and a small window will appear like the one in Figure 16.11.

CAUTION If you wish to use the Maps feature to find directions from your current location, you will need to enable this feature on your iPad by turning on Location Services. Open the Settings app, tap on the Privacy listing in the left column, and in the right column tap Location Services. You'll be provided with a list of apps that can use Location Services—make certain that Maps is switched to On.

FIGURE 16.11

Enter the starting address for driving directions.

After you've typed in an address (or a city or town name), tap the Route button and the path from A to B is displayed on the screen with a nice thick blue line showing the route you'll take. Figure 16.12 shows the route from a suburb in Atlanta to the Atlanta airport.

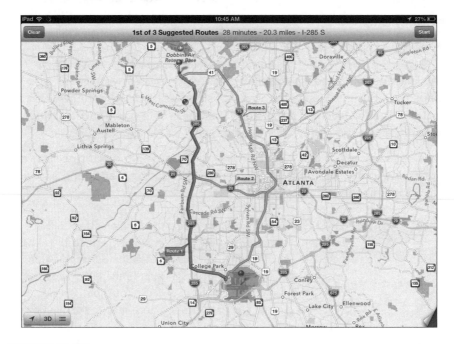

FIGURE 16.12

View your route on the map.

The displayed route is nice, but what if what you really want are actual written driving directions. Fortunately, the Maps app offers this capability. In the lower-left corner of the screen are three tool buttons—Current Location, 3D View, and Directions.

 NOTE If you've enabled the use of Location Services (see previous Caution), tap the Current Location button and the map will zoom in to display the iPad's current location. The 3D View button offers a slightly angled view of the map, but I've honestly never had much use for it. I've been told it's helpful for walkers in an urban area, but I much prefer the standard bird's-eye view.

When you tap the Directions button, you get a pop-up window like the one in Figure 16.13 that provides you with turn-by-turn directions, complete with distances and exit numbers! The route is outlined in blue, and a green pin indicates the starting point and a red pin indicates your destination.

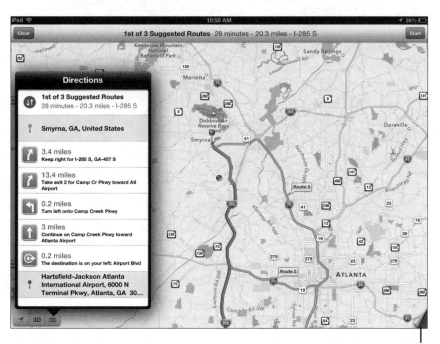

Tap here to see some hidden buttons

FIGURE 16.13

Directions from A to B.

When I'm driving, I usually prefer not to have to look at written directions. Thankfully, I can tap the Start button in the upper-right corner of the screen to get a kind voice that lets me know when exits, turns, and streets are approaching. Figure 16.14 shows how the Maps app offers large, easy-to-read markers for me to glance at so I know what to expect. I can tap the End button at any time to end the guided directions. Keep in mind that step-by-step directions require an Internet connection; this means having an iPad that supports both Wi-Fi and cellular. Because it's unlikely you'll have a Wi-Fi connection in your car, this feature is typically used only with iPads that also come with a data plan from your mobile carrier.

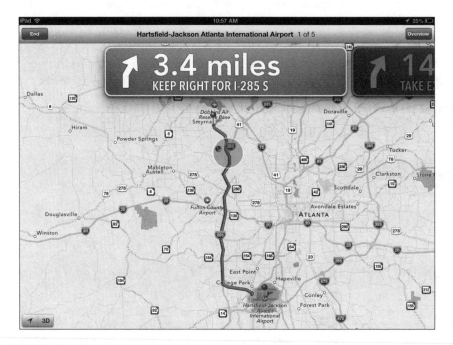

FIGURE 16.14

Following the Maps app's directions.

Finally, tap in the lower-right corner of the screen, where it looks like the page is peeling back (refer to Figure 16.13). The map page will expose some hidden buttons, as shown in Figure 16.15.

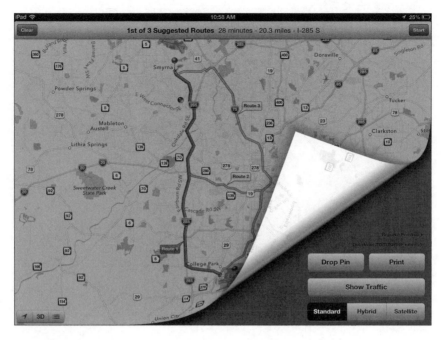

FIGURE 16.15

More options for the Maps app.

The Drop Pin button allows you to place a pin on the map and view the address associated with that location, as shown in Figure 16.16, but it also offers up additional options.

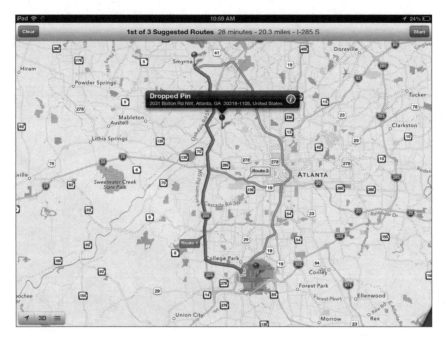

FIGURE 16.16

Drop a pin on the map to see its actual address.

You can tap and hold on the pin to drag it around on the map—release your finger when you wish to drop it in place. As you can see, the pin provides you with the address of where it is dropped, and you can tap the Information icon (small blue circle with an *i* inside) to get more details. You can drop a pin at a particular location on the map and then use it as the destination. I use pins to mark restaurants and other stores I see during a drive and wish to remember the details.

Refer to Figure 16.15 and you'll see the following buttons:

- **Print**—The Print button allows you to print the current map to any printer that supports the AirPrint service.

- **Show Traffic**—If you tap the Show Traffic button, you'll see little construction and traffic accident icons appear on the map, like the ones shown in Figure 16.17.

Alternate routes are shown in a lighter shade of blue

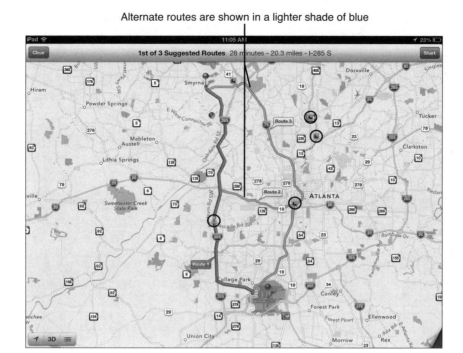

FIGURE 16.17

Accidents and construction can be displayed on the map.

Let's say you see a car accident or construction on your planned route. Notice in Figure 16.19 that there are two additional lines (lighter blue in color) that also link Point A to Point B. If you tap on either of the blue lines, you get an alternate route, as shown in Figure 16.18.

Because I see a traffic accident here…   I can use the alternate route shown here

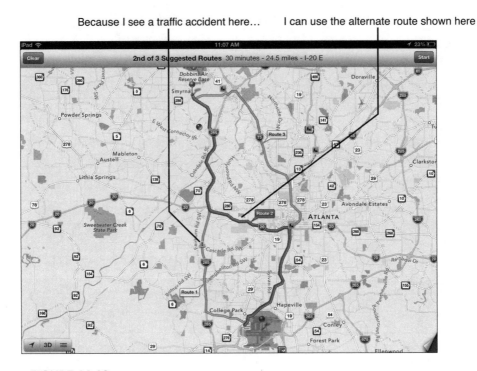

FIGURE 16.18

Find an alternate route from A to B.

The new route is labeled Route 2, and it will still get you from your current location to the Atlanta airport. Likewise, there's a third route you could take (using Interstate 75) if Highway 285 is blocked.

As with the original Route 1, you can tap on the Directions button at any time to get written instructions for the new (alternate) route.

Tap again in the lower-right corner of the screen and you'll see the Satellite button. I don't use this very often, but it's sometimes fun to get a satellite view of a house or famous monument. As you can see in Figure 16.19, using Satellite view, you can look down on the Eiffel Tower in Paris, France!

FIGURE 16.19

Satellite view can provide photo-quality details of your destination.

As with photos, you can zoom in on the satellite image by reverse-pinching (tap your thumb and pointer finger on the center of the screen and then move them apart). This will often give you some surprising details on the visible map.

 TIP One popular alternative to Maps is Google Maps, a free app that offers many of the same features as Apple's Maps. There were some complaints about inaccuracies with Maps during a 2012 update to the application, and to a point, they were valid. Many users prefer the street-level view offered by Google Maps (it provides an image of what you'd see if you were standing and looking left, straight, or to the right), allowing you to see landmarks such as gas stations, statues, street signs, and so on. Try it out! You'll need to determine for yourself which app works best for you.

The Hybrid option (to the left of the Satellite button) simply offers up a mix of the Standard map with the Satellite view, as you can see in Figure 16.20.

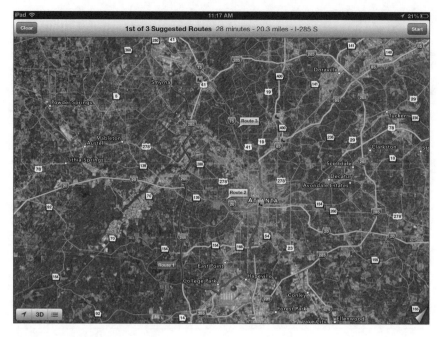

FIGURE 16.20

Hybrid view offers a mix of the Satellite view and Standard map.

TIP Many third-party apps offer the same navigation features found in the Maps app, but they also frequently offer more advanced tools, such as mileage and fuel estimates, recommendations for gas and food stops, and much more. You can search the App Store for alternatives using the Navigation category.

Say Hello to Siri

Before you can use Siri, you'll need to enable it. You might have done so during the iPad setup routine, but if you're not certain, just open the Settings app, tap on the General option on the left side of the screen, and tap the Siri option in the left panel.

When you tap on the Siri option, another page will open as shown in Figure 16.21. If Siri is turned off, tap the toggle button to turn it on.

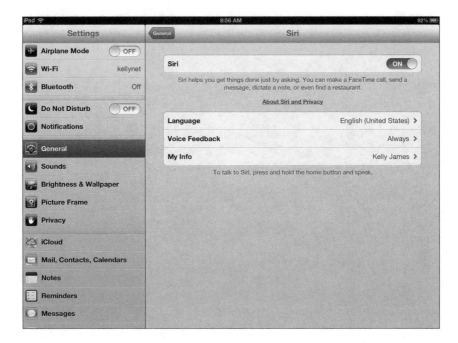

FIGURE 16.21

Siri must be turned on to use the voice-activates service.

Using Siri is fairly straightforward—simply press and hold the Home button for a little longer than one second until you hear a ding-ding sound and see a small microphone appear on screen asking "What can I help you with?" This is shown in Figure 16.22.

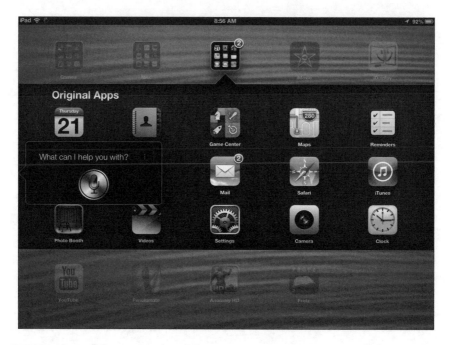

FIGURE 16.22

Ask your question aloud when you see the small microphone icon.

You'll have about five seconds to ask a question before the microphone turns off. You can simply tap the microphone button again to have Siri start listening for your question.

What kinds of questions can you ask? You can request Siri to call a contact using FaceTime (say "Call Donna Kelly with FaceTime."), ask for directions ("I need directions to Rev Coffee in Atlanta, Georgia." or even find out who wrote a certain book ("Who wrote *Gone with the Wind*?). Siri will sometimes answer with a verbal response, but most often will respond with something you must view on the screen. Figure 16.23 shows how Siri responded to my query about the author of *Gone with the Wind*.

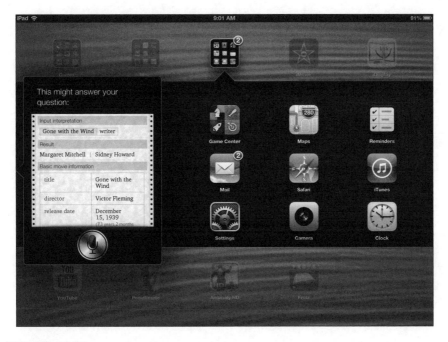

FIGURE 16.23

Siri provides answers in a small window or open an app for you.

If you're looking for a nice summary of all the different things Siri can do for you, I'm going to point you to two different sources of information. The first is the official Siri page on Apple.com. You can find it by visiting http://www.apple.com/ios/siri/.

The second source is much more detailed—visit http://www.tuaw.com/2012/09/14/what-can-you-say-to-siri-in-ios-6/ to read an extensive list of sample queries that can be put to Siri.

When it comes to Siri, the requests I use the most include adding events and reminders (to the Calendar and Reminders apps, respectively), getting addresses for restaurants, and asking for game times for various leagues. You're sure to find your own favorite uses for Siri, so I highly recommend taking Siri for a test.

17

THE TWO iPAD CENTERS

Your iPad has the ability to notify you of many things—new email messages, reminders, birthdays, app updates, and much more. Although many of the apps can pop up alerts on the screen or use the badge system (small numbers on the icon of the app), one really useful feature is built right in to your iPad that can do even more amazing things. It's called the Notification Center, and you may find it just as useful as I do for getting a daily (or hourly) update of all the things that matter to you.

The Notification Center is meant to be a single location for you to see what's going on in your world—weather, email, stock prices, messages, and pretty much anything else that matters to you. It's a great productivity feature I'm hoping you'll find beneficial.

But your iPad doesn't always have to be all about productivity; sometimes you just want to take a break and do something fun—watch a movie, read an eBook, maybe play a game? Yeah, games are great on the iPad, and what's even more fun is playing games with friends… or against friends. And your iPad has a nice tool for finding opponents (friends you know or complete strangers) as well as tracking scores and putting together rankings. It's called the Game Center, and I'll wrap up this chapter by giving you a brief introduction to it.

Exploring the Notification Center

As you've been learning to use your iPad, you may very well have stumbled upon the Notification Center with a swipe of your finger in just the right place. Tap and hold your finger at the very top-center of your iPad's home screen where the time is displayed, as shown in Figure 17.1.

Tap here and hold to bring up the Notification Center

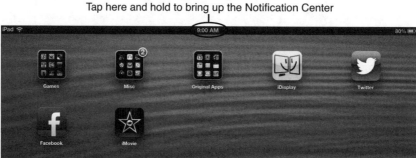

FIGURE 17.1

Tap and hold your finger on the time display.

Now drag down. If you perform this gesture correctly, you should see a small window appear like the one in Figure 17.2. Your window will most likely have different items in it or it might say No New Notifications. However, this is how you will access the Notification Center.

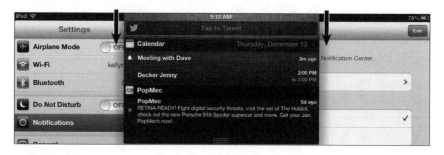

FIGURE 17.2

The Notification Center hides until you need it.

To close the Notification Center, tap on the bottom edge of the Notification Center window (where the small ridges appear) or tap anywhere outside the Notification Center. The Notification Center will disappear.

Now that you've seen where the Notification Center is located, let's take a look at what kinds of information it can display. To do that, I want you to open up the Settings app and browse down the left column to the Notifications option, shown in Figure 17.3.

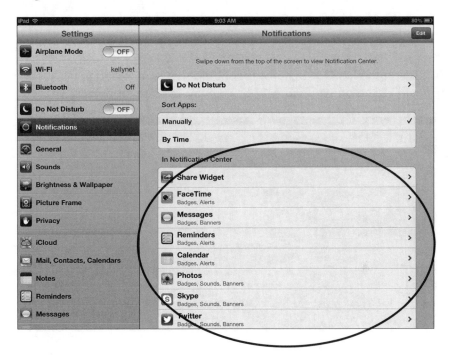

FIGURE 17.3

The Notification Center's setting options.

On the right side of Figure 17.3, you'll notice a long list of apps and options that can be customized for the Notification Center. The first one you'll see there is the Do Not Disturb option. By configuring the Notification Center's Do No Disturb option, you can turn off your iPad's ability to pop up alerts (with a matching sound) on your screen as reminders. If you've not seen these before, Figure 17.4 shows a standard pop-up alert that might appear on your iPad to remind you of a scheduled event you put in your Calendar app.

FIGURE 17.4

A pop-up alert on your iPad looks like this.

To turn on the Do Not Disturb option, tap that option and you'll see a new screen appear like the one in Figure 17.5. You have several options:

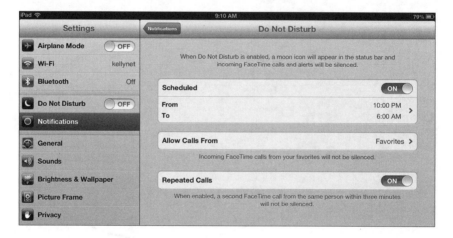

FIGURE 17.5

Configure the Do Not Disturb options.

- **Scheduled**—As you can see, you can define a period of time that the Do Not Disturb feature is turned on—for example, I've set it to 10 p.m. through 6 a.m., so my iPad won't make have any sounds or have alarms going off during that period of time. If I tap the Scheduled option's toggle button to turn it to Off, alerts can pop up at any time.

- **Allow Calls From**—You'll also see that you can override the scheduled Do Not Disturb period so you can receive FaceTime calls from those on your approved list. Tap the Allow Calls From option to specify contacts who can call you using the FaceTime app at any time.

- **Repeated Calls**—Finally, if the Repeated Calls option is set to On, anyone who calls you a second time with FaceTime within 3 minutes will be allowed through, even if they're not on the Allowed Calls list. This is meant to allow for emergency calls, where someone might try to call you again and again to reach you.

Tap the Notifications option in the left column again to return to the screen shown in Figure 17.3. The next section below the Do Not Disturb option allows you to specify the order in which apps provide their notifications in the Notification Center. The Sort Apps section shown in Figure 17.6 is set to Manually, but you can tap the By Time option to have notifications ordered most recent at top to oldest near the bottom.

FIGURE 17.6

Sort your notifications by time or by your own preference.

The Manually option won't make sense to you until you actually configure some apps to use the Notification Center. I'll come back to this in just a moment.

TIP I prefer the By Time option because it's my natural tendency to look at the top of a list first to see what's the most current notification. If you don't have a lot of apps configured to use the Notification Center, it probably won't matter whether you use the Manually or By Time option because all notifications will likely fit on the screen without you needing to swipe to scroll down the list.

Below the Sort Apps options, you'll see a section called In Notification Center, as shown in Figure 17.7.

FIGURE 17.7

The In Notifications Center section lists apps that use the Notification Center.

Any apps listed in this section can send notifications to the Notification Center that you drag down from the top of the screen. However, just because an app appears in this list doesn't mean it will actually have anything to report. I'll return to this list in a moment to show you how to configure individual apps, but right now I want you to scroll down the right side of the screen a bit until you see the next section titled Not in Notification Center, as shown in Figure 17.8.

FIGURE 17.8

These apps will not send anything to the Notification Center.

 NOTE   Your iPad might or might not have some apps automatically configured to use the Notification Center. Don't worry—I'm going to show you how to turn on and off an app's ability to send alerts to the Notification Center. You'll be able to customize your list of approved Notification Center apps easily.

Now that you know how to navigate around the Notification Center's setting options, let's take a look at how to enable apps to send to the Notification Center (and disable them) as well as some of the additional configuration options available.

Configuring the Notification Center

Tap on any of the items in the In Notification Center section and you will see a screen similar to what you see in Figure 17.9.

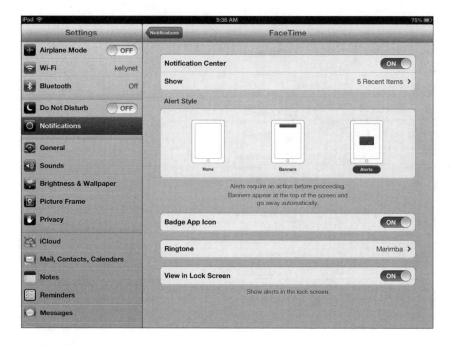

FIGURE 17.9

An app's Notification Center option screen.

NOTE   Every app has slightly different options to configure for the Notification Center, so you'll have to investigate each of them to discover all of the options they provide to you.

Here are the options:

- **Notification Center**—At the very top of the option screen, you'll see the Notification Center toggle button turned to On. If you turn that to Off (by tapping the toggle button with your finger), the FaceTime app will move to the Not In Notification Center section shown in Figure 17.8. That's how easy it is to remove an app's ability to pop up alert windows or even appear in the Notification Center.

- **Show**—If you tap this option, you can choose for the app to list 1, 5, 10, or 20 alerts in the Notification Center. For example, if I have this option set to 5 and six of my contacts call me using FaceTime while I don't have my iPad handy, I can pull down the Notification Center and I'll see the most recent five callers. The first caller won't be shown in the list because the FaceTime Show option is set to 5 Recent Items—most recent to oldest.

NOTE I can always open the FaceTime app to view a list of calls that I've made and calls that I've missed. My other option is to set the FaceTime Show setting to 20 items and hope that I've missed no more than 20 of my contacts calling.

- **Alert Style**—Below the Show option is the Alert Style setting shown in Figure 17.10:

  - **None**—With the None option, the app will not pop up an alert onscreen, nor will it put any information in the Notification Center when you drag it down from the top of the screen.

  - **Banners**—If you select the Banners option, the app will put up a quick banner notification near the top of the screen, as shown in Figure 17.11. It disappears fast (about 5 to 7 seconds after appearing).

  - **Alerts**—The Alerts option will create a pop-up alert like the one shown previously in Figure 17.4. Unlike the banners that disappear, alerts require you to acknowledge the message before it will disappear.

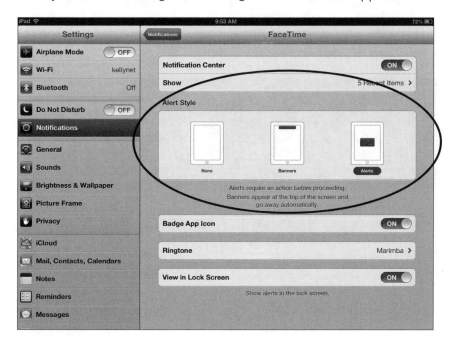

FIGURE 17.10

The type of alert can be configured.

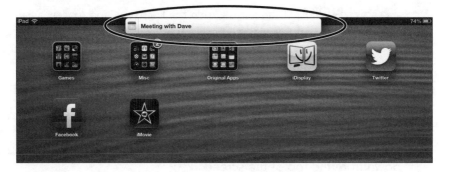

FIGURE 17.11

A banner alert appears near the top of the screen.

- **Badge App Icon**—The Badge App Icon setting is either On or Off. Not all apps use the Badge App feature, but those that do will put a small number on the icon of the app to alert you that something needs your attention. For the Mail app, for example, this number represents the number of unread messages. For the App Store, this number represents the number of app updates available to be installed. Figure 17.12 shows a typical Badge App Icon alert in use.

FIGURE 17.12

The Badge App Icon option provides another type of notification.

TIP Why wouldn't you simply send the app to the Not In Notification Center section if you don't wish to receive any alerts? Good question! Even though I might choose not to have a banner or pop-up alert triggered, I might still want to see the number of missed calls on the FaceTime icon or the number of missed text messages from the Message app. A lot of apps can be quite annoying with the number of pop-up alerts or banners they create, but by setting an app's Alert Style to None and leaving the Badge App Icon to On, you'll still get a visual alert that something's going on with that app.

- **Various options**—Below the Badge App Icon section you'll most often find options that are specific to the app you've selected. For example, Figure 17.13 shows the Ringtone section for the FaceTime app—tapping this option allows you to pick the sound that is played when someone is calling you or when you're calling a contact.

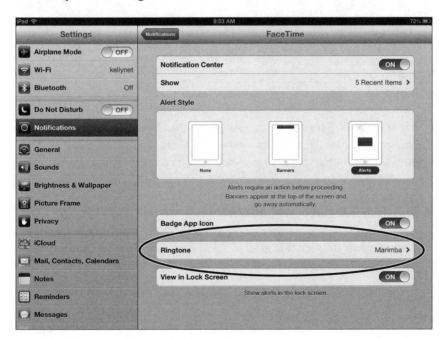

FIGURE 17.13

Select a ringtone for the FaceTime app alert.

Tap Notifications under Settings to return to the previous screen. Tap Calendar to see the Calendar Alerts section shown in Figure 17.14. This section allows you to pick the sound that is played when a Calendar reminder alert is triggered.

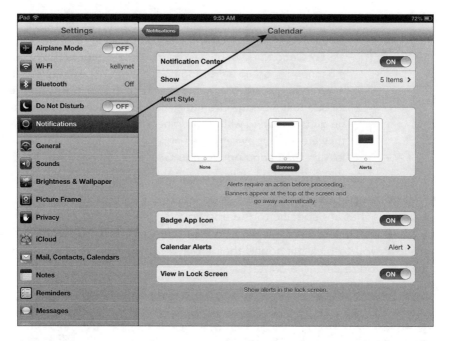

FIGURE 17.14

A different set of options for the Calendar app.

- **View in Lock Screen**—Most every app has the View in Lock Screen option shown in Figure 17.15. If you leave the View in Lock Screen option set to On, alerts from that app (such as a banner alert) can still appear when your iPad is locked and asleep. For example, I selected the Calendar app and turned the View in Lock Screen option to On. My iPad was sleeping (screen turned off) when the alert in Figure 17.16 triggered, turning the iPad's screen on and beeping to get my attention. (Remember, however, that if I had set a Do Not Disturb time period, this alert would not have triggered during that time frame.)

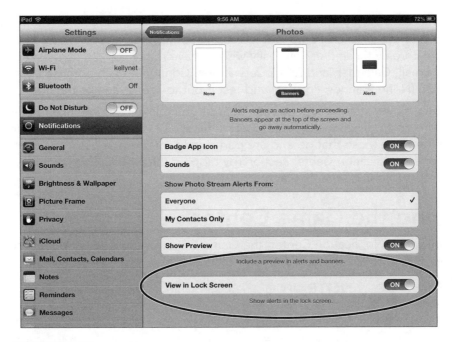

FIGURE 17.15

The View in Lock Screen option.

FIGURE 17.16

Even in sleep mode, some apps can send alerts to the screen.

One of the best ways to use the Notification Center is to first turn off all the apps so they are all listed in the Not In Notification Center section. Then, one by one, turn on only those that you really wish to have notify you. I'd suggest apps such as Email, Calendar, and Reminders at first. Configure each of these apps' Alert Style (None, Banner, Pop-Up) and test it out to see if you like the notifications.

Then, slowly start adding additional apps you think you might like to have access to in the Notifications Center. Most of the apps I use rarely send alerts to the screen, but those that do and are particularly annoying about it get sent to the Not In Notification Center section (by tapping the Notification Center button and turning it to Off). Bye, bye annoying alerts!

Exploring the Game Center

Unlike the Notification Center, the Game Center is an actual app that must be opened in order to take advantage of its features.

 NOTE If you've not yet used Game Center, you'll first be asked to create a nickname and asking if you'd like your profile to be public (available for anyone to see)—set this to On or Off depending on whether you wish other game players to be able to see your game profile and be able to challenge you to games.

Open the Game Center app and you'll be greeted by the Top Game Center Games page, shown in Figure 17.17.

FIGURE 17.17

Find new games and play existing games against friends.

The Game Center allows you to play games on your iPad and share your scores and achievements with anyone you've added as a Game Center friend. When you first start the Game Center app, you won't have any Game Center friends configured, but that's easy to change. Simply tap the Get Friend Recommendations button that appears. After tapping the Get Friend Recommendations button, you'll see a screen like the one in Figure 17.18.

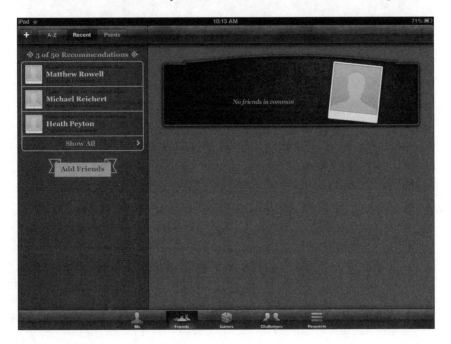

FIGURE 17.18

Invite friends to compete against you.

Tap the Add Friends button to the left and follow the instructions to send an email invite to a friend (or a contact already in your Contacts app). Once they've received and accepted the invite, their names will appear on the list to the left.

Not all games will work with the Game Center, but those games you've installed on your iPad that are compatible will upload your scores to the Game Center. Figure 17.19 shows how players are ranked by the number of achievement points they get from Game Center–approved games.

FIGURE 17.19

Game Center rankings are displayed.

 NOTE Don't even try to catch up with these top-ranked players. Some of them have been playing since 2010 when the iPad was released and many of them have hundreds or thousands of games they've played on their iPad. Makes you really wonder just how much time they have on their hands, doesn't it?

Tap the Games button on the bottom toolbar and you'll be provided with a list of your installed game apps that will work with Game Center. You will also find some recommendations at the top; tap one of the recommendations and you'll be taken to a recommended game.

 TIP If you tap the price button, you'll be taken to the same information page that you would see if you were browsing that game app in the App Store. You can read reviews and a description of the game as well as see some sample screens.

The Game Center allows you to issue challenges to your friends—tap the Challenges button on the toolbar and follow the instructions. You can also tap the Requests button to see any open invites you've sent to your friends.

I'm not as big a game player on my iPad as my son, so the appeal of the Game Center is low for me. But if you're a gamer and have a lot of friends who like to play games on their iPad (or iPhone), this is a great way to have some fun with your tablet.

18

CHARGING AND iPAD PERIPHERALS

You've learned all about the various apps and features that your iPad offers, but now it's time to learn a few bits of information related to third-party products and services. You're going to find that the iPad has its own industry of providers who sell chargers, cases, keyboards, screen covers, and just about anything else you can imagine.

Hopefully you've been using and enjoying your iPad or iPad mini, playing games, reading eBooks, opening email messages, taking photos, shooting videos, sending messages, web chatting, taking notes, and lots more.

You may have been enjoying your iPad so much that you've now discovered a fundamental truth about your new tablet—it runs on batteries that eventually must be charged!

Yes, your tablet is an electronic device, and like all electronic devices its batteries will only last so long before they must be charged up again. Fortunately, the iPad and iPad mini were built with some hefty batteries! I've found it rare that I have to charge my iPad every day. Actually, every three or four days is more realistic, and I'm a heavy iPad user. If you're only using your iPad to check email and maybe read some websites and eBooks, you may very well find that your iPad's batteries are lasting much longer.

The charging port is found at the bottom of the iPad or iPad mini, just below the Home button. As a rule, it's always safer to plug your charger into the wall *first* and then insert the other end of the wire into the tablet; if you plug in your iPad first, and then the plug into the wall you could damage your iPad with a small surge of power. (If you've ever inserted a plug into the wall and seen a small spark, that can cause problems for sensitive electronics like the ones inside the iPad.) Try to never plug in the wire to your iPad and then insert the charger into the wall socket.

Charging time varies from iPad to iPad. With the iPad 1 and 2, I could typically get it fully charged from below 10% to 100% in less than four or five hours using a 10-watt charger. The iPad 3 and 4 seems to take about seven to eight hours to get fully charged. The iPad mini comes with a 5-watt charger and can be completely charged, 0% to 100%, in about three-and-a-half hours. Not bad!

 CAUTION   Some people recommend charging your iPad mini with the 10-watt charger if you have one available. Although your iPad mini will charge faster, some reports out there state that this type of fast-charging may not be good for the iPad mini's batteries. Charge at 10 watts at your own risk!

If you're one of those iPad power users and you're always finding yourself on the road with an iPad at 5% and you've left your charger at home, you might want to consider a third-party power charger, such as those available from Hypershop.com. The HyperJuice Micro costs around $70 and can charge an iPhone and an iPad at the same time using its two USB ports. Figure 18.1 shows the HyperJuice Micro device.

FIGURE 18.1

Consider an external power charger for your iPad.

Many vendors sell external chargers that are similar to the HyperJuice Micro. Just be sure to do your research and read some user reviews before making a purchase.

Peripherals and Add-Ons

There is no shortage of third-party products (and official Apple products) for your iPad and iPad mini. These include printers, keyboards, cases, stands, and much more. You already learned about external power supplies that can quick-charge an iPad's dead batteries, but you may find some of the following items of interest for making your iPad experience more enjoyable.

AirPrint Printers

Many people are finding themselves using their iPads as much or more than they use a separate computer. I haven't tracked my time usage, but I would estimate I spend an equal amount of time using my iPad for writing and research as I do with my laptop. My iPad is much more portable, and its battery life is twice as long as the laptop.

That said, when I need to print something I've found on my iPad (or maybe an attachment received via email), I typically end up forwarding it to my laptop that's connected to a printer. I do very little printing, but I could see this being a major inconvenience for a lot of iPad owners. Fortunately, Apple has a solution.

Your iPad can print to any printer that supports the AirPrint service. This service was created by Apple as a way for third-party manufacturers to add iPad support to their products. Not every printer offers AirPrint (as a matter of fact, it's a very small number that do), so if this feature is important to you, you'll want to examine the list that Apple continuously updates of AirPrint-enabled printers. You can find that updated list by visiting http://support.apple.com/kb/HT4356. The list is organized by manufacturer name, so if you have a favorite brand of printer, click on the name of the company and view the list of available printers that support the AirPrint service.

External Keyboard

The onscreen keyboard is fine for typing tweets and short emails as well as entering data in online web forms, but for typing longer documents (such as a book chapter), you may want to take a look at the external keyboard options available.

At one time, Apple was the only game in town—they used to offer a keyboard with a small stand that also served as a charger. However, this keyboard doesn't appear to be available anymore (except on eBay). Apple still sells the Bluetooth keyboard, however, that connects to your iPad wirelessly. You can see this keyboard in Figure 18.2.

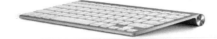

FIGURE 18.2

Apple's Bluetooth keyboard option.

But Apple is no longer the only game in town when it comes to external keyboards. Do a Google search for "iPad external keyboard" and prepare to spend some time sifting through all the available options.

One of the more popular options these days is a case for the iPad that also includes a keyboard built in to the cover of the case. Figure 18.3 shows the Logitech Ultrathin Keyboard Cover. The keyboard covers the screen of the iPad, serving as a cover until you open it up and prop the iPad on the built-in stand.

FIGURE 18.3

The Logitech Ultrathin Keyboard Cover.

Dozens of vendors sell cases with keyboards built in, so be sure to look around. A great place to start is MacMall.com—do a search for "iPad keyboard cases" and you'll find a number of competing products.

Cases

I just mentioned cases, but not every case comes with a built-in keyboard. As a matter of fact, right now exactly 7,243 cases are available for the iPad and iPad mini. Oops, make that 7,244...and counting. Yes, the number of case options available is staggering.

You'll find hard cases, soft cases, gel cases, and Kevlar (bulletproof) cases for both the larger iPads and the iPad mini. I've tried a number or cases, and I prefer hard cases to soft ones, but that's just my personal preference. I'm more likely to drop something *on* my iPad than to drop my actual iPad, so I've steered clear of the soft and gel-style cases and gone with something that has a tough top shell to protect the glass screen.

One thing is for certain, however, when it comes to iPad cases—get one! A case will keep the iPad somewhat protected from spills, drops, and bumps, so it's a worthwhile investment. No case is going to protect your iPad from a 50-foot drop (well, maybe...some case vendors make some mighty big claims), but my iPad has been saved from some near misses all because I've wrapped it in a nice protective shell.

Personal recommendation time: I love my DODOcase from Dodocase.com. From a distance, it looks like I'm carrying a hardback book. The top flips over to reveal my iPad held inside a tough bamboo frame. The thing is handmade (you can pick from a number of styles and colors) and I never stop getting compliments on it. Figure 18.4 shows the DODOcase I purchased—I love orange.

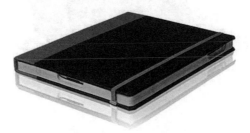

FIGURE 18.4

The DODOcase.

Stands

A number of vendors offer optional methods for holding your iPad. You'll find many options for hand-free operation of your iPad (well, except for using your fingers for gestures). There are stands that hold your iPad at an easy angle for viewing while sitting on a table (the iPad, not you) and there are stands that allow you to attach your iPad to various other surfaces such as inside a car or to a wall.

Figure 18.5 shows one popular minimalist tabletop stand from Grooveipadstand.com—simply insert the bottom edge of the iPad into the groove and your iPad is ready to go.

FIGURE 18.5

A simple stand with a groove for holding your iPad.

Figure 18.6 shows another type of stand that is more protective in nature and surrounds your iPad while still offering hands-free operation. This one is the Luxa2 H4 Holder from Luxa2.com.

FIGURE 18.6

This stand holds your iPad firmly.

If you like to use your iPad while sitting at a table or maybe as a presentation device in small meetings, a stand is a great way to securely hold your iPad at an easy-to-read angle.

AppleTV

Okay, the AppleTV isn't really an iPad accessory, but an argument could be made for it. At $99, it's cheaper than many of the fanciest cases and keyboards for the iPad, and what it offers to the iPad user is an amazing feature called AirPlay.

The AppleTV is tiny—that's it tucked under the TV in Figure 18.7.

FIGURE 18.7

The AppleTV makes a great partner to an iPad.

 NOTE The AppleTV requires a constant Internet connection for it to function properly, and a direct connection to your router or Internet modem will make sure that download speeds are fast. That said, it can communicate via Wi-Fi, but if you've got a slower DSL connection, expect some lag issues.

The AppleTV by itself can do some amazing things—Internet browsing, iTunes access to play your music via iCloud, Photo slideshows, movie purchase and rentals, and much more. For a complete description of all its features, visit Apple.com/appletv.

AppleTV also has what's called AirPlay, which allows you to display whatever is on your iPad screen on your TV! (This is only supported with versions of the iPad 2 and higher).

With AirPlay, any app I open on my iPad, any game I play, any photo or video I watch can be displayed on the larger television screen in my living room. For example, at a recent birthday party for my oldest son, I had a slideshow of photos of him that continuously played on my iPad and displayed on the TV—our visitors (friends and family) enjoyed seeing all the pictures cycle through his birth to his fifth birthday party!

TIP For real-time photo sharing with the AppleTV, I took photos with my iPhone and immediately added them to the album I created in the Photos app via iCloud. My iPad would synchronize (via iCloud) the albums, and the birthday album had instant new photos added to the slideshow. Isn't technology cool?

Lots of accessories haven't been mentioned here: screen protectors (clear sheets for protecting against smudges and spills), attachments for connecting photo and video cameras, and even toy cars that you touch to the screen and drive over the terrain that's displayed (search for Cars 2 Appmates or Hot Wheels Aptivity in the App Store).

As you use your iPad more and more, you may find yourself wanting a case, a stand, or some other accessory that would make using your iPad that much more enjoyable. Rest assured, if you can think of an accessory you'd like to own, someone out there is probably making and selling it!

Insurance

I've never been accused of being accident prone, but that doesn't mean I'm not capable of dropping my iPad or forgetting and leaving it somewhere. The iPad is a big investment, and like any investment, it's deserving of protection. And I'm not talking about cases here. I'm talking about protecting your financial investment against loss, damage, or theft.

Like iPad accessories, you have options when it comes to insurance. The most obvious is the Apple Care service you can purchase when you buy a new iPad. You can find more information about the extended coverage offered by Apple by visiting http://www.apple.com/support/products/.

TIP Your iPad may already be covered by your homeowner or renter insurance for theft or damage (fire, flood, and so on). The only way to know for certain is to contact your insurer and check to see if your policy covers electronics such as the iPad. Be sure to keep your receipt for the iPad you've purchased so you can verify its purchase price.

And there are other options out there besides the one sold by Apple. You'll want to do a Google search for "iPad insurance" and investigate the various companies that offer protection against damage and theft. Not all of them offer the same types of protection, and not all of them have the greatest record based on customer reports. Do your homework, investigate your options, and if you're wanting to purchase some additional backup for your tablet, get a plan that you can afford and that your gut tells you will be honored should you have need to use it.

EIGHT GREAT FREE APPS

You've already learned how to navigate and use the App Store (refer to Chapter 12, "Apps for the iPad," for more details), but if you're like me, the first few times you visit the App Store you're likely to feel slightly overwhelmed. The mixture of free and paid apps, combined with the dozens of categories and specialty collections, can certainly be confusing.

There have been some major upgrades to how the App Store presents its wares; in the early days, it really did feel like hunting for a needle in a haystack, with users being forced to swipe and swipe and swipe, looking through the displays that typically only showed 12 apps at a time. The front-end of the App Store—the Featured page that typically greets you when you first open the app—is much more friendly on the eyes, less cluttered (at least to me), and much more focused on helping you find what you're looking for…usually.

Fortunately, Apple continues to refine the App Store and add new categories that are easy to spot. For example, take a look at Figure 19.1 and you'll see some eye-catching buttons on the Featured page, such as the Games button and the Photo & Video button.

FIGURE 19.1

The App Store and its collection buttons.

Yes, the App Store still puts up banners near the top showing the most popular apps or the ones that Apple wants you to consider purchasing. The New & Noteworthy section also contains some apps that might catch your eye, but for me, it's the prescreened categories that Apple swaps in and out (they change location, and sometimes certain buttons will disappear for a few days or weeks before appearing again) that are really helpful. At certain times in the year, you'll also see buttons related to holidays or back-to-school items. Like I said, check in to the App Store every few days and you're bound to find a collection that appeals to you.

You can spend minutes or hours browsing the free apps that Apple has collected. This may or may not be a good thing for you. I'm not one to spend too long browsing apps; I prefer to get in, find one, and get out. With that said, I'd like to offer up eight free apps that I personally find useful and know others do as well. Some of these you may have heard about, and some not. Note that I've left out games because there are simply too many on my list to narrow it down.

So, in no particular order, here are eight free apps I'd recommend to any iPad owner. Hopefully at least one will catch your eye, but I have a feeling you'll find all of them helpful in some way. You can find all of these apps by searching for the name of the app in the App Store.

Skype

You were introduced to FaceTime back in Chapter 10, "Apps for Instant Communication." It's a great way to video chat with friends and family. However, chatting via FaceTime requires that the person you're calling also has FaceTime on their iPad, iPhone, or Mac computer.

If you'd like to video chat with someone who isn't running FaceTime, there's still a 100%-free solution that will run just fine on your iPad. It's called Skype, and it's free to download and install on all the popular operating systems and just about every brand of smartphone out there. If you have someone you'd like to video chat with using your iPad and they don't have FaceTime, point them to Skype.com and tell them to create an account and install the software on their computer, tablet, or phone.

Unlike FaceTime, which relies on an email address to make the connection, Skype uses account names. So anyone you wish to "skype" needs to provide you with their Skype username/account name. You'll add that to your contacts, and a message will be sent to your friends asking them to approve your request to make calls. (Likewise, if you provide your account name to your friends, when they add you as a contact, you'll get the message asking to approve them.)

You'll want to read all the help options presented to you when you first open Skype, but it doesn't take long. And you'll obviously want to consult the built-in documentation to learn about every feature Skype offers. (For example, with Skype you can also call someone's mobile number or landline number, but this requires you to purchase some Skype credit. Video calls, Skype-to-Skype, are always free, though.)

Figure 19.2 shows Skype running on the iPad. I've pulled up one of my contacts and can tap the Video Call or Voice Call button to call and chat.

FIGURE 19.2

Skype for iPad.

TIP It's considered rude to just dial someone up in Skype, especially if you see that person's status set to Busy or Not Available. A better suggestion that most folks using Skype follow is to use the built-in instant messaging and type a quick "Are you available for video chat?" If your contact is busy, he or she can quickly and easily respond without the interruption of the phone ringing sound that Skype uses when a call is coming in.

Dropbox

You read about iCloud back in Chapter 3, "iCloud and Settings," and although it's a great way to back up and synchronize your iPad data, such as contacts and music, but it does require an Apple iDevice to take advantage of its features. If you're looking for a storage solution that can give you access to your data with your iPad, your home computer, your phone, and even someone else's computer, you'll definitely want to check out Dropbox.

Dropbox is pure cloud storage; the company gives you 2GB of free storage, and you can buy more (just like iCloud) or you can earn additional free space by inviting friends to become users, adding Dropbox as a Friend in Facebook, and a few other tasks. Dropbox doesn't require an Apple device, and besides offering up apps to install on your iPhone and iPad, it allows you to access any files you've stored by opening a web browser, pointing it to Dropbox.com, and logging in with your username and password. This means you can access your files on any computer that has an Internet connection.

What I most enjoy about Dropbox is the ability to create shared folders. For example, I can create a folder called "Photos for Mom and Dad" and then provide Dropbox with the email addresses of those folks I wish to give access to this folder. They will receive a message letting them know they have access; I can store photos, videos, and any other files I wish in there, and my parents (and anyone else I give access) can open the folder by clicking a link and viewing anything inside. They can even download files from the shared folder to their own computer if they want a copy of some photos for themselves.

Figure 19.3 shows the Dropbox app open; I'm viewing folders in my Dropbox account on the left (they're alphabetized) and stored documents on the right (a scan of a coloring sheet my son brought home).

FIGURE 19.3

Dropbox provides plenty of cloud storage for your files.

I've found that Dropbox and iCloud provide me with a suitable level of storage for my files. I back everything up to an external hard drive at least once a quarter (just in case), but having access to all of my files—anytime, anywhere—is well worth the added cost I pay for extra storage space.

Evernote

The best way I can describe Evernote is that it's a digital binder. Evernote works like Dropbox—there's an app for just about every platform and operating system around, including the iPad. Evernote works like Dropbox in that it's available wherever an Internet connection can be found, and changes made to a document on your iPad will synchronize and be available later when you log in to Evernote on your home computer or maybe your mobile phone.

Evernote lets you create notebooks (you provide a name for the notebook) and then you insert notes into them. Notes can consist of typed documents, photos, voice recordings, and even web page clips. The company is constantly adding new features to the service, and I'm constantly surprised at the newest ways I find to use it.

Like collecting recipes? Create a notebook and then store your recipes inside. I have a mixed collection of scanned recipes (ripped from magazines), hand-typed recipes, photos of recipes (usually taken from the back of food boxes or cookbooks that I own), and even a voice recording of my mom explaining the process for creating her special gumbo.

I write books for a living, so every book I write starts out as a notebook. I insert a note that has a draft outline, another note that might contain a photo of a product I'm wanting to include, and dozens more notes that are all web pages I've found and wish to reference once I start writing. If I'm driving in the car and an idea pops into my head, I open up the Evernote app (after pulling over, of course) and tap the Voice Recording button to record my idea before I forget it and lose it forever.

Figure 19.4 shows the Evernote app's user interface on iPad. It's organized like a hanging file system, and you tap on the Notebooks, Tags, or other folder to view your content.

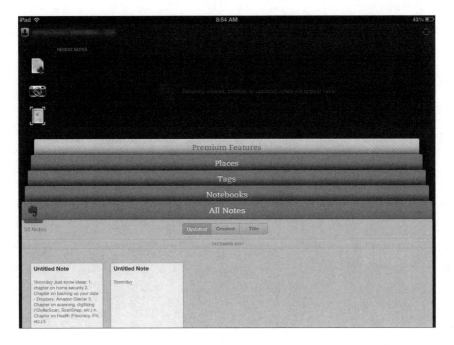

FIGURE 19.4

Evernote for iPad.

Keep in mind that although Evernote is free to use, a premium service (I'm a subscriber) is available that provides additional features not found in the free service, including much more storage space for your notes and such.

eBooks: Kindle and Nook

You saw how iBooks allows you to view and read the eBooks you've purchased from the iBook Store, but your iPad can also give you access to any eBooks you may have purchased from Amazon for your Kindle.

Figure 19.5 shows the Kindle app open and displaying some of the books I am reading (or my wife and kids are reading).

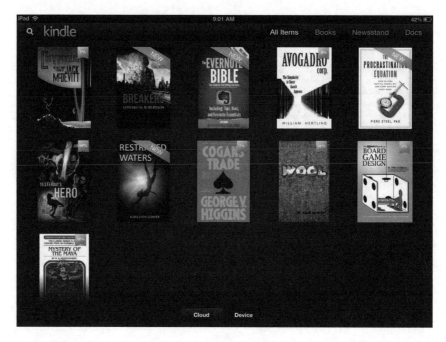

FIGURE 19.5

The Kindle app open and displaying my eBooks.

Any purchases of eBooks you've made from Amazon.com will be available for download to your iPad after you've installed the app and provided your Amazon.com username and password. As with iBooks, you can delete a book at any time and then reinstall it later should you wish to read it again. Amazon keeps a record of your purchases and can put back any eBooks you've deleted from your iPad.

Figure 19.6 shows the Nook app that displays any eBooks purchased from Barnes & Noble. Again, books can be removed and reinstalled at any time, and all that's required is the installation of the Nook app and an account name and password.

FIGURE 19.6

The Nook app for iPad.

Pocket

Do you do a lot of web browsing? Do you often find more web pages to read than you have time for? If so, you're going to love Pocket. When I'm researching for a new book, I often find myself spending hours on my work computer scouring the Internet for ideas, reference material, reviews, and more. And when I'm not working on a book, I'm still always finding websites of interest that I wish to investigate further. The problem is, I don't often have a lot of time to read everything at that exact moment.

Fortunately, I use Pocket on my iPad. It's a free service (you can sign up after downloading the app and opening it by visiting pocket.com) that you install on your web browser. When you find a website you wish to save for later reading, you tap the button on your web browser that the Pocket service installs and that web page will be added to your "I'll read this later" list. And later is what the Pocket app on your iPad is all about. As you can see in Figure 19.7, the Pocket app displays all my saved websites as large rectangular or square buttons that I can click to read the articles. These articles are downloaded to my iPad, so I don't even need a Wi-Fi connection to access them.

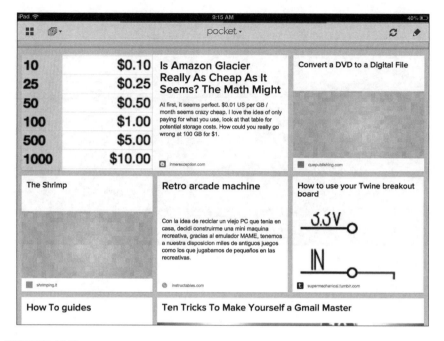

FIGURE 19.7

Pocket for iPad.

After you've read an article, you can tap the check mark above the article to remove it from Pocket, or you can tap the Back button to return to the Pocket app's listing of saved websites.

Pocket isn't meant to be a substitute for your web browser's bookmark system; instead, it's meant to serve as a way to port over your reading list to your iPad so you can read the content when it's convenient for you.

Still, I have found myself keeping quite a number of handy websites stored in Pocket rather than bookmarking them. The ability to access a web article offline when I lack Internet service is great—I can't count the times I've found myself in a waiting room or in line with no Internet access; it's a great time for me to catch up on my web reading.

Pandora

I have a lot of songs stored in my iTunes library, but sometimes I like to listen to new bands that I don't have in my library or songs that I don't own. For this, I love the Pandora app. The Pandora app is one of many music-streaming services (streaming just means that the music is played over an Internet connection).

Figure 19.8 shows the Pandora app—as you can see, I'm currently playing a tune from The Beatles.

FIGURE 19.8

Pandora.

Pandora lets you use the Search box in the upper-left corner of the screen to search for songs, artists, band names, and even music categories such as Blues and Cajun. You create "stations" that can be tapped to start playing music based on your search results. You can create a station that plays music only from a certain band (such as The Beatles) or you can create stations that play a mix of music, such as my Southern Rock station.

Should you hear a song you just don't like, you can tap the Skip button near the top of the screen. However, Pandora's free service only gives you six skips per day (and resets after 24 hours), so use them wisely or upgrade to a Pandora premium service (for a fee).

You also use the Thumbs Up and Thumbs Down buttons to rate songs—this helps Pandora understand your musical tastes so it can make better music suggestions for you. I've found that by using this rating feature that Pandora actually does a pretty good job of figuring out what I prefer to hear and the types of music that I tend to avoid.

Flipboard

You learned about Facebook and Twitter in Chapter 11, "Social Apps," and when you want to check in on your friends and colleagues, you open up one of those apps and see what's going on. But there's a much faster way to do this, as well as a more eye-catching method, called Flipboard.

Flipboard pulls in all the Facebook and Twitter updates from your contacts as well as any RSS feeds (websites and blogs that you subscribe to) that you wish to configure Flipboard to access. If you have a mobile phone running Instagram, you can view your friends' photo uploads as well! In addition to items from friends, family, and co-workers, you can also add in newsfeeds by category, such as Science, Art, Music, and many more.

All of this is then presented to you in a digital magazine format. Photos from friends are presented as figures in a manner you'd see in a magazine. Tweets and posts and much more become available in a single app that presents the data to you with a swipe like you're turning a page.

Figure 19.9 shows the Flipboard app on the iPad.

FIGURE 19.9

The Flipboard app.

You can tap a block to open up a category or a Facebook feed, or tap the More block to see additional items that Flipboard wishes to share with you. And while you're viewing items, if you see something you wish to share, you can tweet it or post it to Facebook from right inside the Flipboard app!

iTunesU

In addition to reading lots of books on my iPad, I also enjoy using my iPad to learn new things. The iTunesU app works just like the iBooks app, with the exception being the books you read in iTunesU are more akin to textbooks you'd find in a college-level program.

Figure 19.10 shows the iTunesU app opened up and displaying some e-textbooks I've downloaded.

FIGURE 19.10

The iTunesU bookshelf.

If you've ever wanted to learn (or relearn) something from school, such as chemistry, statistics, or maybe a foreign language, you may very well find a great book in the iTunesU catalog.

After downloading the free app from the App Store and opening it up, tap the Catalog button in the upper-left corner of the screen and prepare to be amazed by the sheer volume of information available. You'll find coursework here from Harvard, Stanford, and many more universities, with all sorts of categories, such as Engineering, Business, History, and more.

Many of these e-textbooks are actually used by students enrolled in colleges and universities, so you won't be getting the lectures they get, and you certainly won't be able to raise your hand with a question, but if you're wanting to read the same textbook that many of today's college students are using, the iTunesU app is one of the best ways to get access to the information you wish to learn.

Finding More Free Apps

I mentioned earlier that Apple offers the Great Free Apps button, usually found near the bottom of the Featured page. That's one great place to start your hunt for more free apps, but it's not the only place.

Google is a great starting point—just type in "free iPad apps" and you're probably going to be overwhelmed quickly. Instead, use "free iPad apps" along with other keywords such, as "foreign language" or "RPG" (role-playing game), to find more specific options.

You can also find magazines devoted to the iPad that are great sources for finding the latest free apps released, often with reviews and blunt assessments of the pros and cons.

Word of mouth, however, is probably one of the best ways to find free apps. I cannot count the number of free apps I've installed over the past few years because a friend or family member recommended them. Never underestimate keeping your ears open and listening to discussions on the latest hot apps for the iPad—you'll often find enough free apps that you may wonder why you'd ever need to pay for an app. (But keep reading, as I'll answer that question in the next chapter.)

EIGHT GREAT PAID APPS

When I first purchased my iPad, I loaded it up with all the free apps I could find. Although many of these apps were great, the reality was that most of them just didn't hold my attention for more than a day or so. Free apps can be great, and the old phrase "You get what you pay for" doesn't always hold true because I've found some amazing free apps over the years. But I've also found some incredible apps that weren't free, and to this day a number of them have earned back their initial cost thousands of times over in saved time and aggravation and usefulness.

The nice thing about paid apps for the iPad is that, for the most part, they average between $0.99 and $4.99 in price. This is far better than the cost of computer software, which always seems to cost $19.99 or $39.99 or even into the hundreds of dollars. For a small investment, you can often find an app that exceeds your expectations. I have a small number of apps I fully believe should cost more for what I've received. Still, it's hard to feel too bad when you spend $1.99 on an app and discover after a few weeks of use that it just doesn't meet your needs. The small investment is often a suitable risk to try out an app that might not have a free "lite" version available for testing purposes.

In Chapter 19, "Eight Great Free Apps," I provided you with eight free apps that I've used and recommend to my friends, family, and colleagues. In this chapter, I'm going to provide you with eight recommendations of paid apps. Hopefully, as with the free apps, you'll find one or more of these paid apps useful.

All of these apps are currently available in the App Store, and if you don't like these eight paid apps, you have a couple hundred thousand apps left to investigate!

 NOTE Some apps, especially games, will often be listed as "Free." Only later will you discover that the app is free because it has what are called in-app purchases. With games, for example, in-app purchases often include special features or powers that give you an edge in the game. Other in-app purchases often include extra functionality such as a sketch app that sells different types of textures, background colors, or shapes for the pen or brush. Always read the app's information page to determine if there are in-app purchases; you'll almost always see a listing on the information page called "Top In-App Purchases" that shows you what in-app purchases other owners of the app are buying. That's your clue that although the app is free to download, it's not always free to use.

GoodReader

For every type of media you wish to view, there's an app. Want to read PDF files? There are PDF viewers (many free, some paid). Want to watch videos on your iPad that aren't supported by the Videos app? Just search the App Store for the movie format (such as WMV—Microsoft's standard video format) and you'll find plenty of solutions. The same goes for different image types (TIFF, GIF, JPG, and so on) and eBook formats (ePub, Mobi, and so on).

If you have something you want to read, you just need to go find an app that supports it. Or...you can grab GoodReader.

Without a doubt, one of my most used apps on my iPad is GoodReader—I use it to watch videos, read eBooks, view photos, and much more. It's a solid multipurpose app that continues to surprise me with new features it supports.

I mentioned Dropbox in Chapter 19, and GoodReader allows me to create a permanent connection to my Dropbox account. This means I can view all my Dropbox folders that contain a mix of content and tap my files to open them in GoodReader. I can even choose to download a copy from the Dropbox connection so that if I lose my Internet connection, the file is still available on my iPad.

Figure 20.1 shows the basic look of GoodReader.

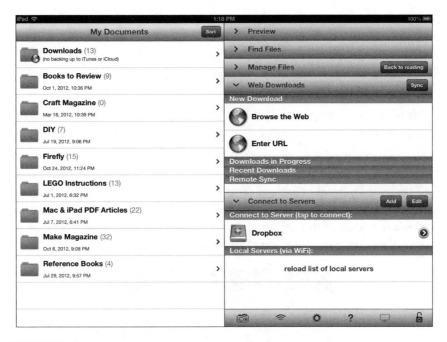

FIGURE 20.1

GoodReader for iPad.

You'll notice that the left side of the screen shows folder I've created to organize my files. On the right are the various options offered by GoodReader. I can use the Web Downloads section to enter a URL for a file or PDF and download directly to GoodReader. The Connect to Servers section lets me create connections to other services (such as Dropbox) for moving files over to GoodReader.

I store a lot of stuff on my iPad with GoodReader—LEGO instructions for my son's collection, all the episodes of my favorite science fiction TV series (*Firefly*), digital copies of *Make* magazine, and much more.

GoodReader allows you to annotate your documents, write in the margins, highlight, and much more. It's currently priced at $4.99 and is one of the best investments I've made for my iPad.

Pages

I try to avoid using my home office computer as much as possible. Whenever I can, I prefer to use my iPad to write, play, check email, and anything else I can avoid using the desktop computer that's not at all portable.

One of the tasks that often brought me back to my desktop computer was creating PDFs—brochures, proposals, and other documents that would have a mix of text and images. Although the software I used on my computer did the job, it was bloated with features and quite slow to work with. Thankfully, I rarely have need to use that software anymore now that I've installed Pages on my iPad.

Pages is Apple's version of the word processor. It has all the features I need and, so far, I haven't yet discovered something I need to do that it can't handle.

Pages comes with a mix of templates such as a Formal Letter, Resume, Term Paper, Recipe, Thank You Card, and Flyer…plus many more. You can type your text, move images around (and resize them), and have the text shift to accommodate an embedded image. Colors and fonts and other features are hidden on a toolbar that disappears until you need it, giving you a better view of your final document, as shown in Figure 20.2.

FIGURE 20.2

Pages lets you create eye-catching documents.

The only problem I have with Pages is that it functions best when you're using an external keyboard instead of the onscreen keyboard. (You can learn more about external keyboard options in Chapter 18, "Charging and iPad Peripherals.") With a separate keyboard, you can type as fast as you like and save all your work easily on your iPad until you're ready to print or email it out.

Pages is currently $9.99 from the App Store, and is one of the easiest word processing apps I've ever used—it even saves to iCloud so I can access my documents from my iPhone! It doesn't have all the bells and whistles you're probably used to in a computer-based word processing application, but ask yourself when was the last time you actually used a macro or a mail merge or any of those hundreds of fonts? If you're like me and want a simple, easy-to-use word processing app that can create some eye-catching documents, then Pages is the app for you.

PDFpen

Although I use GoodReader to read a lot of PDF files, when I actually need to work with an existing PDF (signing a contract, for example), I turn to PDFpen.

PDFpen lets me create new PDF documents (just as I can do with Pages), but for me the real power is editing with PDFpen. When I get a book chapter and I need to provide some editing commentary, I open the PDF in PDFpen and use the markup tools to highlight, scratch out, add notes, and draw boxes around items of interest.

For contracts, I have a scanned image of my signature stored in the Photos app that I can open and paste (and resize) to fit on any signature line. I cannot tell you how many times this has saved me when a contract needed an immediate signature and I didn't have time to print, sign, and fax back a document.

Another great thing about PDFpen happens after you install it. Should you find a PDF attachment (in an email) or a PDF file for download on a website, when you tap the item to open it you'll see PDFpen listed as one of the options to use to open the PDF document. When you open it in PDFpen, a copy is automatically saved in PDFpen so you won't need an Internet connection later to access it.

Figure 20.3 shows PDFpen and the markup tools available.

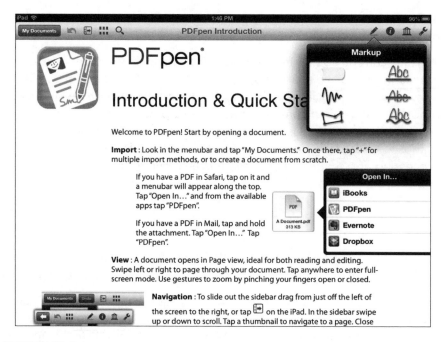

FIGURE 20.3

PDFpen for iPad offers markup tools and editing features.

PDFpen is currently $14.99 for the iPad. It supports iCloud, but it can also move your documents to other services such as Dropbox and Google Docs. I'm always finding PDFpen saving the day—a few weeks ago my son's school emailed me some PDF forms at 4:30 p.m. that were due by 5 p.m. and that I'd forgotten to send in with him that day. Rather than head home for the documents, I opened them with PDFpen, filled them out, and emailed them back in less than 15 minutes. I am invincible!

iDisplay

Most desktop computers have the ability to use two or more monitors to provide more screen space to users, but this isn't all that convenient for laptop users. The idea of carrying a second LCD flat screen to the coffee shop is just silly. Or is it?

With iDisplay, my iPad quickly becomes a second monitor while I'm using my MacBook Air. The screen isn't as big as my laptop screen, but I still find having the ability to drag a web page or other open document to the iPad's screen so I can view it while working on something else invaluable.

Of course, iDisplay will work on a Mac or Windows computer as long as it's running the iDisplay software. It uses a Wi-Fi connection, and the app is free for your desktop or laptop computer. You open and run the application on your desktop or laptop first. Next, you open the iDisplay app on your iPad—it will list any computers it sees that are running iDisplay. Make the connection, and your iPad can now be placed to the right of your computer to serve as a second screen.

As you can see in Figure 20.4, half of this chapter is displayed on my iPad screen. The other half is on my laptop's screen—you'll just have to trust me that it's there.

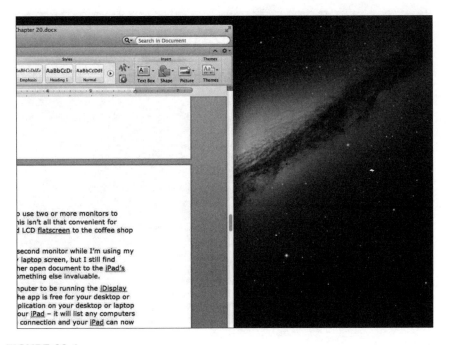

FIGURE 20.4

The iDisplay app turns your iPad into a second screen.

iDisplay currently costs $4.99 from the App Store. If you find your laptop or desktop computer screen just doesn't offer enough viewing space when you need it, consider turning your iPad into a second screen temporarily.

Paper by FiftyThree

I have a lot of friends who love the Moleskine brand notebooks. They're small, easy to carry, and they're fairly rugged and hold up over time. I use them occasionally, but for me, I prefer Paper by FiftyThree.

The app called Paper by FiftyThree is one of those apps that's free to download and install, and you can actually use it as much as you like without ever paying an extra cent. However, it does have some in-app purchases that make this app a real standout for me.

Figure 20.5 shows the scrollable collection of notebooks—create as many as you like (each starts with 10 pages, but you can add and delete pages at the touch of a button) and customize their covers with textures, colors, and even photos or artwork from your iPad's albums!

FIGURE 20.5

Paper by FiftyThree lets you create custom notebooks.

You create a new notebook by tapping the + button shown in Figure 20.5. After the new journal appears, tap the small "i" icon on the journal's cover and enter the name of the journal and select a cover from the scrolling list shown in Figure 20.6.

FIGURE 20.6

Name a new journal and select its cover.

After you create and name a notebook, tap its cover to open it. You swipe to move from page to page and then tap a page to open it in full screen. Figure 20.7 shows a single page along with the tools that Paper by FiftyThree offers. The Eraser and Drawing Tool are hidden until you need them—swipe up from the bottom of the screen to see the tool palette, and then swipe down to hide the palette again.

The free version of the app only comes with the Eraser and the Drawing tool (to the right of the Eraser). The other items can be purchased individually ($1.99 each) or as a package deal called The Essentials ($6.99). The small circle on the toolbar is the Mixer ($1.99) and allows you to mix up your own colors.

FIGURE 20.7

An open notebook page and the toolbar.

I find myself using Paper by FiftyThree most often to create custom sketches that I need my publisher's art department to re-create for me (but in a much more polished and professional manner). I've also found the app quite handy at keeping my five-year-old son busy during any kind of wait where game sounds would be unwelcome.

Clear

My wife has always made fun of me because I'm a list person. I would create these lists on paper with everything I needed to do for both home and work, and over time the items would get crossed out. It's an extremely motivating method that worked for me. The problem is that I often had two or three sheets going at any given time and sometimes I'd lose one.

A friend introduced me to the app called Clear, and my list making has never been the same. I'm done with paper lists. Now, with a simple swipe of my finger, I can create a new to-do item. When the item is completed, another swipe deletes it from the list. The eye-pleasing color gradient is supposed to serve the purpose of ordering items by priority (red is highest priority at top, whereas the light orange item near the bottom is low priority).

There's one caveat about using Clear, however—it's really an iPhone app. It can also be a little troublesome to find using the Search tool because so many apps have the word "clear" in their title or description. When you search for it in the App Store, search for "Clear Realmac" and tap the iPhone apps as shown in Figure 20.8.

FIGURE 20.8

Search the app store for an iPhone app called "Clear Realmac."

Figure 20.9 shows the Clear app open with some items in it.

FIGURE 20.9

Clear for iPad is great for making a To Do list.

What I've discovered about Clear is that people love it... or hate it. It doesn't have a lot of bells and whistles—it doesn't interrupt you with pop-up alerts and it doesn't have a lot of configuration options. Instead, it's a simple list that is extremely easy to add and remove items from, and it has an interesting method for creating, reorganizing, and removing items. It does offer a folders option for creating different types of lists (such as a home to-do list versus a work to-do list), but I don't use it in that manner. For me, I just keep adding the stuff that needs to be done, and I delete off the list what is completed. It's a never-ending list, but that's life—and Clear is my absolutely favorite to-do app.

Clear is $1.99—at that price, you won't lose a lot of coin for giving it a try. Clear was originally created for the iPhone, and it looks great on that device as well. And with iCloud support, you can synch your items in Clear between iPad and iPhone easily.

iMovie

I shoot a lot of video using my iPhone (and sometimes my iPad), but I am horribly lax when it comes to actually editing my videos into anything worth watching. I have two small boys (ages 5 and 2) who love to watch themselves on my iPad or on the TV (using my Apple TV and the AirPlay feature that puts whatever's on my iPad's screen on the TV screen).

For a while, I would just cycle through all the videos stored on my iPad (or in Dropbox) and play them randomly, letting my boys laugh at their antics. But then someone showed me how easy it is to edit these videos down to their best parts, blend them together, and package it all with animated openings and text and special effects using iMovie.

Now I'm an iMovie fanatic, and my boys are able to specify certain videos they'd like to watch because I've added titles and special effects that they can remember. "Daddy, play the Falling Down video!" (The single video containing all the snippets I filmed of my boys as they learned to walk.)

iMovie is fantastic. You can create movie trailers for your larger videos. Are you familiar with the Ken Burns effect? It's in there, allowing you to add photos, move and change scale, and provide a semblance of animation. You can split videos up, blend them together, add sound effects, add music and voiceovers, and much more. It comes with a $4.99 price, but it's worth every penny in my opinion, and I use it constantly.

Figure 20.10 shows the basic iMovie interface.

FIGURE 20.10

iMovie for iPad turns you into a semi-pro movie director.

The first few times you use iMovie can be a little confusing until you figure out how to navigate and use the tools available. Use the Help options when you can, but turn to the Internet with a Google search for "iMovie tutorials" and you'll be in good hands. You can find hundreds of videos and documents out there that will make you an iMovie expert and take your videos to the next level.

Angry Birds (Anything)

I hesitated to include any games in this chapter, but if there is collection of games that has more than earned its spot on the best paid apps, it has to be the *Angry Birds* group of games.

There's the original—*Angry Birds*. The bad pigs have stolen the birds' eggs and built a series of forts and defenses to keep the birds out. You fling a variety of birds with various powers (one drops an egg that explodes and can destroy walls) to try and defeat all the pigs. Yeah, that's the game in a nutshell. And it's sold gazillions of copies and made more money than most countries can print. Why is it so popular? I can't explain it, other than to tell you to try it out if you dare.

Figure 20.11 shows the original *Angry Birds*.

FIGURE 20.11

The original Angry Birds *game.*

But the fun doesn't stop there. Since the release of the original version, the app's developers have continued to release game after game—*Angry Birds Seasons* (with free holiday updates for St. Patrick's Day, Halloween, and many more), *Angry Birds Space* (birds fly around planets and use gravity to take out defenses), *Angry Birds Rio* (a tie-in to the animated *Rio* movie for kids), and now...*Angry Birds Star Wars*. Yes, the birds play the roles of Luke Skywalker, C-3PO, and many more good guys—and the pigs wear Darth Vader and Stormtrooper helmets. It's crazy, and my oldest son is an expert at all of them.

Where will it end? Who knows? A spin-off game was just released called *Bad Piggies*, which puts you, the player, into the roll of the pig trying to escape safely with an egg.

Should you try out an *Angry Birds* game, consider yourself warned. The games are addictive, the music will get in your head and stick there, and the constant free updates with new levels makes purchasing the $0.99 full versions (versus the free versions, which have annoying advertisements at the top of the screen) a good investment for long-term play.

Finding More Paid Apps

Paid apps are never hard to find. Most of the apps on the Featured page of the App Store are paid apps; given that Apple gets a nice piece of every sale, it makes sense that most of the apps they display will be paid apps and not free apps.

Still, Apple and the App Store do a great job of promoting the most popular paid apps. And they're popular for a reason! Word of mouth can quickly kill a paid app that doesn't deliver on its promises, but it can also create legends in the paid app world when users return to the App Store to give an app praise (using the review feature).

Obviously you can use the App Store's category option and the various specialty collections displayed on the Featured page, but don't discount the numerous websites that review apps. Just Google "iPad app reviews" and you'll find dozens of websites dedicated to reviewing paid apps. Try to find the sites that actually pay for the apps and can provide unbiased opinions rather than those sites that receive the apps for free to review.

Magazines and blogs are also a great place to find reviews of paid apps. And just as with free apps, you'll often find that a recommendation from someone you know will lead you to a paid app that gets added to your list of favorites.

Index

CHECK OUT THESE OTHER
ABSOLUTE BEGINNER'S GUIDES
FROM QUE PUBLISHING

Windows 8
ABSOLUTE BEGINNER'S GUIDE
no experience necessary!
Paul Sanna

ISBN: 9780789749932

Computer Basics
ABSOLUTE BEGINNER'S GUIDE
no experience necessary!
Sixth Edition
Michael Miller

ISBN: 9780789750013

Project Management
ABSOLUTE BEGINNER'S GUIDE
no experience necessary!
Third Edition
Gregory M. Horine

ISBN: 9780789750105

Excel 2013
ABSOLUTE BEGINNER'S GUIDE
No experience necessary!
Tracy Syrstad

ISBN: 9780789750570

PowerPoint 2013
ABSOLUTE BEGINNER'S GUIDE
No experience necessary!
Patrice-Anne Rutledge

ISBN: 9780789750631

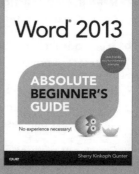

Word 2013
ABSOLUTE BEGINNER'S GUIDE
No experience necessary!
Sherry Kinkoph Gunter

ISBN: 9780789750907

No experience necessary!

iPad® and
iPad® mini

**ABSOLUTE
BEGINNER'S
GUIDE**

No experience necessary!

que   James F. Kelly

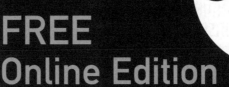

**FREE
Online Edition**

Your purchase of *iPad and iPad mini Absolute Beginner's Guide* includes access to a free online edition for 45 days through the **Safari Books Online** subscription service. Nearly every Que book is available online through **Safari Books Online**, along with thousands of books and videos from publishers such as Addison-Wesley Professional, Cisco Press, Exam Cram, IBM Press, O'Reilly Media, Prentice Hall, Que, Sams, and VMware Press.

Safari Books Online is a digital library providing searchable, on-demand access to thousands of technology, digital media, and professional development books and videos from leading publishers. With one monthly or yearly subscription price, you get unlimited access to learning tools and information on topics including mobile app and software development, tips and tricks on using your favorite gadgets, networking, project management, graphic design, and much more.

Activate your FREE Online Edition at
informit.com/safarifree

STEP 1:   Enter the coupon code: JWOXEBI.

STEP 2:   New Safari users, complete the brief registration form.
           Safari subscribers, just log in.

If you have difficulty registering on Safari or accessing the online edition,
please e-mail customer-service@safaribooksonline.com

Addison Wesley   Adobe Press   ALPHA   Cisco Press   FT Press   IBM Press.   Microsoft Press   New Riders   O'REILLY

Peachpit Press   PRENTICE HALL   que   Redbooks   SAMS   SAS Publishing   vmware PRESS   WILEY   wrox